Federal Equal Employment Opportunity

David H. Rosenbloom

The Praeger Special Studies program—utilizing the most modern and efficient book production techniques and a selective worldwide distribution network—makes available to the academic, government, and business communities significant, timely research in U.S. and international economic, social, and political development.

Federal Equal Employment Opportunity
Politics and Public Personnel Administration

PRAEGER SPECIAL STUDIES IN U.S. ECONOMIC, SOCIAL, AND POLITICAL ISSUES

Praeger Publishers   New York   London

Library of Congress Cataloging in Publication Data

Rosenbloom, David H
   Federal equal employment opportunity.

   (Praeger special studies in U.S. economic, social,
and political issues)
   Bibliography: p.
   Includes index.
   1. Civil service—United States—Personnel
management.   2. Affirmative action programs—
United States.   3. Discrimination in employment—
United States.   I. Title.
JK765.R67   353.001'3   77-954
ISBN 0-275-24420-2

PRAEGER PUBLISHERS
200 Park Avenue, New York, N.Y. 10017, U.S.A.

Published in the United States of America in 1977
by Praeger Publishers, Inc.

789   038   987654321

Printed in the United States of America

To Leah Naomi, Sarah Tamar, and Barbara

In recent years there has been a growing concern with equal employment opportunity in the public sector and with the possibility of making public bureaucracies representative institutions. This study differs from related ones in that it concentrates on the politics of the Federal Equal Employment Opportunity Program. In so doing, it sheds light on the nature of bureaucratic politics in the federal government and provides a lesson in how administration may be infused with politics. It shows the extent to which organizational and administrative choices may be political choices and how agencies can use their control over the implementation of policies to protect their "cultures" and values. The analysis suggests that the equal employment opportunity (EEO) policy arena is dominated by a contest between those who seek to maintain the merit system as it has traditionally existed and those who seek a far more representative federal service. It is argued not only that "representationists" have made substantial inroads on federal personnel policy, but that representation will occupy a key position in the public personnel administration of the future. In addition, this book differs from others in its attempt to explore fully the nature of the contemporary EEO "problem" and to evaluate EEO policies from the perspective of their contributions to its resolution. Hence, it is also a study in public policy, but implicit in the central argument is the belief that the organizational politics of EEO policy will continue to dominate its content.

This study is an outgrowth of my experience as an American Society for Public Administration (ASPA) fellow with the Office of Federal Equal Employment Opportunity of the U.S. Civil Service Commission (CSC) during the 1970-71 academic year. I am indebted to both ASPA and the CSC for this experience. Among those to whom special thanks are due are Ms. Helene Markoff, a former director of the Federal Women's Program, and Professor Peter N. Grabosky for his assistance with the material contained in the first chapter. I am also grateful to Susan Brannigan, Jeanette Featherstonehaugh, Peter Carl Flood, and Gail A. Nicholas for their valuable aid in preparing the manuscript for publication.

Thanks are also due to *Social Science Quarterly* for permission to use parts of Peter N. Grabosky's and my article, "Racial and Ethnic Integration in the Federal Service" (56 [June 1975]: 71-84), in Chapter 1; to the *Western*

Political Quarterly for permission to use parts of my article, "The Civil Service Commission's Decision to Authorize the Use of Goals and Timetables in the Federal Equal Employment Opportunity Program" (26 [June 1973] : 236-51), in Chapter 5; and to *Midwest Review of Public Administration* for permission to use parts of my article, "Implementing Equal Employment Opportunity Goals and Timetables in the Federal Service" (9 [April/July 1975] : 107-20), in Chapter 5.

CONTENTS

LIST OF TABLES

LIST OF ABBREVIATIONS

ACLU	American Civil Liberties Union
ADP	Automatic data processing
AEC	Atomic Energy Commission
AFGE	American Federation of Government Employees
ARB	(CSC) Appeals Review Board
ASPA	American Society for Public Administration
BAR	(CSC) Board of Appeals and Review
BMIS	(CSC) Bureau of Manpower Information Systems
BPI	(CSC) Bureau of Personnel Investigations
BPME	(CSC) Bureau of Personnel Management Evaluation
BPS	(CSC) Bureau of Policies and Standards
BRE	(CSC) Bureau of Recruiting and Examining
CAB	Civil Aeronautics Board
CCR	(U.S.) Commission on Civil Rights
CSC	(U.S.) Civil Service Commission
DOD	Department of Defense
DOT	Department of Transportation
EEO	Equal employment opportunity
EEOC	Equal Employment Opportunity Commission
EPO	Employment policy officer
FCC	Federal Communications Commission
FEB	Fair Employment Board
FEO	Fair employment officer
FEP	Fair Employment Program
FEPC	Fair Employment Practice Committee
FSA	Federal Security Agency
FSEE	Federal Service Entrance Examination
FTC	Federal Trade Commission
FWP	(EEO) Federal Women's Program
GAO	General Accounting Office
GPO	Government Printing Office
GS	General schedule
GSA	General Services Administration
HEW	Department of Health, Education, and Welfare
HUD	Department of Housing and Urban Development
ICC	Interstate Commerce Commission
MV	Measure of variation

NAACP	National Association for the Advancement of Colored People
NASA	National Aeronautics and Space Administration
NCSL	National Civil Service League
NFFE	National Federation of Federal Employees
ODM	Office of Defense Mobilization
OEM	Office of Emergency Management
OFEEO	Office of Federal Equal Employment Opportunity
OMB	Office of Management and Budget
OPM	Office of Production Management
PACE	Professional and Administrative Careers Examination
PCEEO	President's Committee on Equal Employment Opportunity
PCGEP	President's Committee on Government Employment Policy
PCSW	Presidential Commission on the Status of Women
SBA	Small Business Administration
SM	Scientific management
SSP	(EEO) Spanish-Speaking Program
VA	Veterans Administration

Federal Equal Employment Opportunity

The U.S. federal bureaucracy is a vast and complex organization. It is composed of an array of units, including departments, agencies, bureaus, commissions, institutes, and corporations. Their diverse missions and objectives range from providing for the common defense and overseeing the national economy to assuring that all Americans have a nutritious diet and administering a nationwide system of public parks. Some of its units, such as the Departments of State and Defense, are well known, but the existence of others, including the Railroad Retirement Board, the American Battle Monuments Commission, and the Board on Geographic Names, would come as a surprise to many citizens. Its human composition is equally varied. Its employees, distributed throughout the 50 states and many foreign lands, include doctors, lawyers, accountants, scientists, typists, postal carriers, program managers, and others who are engaged in a host of additional occupations as well. Federal employees are overwhelmingly anonymous to the American public and their image is somewhat negative.[1] They play a crucial role in governance, however, and who they are and how they are selected are among the most important questions one could ask about the federal government and politics in the United States.

Unfortunately, this reality has been obscured by several factors. For instance, the basically unfavorable image of federal bureaucrats that is held by the general public has contributed to the notion that they are inefficient paper shufflers wrapped up in red tape, rendered inarticulate by obtuse, arcane, and unnecessary verbiage, and consequently unable to perform any positive functions. An earlier generation of political scientists and administrative theorists arrived at a similar conclusion through a different approach. Traditionally, they drew a rather rigid distinction between politics and administration,[2] conceiving

1

of these as two distinct functions that could not be combined without a resulting loss of efficiency,[3] and denied that public administrators could legitimately exercise policy-making or other political functions. Sociologists, too, have fostered the idea that the human composition of bureaucracies is of secondary importance or even inconsequential. By concentrating on the structural aspects of bureaucratic organizations and how these influence behavior, they have sometimes come to view the individual bureaucrat as little more than a powerless and interchangeable cog in a complex organizational machine.[4] Finally, in their almost reflexive, incessant attacks on "the bureaucracy," American politicians, while accepting the reality of bureaucratic power, have also furthered the belief that this power is seldom used for legitimate purposes.[5]

More recent approaches, however, have begun to stress the positive side of public bureaucracy, its full politicality, and the extent to which the social background of bureaucrats affects their behavior. Thus, today most political observers would probably agree with Wallace Sayre that

> the staffs of the executive branch agencies have come to exercise an important share of the initiative, formulation, the bargaining and the deciding process by which governmental decisions are taken. They are widely acknowledged to be the leading "experts" as to the facts upon which issues are to be settled; they are often permitted to identify authoritatively the broad alternatives available as solutions; and they frequently are allowed to fix the vocabulary of the formal decision. These powers are shared and used by the career staffs in an environment of struggle and competition for influence, but the relatively new fact to be noted with emphasis is that others who share powers of decision—the President, Congress, the political executives, the congressional committees and staffs, the interest groups, the communications media—now rarely question the legitimacy of the career staff spokesmen as major participants in the competition.
>
> Great power also belongs naturally to those who carry out decisions of public policy. In this stage, the career staffs have had a paramount role. The choices of means, the pace and tone of governmental performance, reside largely in the hands of the federal service. Constraints are present, and most of these uses of discretion by the career staffs are subject to bargaining with other participants, but the civil servants have a position of distinct advantage in determining how public policies are executed.[6]

Indeed, so central are the political and policy-making roles of the federal service that at least one contemporary observer has gone so far as to argue that government would come to a standstill if federal bureaucrats suddenly began acting in the apolitical fashion so highly desired by administrative theorists of an earlier generation.[7]

For those accustomed to thinking about the federal government in terms of three separate branches, with the bureaucracy being "under" the president, the political nature of the federal service may be somewhat difficult to grasp. It should therefore be noted that, whatever the formal lines of political authority running to and through the bureaucracy, in practice a great deal of political power is formally and informally delegated to it by the other branches. Thus, within broad guidelines established by Congress and the president, federal agencies have authority to regulate many areas of American life. For instance, the nature, quality, and price of domestic shipping and transportation are largely determined by the Interstate Commerce Commission (ICC), the Civil Aeronautics Board (CAB), and the Department of Transportation (DOT); the Department of Agriculture makes policies that affect the supply, price, and purity of the food we eat; the Federal Communications Commission (FCC) oversees television and radio programming; the Department of Housing and Urban Development (HUD) has a considerable impact on the nature of urban environments and housing throughout the nation; and so on. The Equal Employment Opportunity Act of 1972 presents a typical example of the process through which administrative agencies gain a great deal of political power. The objective of the act is to eliminate discrimination based on race, ethnicity, religion, or sex from various walks of American life and to insure that all citizens have an equal opportunity for advancement through employment and education. It is administered by several agencies and, by and large, leaves the choice of means for implementation and enforcement to their discretion. Despite considerable opposition to the approach, several of these agencies, most notably the Department of Health, Education, and Welfare (HEW), have chosen to rely on the use of numerical goals (similar to quotas) for insuring that members of minority groups and women receive equal educational opportunities and equal opportunity for employment by educational institutions. Moreover, HEW has issued guidelines for the equal treatment of students by schools and universities and has even offered criteria for the selection of nonracist and nonsexist textbooks. As a result, HEW's reach currently extends to some of the most important personnel and policy choices made by educational institutions; it is consequently in a position to exercise a great deal of control over the nature of education in the United States. Whatever the desirability of this situation, it illustrates that when Congress allows administrative agencies to "fill in the details," as it frequently does, federal bureaucrats *must* exercise a great deal of political discretion in simply attempting to do their jobs. Furthermore, because they must defend the choices they make and organize support for them, bureaucrats and the federal service as a whole are inevitably and deeply entrenched in political processes.

Federal bureaucrats, then, make public policies that in one way or another touch the life of every American. Consequently, in recent years more attention has been paid to who they are. The earlier sociological tradition of considering bureaucrats to be automatons has been increasingly rejected in favor of one which argues that "the behavior of government bureaucrats varies with the non-governmental social background and interests of those controlling the bureaucratic structure."[8] Indeed, the question of the human composition of public bureaucracies has risen to the forefront of political concerns in the contemporary world. The intensity of this matter is well conveyed by Samuel Krislov:

> The failure of a white, middle-class administered poverty program to stir up much except controversy is related to its social bearing. In New York City an educational crisis is best understood as a conflict of values between a rabidly suspicious Black community and a bureaucracy—largely Jewish—which finds departures from its own sense of academic priorities personally threatening. In Nigeria a civil war has emerged from the fantastic success of the Ibos in securing bureaucratic power over other tribes through personal efficiency—an efficiency which could only be dealt with by the massacre of the Ibos. Fear of similar conflict reluctantly led the Tunku, Abdul Rahmin, premier of the Malaysian states, to suggest dismemberment of the Union so that the energetically successful Chinese concentrated in Singapore would not arouse the animosity of his compatriots. In short, throughout the world, bureaucracy is the blood, bone, and sinews of political power.[9]

Consequently, in the view of some, "Who writes the [bureaucratic] directive—his or her style, values, concept of role—is as significant as who gets to be president, congressman, senator, member of parliament, or cabinet member."[10]

These concerns reach to the heart of the importance of the Federal Equal Employment Opportunity Program. For the program plays an increasingly large role in determining who gets positions in the federal bureaucracy and at what level. It therefore bears directly upon the distribution of political power, authority, and influence in the United States. Hence, it is not surprising that federal EEO policy has been the center of a great deal of interest and political conflict over the past three decades, or that it remains a hotly contested program and policy area at the present time. It also stands to reason that a proper place to begin an exploration of the Federal EEO Program is with a thoroughgoing analysis of the social composition of the federal service and its political ramifications.

THE SOCIAL COMPOSITION OF THE FEDERAL SERVICE

Who, then, are the federal bureaucrats and why is the social composition of the federal service such that an EEO program has been developed at all? One could address these matters in several ways, for, depending on the political and social context of the nation and the historical period involved, different responses are appropriate. The fact cannot be overstressed that not only is the social composition of a national bureaucracy of great political consequence, the ways in which it is viewed are also highly political. For example, in some nations, including Northern Ireland and Lebanon, religion is of major concern when considering the social composition of the national bureaucracy. In others, such as Canada and Belgium, language is of paramount importance. In still other circumstances, the social class background of civil servants, their educational attainments, their ages, their occupations, and the regions from which they are drawn could be of importance. In the United States, three elements of the social composition of the federal service have been politicized at one time or another. Today the major elements are 1) race and ethnicity, and 2) sex. In the past, the social class background of federal servants has also been the basis of political controversy and political action.

Race and Ethnicity

There are several plausible ways of assessing the racial and ethnic composition of the federal service. At the outset it must be noted that these are inherently limited by the fact that the federal government classifies its employees according to the following racial and ethnic groups: blacks, Spanish-surnameds, American Indians, Orientals, and all others. This approach has been adopted for political reasons, and while it might be administratively and analytically rational to maintain data in terms of religious affiliation and to include other ethnic groups, such as Italians, Poles, and so forth, in the classification system, the government has not seen fit to do so.

The first step in analyzing the available data on the racial and ethnic composition of the federal service is to consider the information presented in Table 1. The table shows the number and percentage of employees in the different general schedule (GS) grades who belong to the various racial and ethnic groups. The general schedule is the government's most politically and administratively important career pay system, and it includes about half of all federal employees. It is evident from the table that although members of the minority groups under consideration constitute a sizable proportion of all federal servants in the general schedule, they are heavily concentrated in the lower levels. Thus, whereas grade GS-1 is about 47 percent minority, grade GS-18 is only about 4 percent minority. Minorities constitute about 17 percent of all general schedule employees, but they hold less than this proportion of the positions in all the grades above GS-8. This pattern is especially prevalent among blacks, who constitute 37 percent of the employees in grade GS-1 and only 2.4 percent of those in grade GS-18. At the same time it should be noted that, unlike other minority groups, Orientals tend to be concentrated in the middle rather than in the lower or upper grades. Nonminority employees, on the other hand, have a pattern which is the

TABLE 1

Racial and Ethnic Composition of the Federal Service, 1974

Pay System	Total Full-Time Employees	Total Minority Employees		Black		Spanish-Surnamed		American Indian		Oriental		All Other Employees	
		Number	%	Number	%	Number	%	Number	%	Number	%	Number	%
Total all pay system	2,433,483	510,061	21.0	390,361	16.0	78,972	3.2	19,663	.8	21,065	.9	1,923,422	79.0
Total general schedule or similar	1,354,451	230,126	17.0	171,658	12.7	33,125	2.4	13,265	1.0	12,078	.9	1,124,325	83.0
GS-1-4	317,605	90,642	28.5	69,700	21.9	12,056	3.8	6,625	2.1	2,261	.7	226,963	71.5
GS-5-8	412,483	87,062	21.1	68,413	16.6	11,377	2.8	3,658	.9	3,614	.9	325,421	78.9
GS-9-11	308,315	33,392	10.8	22,075	7.2	6,208	2.0	1,932	.6	3,177	1.0	274,923	89.2
GS-12-13	233,384	14,866	6.4	8,994	3.9	2,718	1.2	822	.4	2,332	1.0	218,518	93.6
GS-14-15	77,321	3,953	5.1	2,327	3.0	736	1.0	221	.3	669	.9	73,368	94.9
GS-16-18	5,343	211	3.9	149	2.8	30	.6	7	.1	25	.5	5,132	96.1

Source: U.S. Civil Service Commission, *Minority Group Employment in the Federal Government* (Washington, D.C.: Government Printing Office, May 1974), Table 1-001, p. 3.

reverse of that for minority groups: they constitute a far greater proportion of the employees at the top levels than at the bottom.

Representation

Another way of addressing the racial and ethnic composition of the federal service is to assess the extent to which it reflects the racial and ethnic composition of the society as a whole. The most common approach for so doing is to compute the ratio of the percentage of minority group members in the federal service and its various components to the percentage of members of these groups in the society as a whole. The resultant figure is generally called the index of representation, which equals

$$\frac{\text{percentage of minority group members in the federal service, agency, and so on.}}{\text{percentage of minority group members in the entire national population}}$$

Using this index, a value of 1.0 signifies perfect proportional representation; values less than 1.0 indicate that minorities are underrepresented; and values greater than 1.0 indicate that they are overrepresented. Table 2 presents the indexes of representation for each of the minority groups under consideration in the general schedule in 1975. It shows that, with the exception of the Spanish-surnamed group, minorities are actually overrepresented in a proportional sense in the general schedule, and that some of them are very much so. As discussed earlier, however, they are heavily concentrated in the lower levels and underrepresented in the higher and more politically important levels.

TABLE 2

Proportional Representation of Racial and Ethnic Groups in the General Schedule, 1975

Group	Percent in GS	Percent in Society	Index of Representation
Blacks	12.6	11.1	1.14
Spanish-surnameds	2.5	4.5	.56
American Indians	1.1	0.4	2.75
Orientals	0.9	0.5	1.80
All others	82.9	84.4	.98

Source: *The World Almanac, 1975* (New York: Newspaper Enterprise Association, 1975); U.S. Bureau of the Census, *Statistical Abstract,* 1974, pp. 26, 30; U.S. Civil Service Commission, *Civil Service News,* April 6, 1976, table 1 a.

Although historical data are not available for the other groups, Table 3 displays the evolutionary trend with regard to blacks in the federal service as a whole. It shows that blacks went from a position of proportional underrepresentation in 1940, a year before the Federal EEO Program began, to a position of overrepresentation by 1960. To the extent that these changes can be attributed to the program itself, it appears that it has had a substantial impact.[11]

The information presented thus far leads to an important conclusion: Although the misrepresentation of members of minority groups in the bureaucracy was, at one time, a major problem involving the social composition of the federal service, as defined by political authorities and the political community in general, the problem today involves the maldistribution of these citizens throughout the grade structure. In other words, the problem of minority entry into the federal service as a whole has been more or less resolved; the present problem concerns their concentration in the lower grades. This basic change in the nature of the EEO "problem" has had important policy repercussions: the program has shifted in emphasis from recruitment of minorities to insuring their advancement through the ranks.

The index of representation is useful, but it must be applied with caution since it possesses some significant limitations in describing the social composition of the federal service. It is largely based upon the belief that,

> while an oversimplification, a normal distribution of racial minorities should occur in employment, unless specific overt actions are taken to increase or decrease this distribution. For example, the percentage utilization of Negroes in the federal government should be approximately equal to the percentage of Negroes in the total population.[12]

TABLE 3

Black Representation in the Federal Service, 1940-75

Year	Black Federal Employment (%)	Black Population in United States (%)	Index of Representation
1940	4.2	9.8	.42
1950	9.3	10.0	.93
1960	11.7	10.6	1.10
1970	15.0	11.2	1.33
1975	15.9	11.1	1.43

Source: Don Hellriegel and Larry Short, "Equal Employment Opportunity in the Federal Government: A Comparative Analysis," *Public Administration Review* 32 (November/December 1972), Table 1, p. 854.

Unfortunately, this logic ignores several intervening variables that may make the findings obtained misleading. For instance, the distribution of groups within the working-age population could be of importance. Thus, in 1969, 46.8 percent of all Spanish-surnameds, as compared to only 25.6 percent of all other Americans, were under the age of 18 years. Similarly, attention should be paid to the geographical distribution of groups and how well this coincides with the distribution of government jobs. One would also have to look at the population with requisite educational levels and occupational skills in some instances. Finally, the essence of minority group status may well be an adherence to a substantially different culture, and not all cultures place an equal prestige value on public employment. Consequently, some groups are more predisposed to seek bureaucratic employment than are others. In theory there is perhaps no reason why all of this cannot be taken into account in a representational index; in practice, however, the necessary data simply do not exist.

A more fundamental limitation of the index is that it does not provide adequate information concerning the overall degree of *integration* in a civil service or a bureaucratic agency. It may be able to tell us whether blacks and other groups are over-, under-, or perfectly represented in a proportional sense, but unless every group under consideration is perfectly represented, there is little if anything one can say concerning the general racial and ethnic integration of the bureaucracy. What, for example, can be said if we are confronted with the following data? "In General Schedule positions in the Department of the Interior the index of representation for blacks is .4, for Spanish-surnameds, .8, for American Indians, 42.3, and for all other employees it is .9; whereas in similar positions in the Justice Department the respective figures are .9, 1.2, .3, and 1.0." Obviously, a different approach is necessary when considering the social composition of various agencies and the determinants of this composition.

Integration

One of the few methods for measuring integration in public bureaucracies is called the measure of variation (MV).[13] It measures the heterogeneity of specified social characteristics found in a group of people and transforms this value into an index. It varies from 0 to 1.0, and the closer it is to 1.0 the more equally represented are the groups under analysis. Using this measure, it is possible to obtain a single summary figure for the degree of integration—in the sense of heterogeneity—in an agency, an entire bureaucracy, and in individual occupations, grades, or grade groups. Moreover, it is possible to measure changes in levels of integration over a period of time and to investigate their causes.

Table 4 presents the integration of grade groupings for the period 1967-1975. Several aspects of racial and ethnic integration in the federal service are evident from the table. First, as would be expected from the data in Table 1,

TABLE 4

Integration in the Federal Service by Grade Groupings, 1967-73

| | Measure of Variation (MV) | | | | | | | |
Grades (GS)	1967	1969	1970	1971	1972	1973	1974	1975
1-4	.50	.52	.54	.53	.54	.54	.55	.51
5-8	.33	.36	.38	.39	.40	.42	.44	.44
9-11	.16	.19	.20	.20	.21	.22	.24	.24
12-13	.09	.11	.12	.12	.13	.14	.13	.16
14-15	.06	.08	.09	.10	.11	.12	.10	.13
16-18	.04	.04	.06	.07	.08	.09	.08	.08
All	.30	.31	.32	.33	.34	.35	.36	.37

N = Number on which sample is based = 19 agencies.

Note: The agencies analyzed contain about 96 percent of all general schedule employment and 50 percent of all federal employment. The only sizable agency omitted is the post office, which has its own grade system and is less interesting from a policy perspective.

Source: Compiled by the author.

the lower grades are far more integrated than the upper grades. Indeed, by 1967, grades 1-8 were actually more integrated, in the sense of being heterogeneous, than is the United States as a whole, for which an MV value of about .30 is obtained. Compared to the society at large, grades GS 9-11 are fairly well integrated, whereas grades 12-18 are poorly integrated. Thus, the degree of integration varies inversely with grade level, but more importantly, there is a sharp drop in integration at the primary policy-making levels. From the perspective of the political consequences of the social composition of national bureaucracies, the importance of this fact cannot be overemphasized.

Table 4 also indicates that the federal service as a whole, and each of the grade groups except the lowest, is becoming more integrated. Moreover, the amount of increase in terms of raw differences in the MV has been roughly the same for each of these grade groups. This indicates that although upward mobility for minority groups has become more important in terms of the thrust of the Federal EEO Program in recent years, there has not been a drop in integration at the lower levels during the period under consideration. Insofar as the major aim of the program is to further integration in the federal service, these data indicate that the program's objective is being served. There is, nevertheless, still a very long way to go before grades GS 12-18 can be considered to be well integrated.

Turning from a consideration of the federal service in terms of grades to an analysis of agencies, we can further describe the social composition of the federal service. Table 5 presents MV scores for 19 agencies in 1967 and 1974. It indicates that there are considerable differences in levels of agency integration

TABLE 5

Racial and Ethnic Integration of Selected Federal Agencies, 1967, 1974

Agency	MV 1967	MV 1974	Increase in Integration (MV 1974–MV 1967)
General Accounting Office	.31	.35	.04
NASA	.09	.15	.06
Small Business Administration	.30	.31	.01
Equal Employment Opportunity Commission	.72	.76	.04
Government Printing Office	.63	.63	.00
Civil Service Commission	.46	.57	.11
Defense (entire)	.25	.28	.03
Army	.27	.28	.01
Navy	.08	.26	.18
Air Force	.22	.26	.04
Justice	.22	.29	.07
HEW	.49	.56	.07
HUD	.37	.47	.10
Commerce	.34	.40	.06
State	.54	.62	.08
Transportation	.14	.23	.09
Treasury	.29	.36	.07
Agriculture	.17	.22	.05
Interior	.38	.42	.04
Labor	.48	.57	.09
Veterans Administration	.47	.60	.13
General Services Administration	.45	.55	.10

Source: Compiled by the author.

and in amounts of change during the six-year period. The range of increase is from .00 in the Government Printing Office (GPO) to .18 in the Department of the Navy. The mean increase for all agencies was .07. On the whole, the more-integrated agencies in 1967 registered the greatest increases over the period. However, the experience of the Small Business Administration (SBA), DOT, and especially the Department of the Navy indicates that it is possible for agencies that are not highly integrated to rapidly increase their levels of integration. In order to explain the variation in agency scores, the impact of agency size and growth on agency integration should be explored.

Size

Organizational theorists have considered size to be an important explanatory variable and have found it to be a significant correlate of some forms of organizational behavior, including the formalization of authority structures and employee satisfaction.[14] One could hypothesize that the larger an agency, the less likely it is to be integrated. This is so because the larger the agency, the less important to its overall integration will be the addition of each minority group employee; given the fact that an overwhelming number of positions existed before the equal employment program was effectively implemented, large agencies are consequently more likely to be less integrated. Implicit in this line of reasoning are two assumptions concerning turnover. First, turnover rates in the general schedule positions of the agencies under consideration could be so small as to be inconsequential. Second, if turnover rates were significant, they might be expected to be higher in smaller agencies than in larger ones because large agencies tend to be established organizations with more stable general schedule work forces. If this were the case, smaller agencies would have a greater opportunity to change the composition of their work forces. Unfortunately, sufficient data are not available to evaluate these assumptions, although those available do suggest that turnover, while uneven, can be substantial.[15] However, the expected negative relationship between agency size and integration is borne out by the findings reported in Table 6. These results suggest that special efforts may be necessary in the larger agencies to increase levels of integration.

Growth

It is also logical to assume that agency growth can have an impact on levels of social integration. It is generally considered easier to increase the proportion

TABLE 6

Relationship Between Agency Size and Agency Integration, 1967-74

Year	Correlation Coefficients (r)
1967	-.24
1969	-.27
1970	-.29
1971	-.31
1972	-.30
1973	-.30
1974	-.26

N = 19 agencies.
Source: Compiled by the author.

of new positions going to minority group members than to increase the minority component primarily by replacing nonminorities. This is especially true in view of the difficulties involved in making removals for reasons other than reductions in force in the federal service. Furthermore, minorities historically have made their greatest employment gains during periods of expanding employment and have suffered disproportionately from umemployment during periods of contracting employment. Upon analysis, however, no evidence to support this expectation can be found. Correlations between raw agency growth and raw MV change, between raw agency growth and percent MV change, between percent agency growth and percent MV change, as well as between percent agency growth and raw MV change, show no meaningful associations. These results may be attributed to several factors. For instance, to some extent agency growth is a function of merger and reorganization and therefore does not necessarily require new hiring. In addition, some agencies, including the State Department, the Department of the Interior, the Department of Defense (DOD), and National Aeronautics and Space Administration (NASA), declined in size but not in integration.

It is apparent that most of the variance in agency integration remains unexplained by the structural factors of size and growth. To a considerable extent, agency integration appears to be related to mission and work process. The most integrated agencies tend to fall into one of two categories. First, agencies such as the Departments of Labor, HEW, HUD, and the Equal Opportunity Commission (EEOC) have missions which stress a commitment to equality and helping the disadvantaged. This commitment is evidently reflected in their internal personnel policies and/or is related to their ability to attract qualified minority group members. This could also be said to be true of the CSC, which currently administers the Federal EEO Program and the SBA, which has recently been concerned with aiding minority capitalism. A second category of highly integrated agencies includes, among others, the General Services Administration (GSA) and the GPO, which have a large proportion of positions in the lower grades and engage in factory-type operations or tasks in which minority group members are often concentrated.

Agencies having low levels of integration also tend to fall into two major categories. Some, such as NASA and DOT, have far more positions in their upper levels than in their lower grades. Given the information in Table 4, this would obviously militate against the achievement of a high level of integration. Others, such as the Department of Agriculture and the Navy, are less integrated perhaps because of past discrimination and lack of concern with minority groups. There are, of course, some agencies which do not fit these tendencies, such as the State Department, and others which fit more than one, such as the Veterans Administration (VA), which has about four times as many positions below GS 10 as it does above that grade; it also has a significant number of minority group members among its clientele.

Integration in the Higher Grades

It is important to qualify these findings with regard to agency integration by pointing out that few agencies are well integrated in the higher grades. Table 7 presents the integration levels of grades GS 14-18, which are the primary policy-making grades in the career service for the agencies under consideration. It indicates that although there is considerable variation, and while most agencies are becoming more integrated at these levels, the overwhelming number of agencies are still poorly integrated at their policy-making levels. In fact, only EEOC, HEW, Labor, and HUD can be considered at least reasonably well integrated. For the most part, then, there are few exceptions to the dominant pattern found in the racial and ethnic composition of the federal service: members of minority groups are overwhelmingly found in lower levels in most agencies, and

TABLE 7

Racial and Ethnic Integration of Grades GS 14-18 Among Selected Federal Agencies 1967, 1974

Agency	MV 1967	MV 1974
General Accounting Office	.01	.04
NASA	.03	.05
Small Business Administration	.06	.18
EEOC	.71	.76
Government Printing Office	.00	.18
Civil Service Commission	.06	.16
Defense (entire)	.03	.06
Army	.03	.07
Navy	.03	.06
Air Force	.03	.07
Justice	.03	.09
HEW	.10	.24
HUD	.12	.26
Commerce	.06	.13
State	.07	.12
Transportation	.02	.09
Treasury	.03	.08
Agriculture	.02	.07
Interior	.09	.13
Labor	.16	.28
Veterans Administration	.17	.20
General Services Administration	.02	.11

Source: Compiled by the author.

they are generally excluded from policy-making positions. Hence, policymaking in the career component of the federal service tends to take place in a social environment which is considerably different from that of the nation as a whole.

Tipping

Another interesting question concerning the racial and ethnic composition of the federal service is whether some agencies have "tipped," in the sense of becoming less integrated as a result of the addition of more minority group members. This phenomenon is potentially of great importance to the Federal EEO Program because it may force a policy choice between, on the one hand, seeking a representative, integrated federal service and, on the other, stressing increased minority employment as the primary objective. To the extent that "tipping" is prevalent, integration may require special efforts to recruit and retain nonminorities.

In analyzing this aspect of the EEO problem, it is important to note that the concept of tipping involves two different ideas. Generally, according to Krislov, when more than 50 percent of the personnel within agency grades or offices are drawn from minorities, nonminorities begin to leave at a rapid rate.[16] Tipping can also occur as a result of increases in the number of minority group employees even if there is no effort by nonminorities to leave the grades or offices involved. In the latter instance, the nonminority component would be decreasing as a proportion of all employment, but not in terms of raw numbers. Tipping in this sense could be said to occur when the unit becomes less heterogeneous as a result of increased minority group employment.

Using the MV, it is possible to locate two cases of tipping in the latter sense. Between 1972 and 1973 the MV score for the Government Printing Office decreased from .64 to .63, while that of the EEOC declined from .78 to .76. Upon analysis, it is evident that the decrease in integration in the Government Printing Office was due to an increase in the number of black employees from 1,004 in 1972 to 1,186 in 1973, representing a rise in agency general schedule employment from 48.5 to 51.4 percent.[17] At the same time, the number of nonminority employees increased from 1,046 to 1,095, but their representation in the agency's general schedule positions dropped from 50.5 to 47.5 percent. The representation of Spanish-surnamed individuals, American Indians, and Orientals, taken together, remained virtually constant. Thus, the Government Printing Office's general schedule work force can be said to have tipped by becoming less integrated as a result of increased black employment. Similarly, increased black employment in the EEOC was also associated with declining integration. Blacks increased from 594 (48.3 percent) to 786 (49.7 percent), while the number of nonminority persons in the agency's general schedule work force increased from 442 to 567; in proportional terms, the latter declined from 35.9 percent to 35.8 percent. In this case, however, other minority group

employment also decreased as a proportion of agency general schedule employment from 15.8 percent (195) to 14.5 percent (229). This suggests that tipping
can also occur where one minority group makes proportional gains at the
expense of another, and that interminority group competition for federal service
positions can be of considerable importance to current EEO objectives. This
matter will subsequently be explored in greater detail.

Whether these cases of tipping will be reversed in the future remains to
be seen. Although black employment in both agencies reached the 50 percent
mark by 1974, their MV scores remained constant, which suggests that agencies
may hover around a tipping point for a period. However, the findings presented
here strongly suggest that the federal EEO problem is entering a new stage. In
general, the problem of minority entrance into agencies has been resolved. In
its wake, however, is the related matter of minority *impaction* in the lower
grades and, increasingly, in certain agencies as a whole. This tendency may ultimately have profound consequences for the nature of federal EEO.

WOMEN

The sexual composition of the federal service has also been of political
importance at various times in American history. Today, the pattern of female
employment is somewhat similar to that of minority groups. Table 8 presents
the employment of women in the white-collar component of the federal service
for the year 1974, the latest year for which data are readily available. It indicates
that women, like members of minority groups, are disproportionately concentrated in the lower grades. Thus, although women constitute about 35 percent of
the federal white-collar work force, they hold less than 2 percent of all the
positions in the highest career grade (GS-18). Moreover, they hold only about
10 percent of all positions over grade GS-9. As in the case of minority groups,
the relative exclusion of women is very pronounced in the most important
policy-making positions in the career structure. Given the fact that their overall
representation in the federal service is similar to their representation in the
nation's work force, it is evident that the major EEO problem concerning
women is not their entry into federal positions, but rather their promotion and
advancement within it.

A more sophisticated picture of the sexual composition of the federal
service may be obtained by examining the employment of women in the major
agencies. Table 9 shows the percentage of women employed by 20 major federal agencies in 1966 and 1974. It indicates that there is considerable variability.
The work forces of some agencies, including HEW, the CSC, and the VA, are
over 50 percent female. Other agencies, such as NASA, DOT, the Department
of Agriculture, and the General Accounting Office (GAO), employ a considerably
smaller proportion of women than does the federal service as a whole. To
some extent, it appears that female employment, like minority employment,

TABLE 8

Full-Time White-Collar Employment of Women According to GS and Equivalent Grades, 1974

GS and Equivalent Grade	Total	Women	
		Number	Percent
1	3,950	2,840	71.9
2	32,301	24,858	77.0
3	111,522	86,341	77.4
4	173,593	129,823	74.8
5	183,708	119,281	64.9
6	83,399	55,923	67.1
7	131,932	57,178	43.3
8	30,837	15,157	49.2
9	148, 241	45,172	30.5
10	21,682	5,140	23.7
11	148,785	23,228	15.6
12	137,373	12,555	9.1
13	108,406	5,854	5.4
14	52,653	2,215	4.2
15	29,091	1,078	3.7
16	5,082	130	2.6
17	1,654	33	2.0
18	451	7	1.6
Total	1,404,660	586,813	41.8

Source: U.S. Civil Service Commission, Civil Service News, October 6, 1975, table c.

is related to factors of mission and structure. For example, among those agencies employing a high percentage of women are HEW, the Department of Labor, and the CSC, all of which have broad social missions aimed at women as a group. Agencies with a large proportion of positions in the lower half of the GS also tend to employ a greater proportion of women. This is true, for instance, of the GPO and the VA. Conversely, NASA, which has more than two-thirds of its positions above GS-9, employs a very low proportion of women. DOT displays a similar pattern. In general, it also appears that, unlike the case of minority groups, the larger agencies (Treasury, Army, Navy, Air Force, HEW, and VA) tend to employ a higher proportion of women. The Department of Agriculture and DOT, however, are important exceptions to this generalization.

Finally, it should be noted that the sexual composition of the federal service has not changed much in recent years. Between 1966 and 1974 the proportion of women in the federal service grew slightly, but as Table 9 indicates, only a few agencies increased the proportion of women in their work forces.

TABLE 9

Female Employment in White-Collar Positions
According to Agency, 1966-74

Agency	1966 Percentage of Women	1974 Percentage of Women	1966-74 Percent Change
GAO	27.0	25.2	-1.8
GPO	53.3	48.7	-4.6
State	35.4	34.8	-0.6
Treasury	42.5	43.8	1.3
Army	46.7	42.3	-4.4
Navy	43.6	38.6	-5.0
Air Force	49.8	42.8	-7.0
Justice	35.1	33.4	-1.7
Interior	29.7	30.4	0.7
Agriculture	25.4	23.0	-2.4
Commerce	31.7	34.7	3.0
Labor	46.7	45.1	-1.6
HEW	57.7	60.1	2.4
HUD	40.7	40.3	-0.4
CSC	52.6	56.1	3.5
GSA	39.2	39.5	0.3
NASA	23.2	18.2	-5.0
SBA	47.6	47.0	-0.6
VA	49.6	55.4	5.8
DOT	--	16.7	--

Source: U.S. Civil Service Commission, *Federal Civilian Employment of Women,* 1969, table c, pp. 20-91 and *Civil Service News,* October 6, 1975, table c.

In addition, there have been only modest increases in the proportion of women employed in the policy-making grades.

MINORITY OR MINORITIES?

Thus far it has been observed that the central problem currently confronting federal EEO is politically defined and does not involve proportional underrepresentation of members of minority groups and women in the federal service; rather, it concerns their maldistribution throughout its ranks and component parts. In addition, it has been noted that such elements as agency structure and mission have a bearing on these patterns. Furthermore, it has been shown that although considerable progress toward racial and ethnic integration has been made throughout the federal structure, women have made only limited

TABLE 10

Percentage Distribution of the Federal Work Force
According to Sex and Social Background Within Grade
Groupings, and Equivalent Grades, 1972
(percentage distribution)

Grade Grouping	Total		Minority		Nonminority	
	Men	Women	Men	Women	Men	Women
GS 1-4	24.0	76.0	8.0	20.5	16.0	55.6
GS 5-8	43.2	56.8	7.5	12.2	35.6	44.6
GS 9-11	82.2	17.8	6.5	3.0	75.8	14.8
GS 12-13	93.9	6.1	4.9	0.7	89.0	5.4
GS 14-15	96.9	3.1	3.7	0.4	93.2	2.8
GS 16-18	98.2	1.8	3.3	0.2	94.9	1.7
Total	59.7	40.3	6.7	9.3	53.0	31.0

Note: Percentages are rounded off independently and not forced to add to totals. More recent data are unavailable.

Source: U.S. Civil Service Commission, *Federal Civilian Personnel Statistics.* November 30, 1972, p. 5.

gains at best. This suggests that women are categorically different in terms of federal employment and that the program should (and does) recognize this fact. Further evidence of this can be seen in Table 10, which indicates that women, whether members of minority groups or not, are heavily concentrated in the lower ranks and almost entirely excluded from the highest grades. Thus, it appears that women as a group face the greatest difficulties with regard to moving up the federal employment ladder. Moreover, Table 10 indicates that minority women have not benefited "doubly" from federal EEO efforts.

Hence, there is strong evidence that the EEO problem for women is different from that of men. But is each minority group also different from every other group, or can all members of minority groups be treated as a single categorical unit? Table 11 suggests that the employment patterns of blacks, Spanish-surnameds, and native Americans may be similar. Members of these groups are heavily concentrated in the lower grades. However, this is not true of Orientals, whose employment pattern in this regard is closer to that of the "Other" group. Indeed, their distribution in the upper levels compares favorably proportionally speaking, to that of the majority group. It is desirable, therefore, to explore two questions which are of fundamental importance to the nature of federal EEO efforts: 1) Is there substantial competition between racial and

TABLE 11

Distribution of Ethnic and Racial Groups
in the General Schedule, 1975

Group	Percentage of Group Grades 1-8	Percentage of Group Grades 9-18	Group as Percentage of Total GS Employment
Black	79	21	12.6
Spanish-surnamed	69	31	2.5
Native American	78	22	1.1
Oriental	47	53	0.9
Other	49	51	82.9
All	54	46	100.0

Source: U.S. Civil Service Commission, *Civil Service News*, April 26, 1976, Table 1A (unpaged).

ethnic minority groups for federal positions? 2) If not, are the employment patterns of different racial and ethnic groups sufficiently unrelated to indicate that minority employees do not constitute a single bloc?

There are several reasons for assuming that either of these possibilities exists. First, one of the reasons that EEO programs are deemed necessary is the fact that there is a tendency on the part of the society at large to consider some less desirable jobs as primarily "minority jobs." Indeed, the concept of a "black job" has been an important element in fostering racism in the United States, one which, as we shall see in the third chapter, has had considerable application in the federal service. To the extent that such an attitude prevails generally, job competition among minorities is largely restricted to competing against members of their own or other minority groups. Second, minority groups are considerably different from one another in terms of degree of disadvantage and nature of subculture. It is to be expected, therefore, that although they share some common interests and difficulties as minorities, there are also significant areas in which they might have conflicting needs and objectives. Indeed, as Table 11 suggests, Orientals have far less need for EEO policies stressing upward mobility in the federal service than do blacks and native Americans. Overall, Orientals are at least as different from native Americans in terms of subculture and socioeconomic status as they are from the majority group. Again, the decision to define them as a group to which federal EEO efforts are particularly directed has been a political one, and it may be that it cannot be supported on the basis of current employment patterns or social status. The Spanish-surnamed population has not suffered the same degree of cultural destruction as have native Americans and blacks; the latter groups differ radically in many other respects as well. Finally, and more generally, to the extent that assimilation and upward mobility in the United States involve progress along an "urban frontier,"[18] one minority group tends to compete with another for housing, jobs, and, more recently, education. It is important to emphasize that none of this is intended to suggest that competition between individual minority groups and the majority group does not take place at the same time, but rather that competition on another level must be explored as well.

These questions can be investigated by comparing the relationship between changes in the proportion of each racial and ethnic group in the various agency grade levels with changes in that of every other group. Such an analysis is based on the general schedule work forces during the period 1967-73 for those agencies previously considered. In terms of federal EEO, the most important findings presented are those involving the relationships between blacks and the other groups and between the majority group and each of the minority groups. Those findings concerning competition between native Americans and Orientals are of less importance, largely because these groups constitute a relatively small proportion of the U.S. population and there are relatively few of them in the federal service.

Table 12 reflects relationships between changes in the proportion of blacks in the grade groups in the agencies under consideration and changes in the proportions of other groups. It is evident that the overwhelming degree of competition has been between blacks and the majority group. Nevertheless, Table 12 also suggests that there is probably some competition between blacks and the other minority groups in grades GS 1-11. This might be expected to occur at the GS 1-4 level since it is there that the idea of a "minority job" would be of greatest importance. In grades GS 5-8, and especially grades 9-11, any competition that exists can be considered damaging to the objectives of the Federal EEO Program because it is at these levels that the major effort towards upward mobility for minorities has been made. The competition between blacks and Orientals in grades GS 12-13 may be a reflection of the unique distribution pattern of the latter minority group. It should be stressed, however, that given the size and significance levels of these findings with regard to interminority group competition in this context, they must be taken as tentative rather than conclusive.

In any event, the only meaningful, positive relationships between black employment and that of other groups occur in grades GS 12-18, with respect to Spanish-surnameds. This indicates that at these levels the two groups have harmonious patterns. Perhaps this is partly due to the almost total exclusion of both groups from such positions prior to 1967. In other words, their relative absence made competition, as conceptualized here, less likely because it was practically impossible for their employment proportions to decrease between 1967 and 1973.

Table 13 presents the relationships between the majority group's proportional changes and those of each of the minority groups. It indicates that, for

TABLE 12

Relationships Between Changes in Black Employment and Changes in the Employment of Other Racial or Ethnic Groups, 1967-73

| GS Levels | Correlation Coefficients (r) Black Changes and Those of | | | |
	Spanish-Surnameds	Native Americans	Orientals	All Others
1-4	−.26	−.31	−.31	−.87[b]
5-8	−.16	−.32	.18	−.98[b]
9-11	−.33	−.33	−.08	−.87[b]
12-13	.55[a]	−.05	−.51[a]	−.94[b]
14-15	.24	−.08	−.29	−.83[b]
16-18	.63[b]	−.06	.14	−.94[b]

N = 21 agencies

  a P < .01
  b P < .001

Note: Correlation coefficients below .36 are not significant at .05.
Source: Compiled by the author.

the most part, relationships are competitive—majority gains occur in conjunction with minority losses, and vice versa. This is especially true with regard to blacks throughout the general schedule and Spanish-surnameds in the upper levels. Yet the competition also has an uneven quality and in some cases is even nonexistent. This suggests, as do some of the findings reported in Table 12, that to some extent the relative fortunes of the various groups are disconnected. The black versus majority group competition is clear, but beyond that overall patterns are not apparent, perhaps because, as suggested earlier, each agency acts as a relatively separate unit responding to different forces and circumstances.

Table 12 implies that there may be some interminority group competition. However, on the whole the data more strongly suggest that patterns of minority group interaction in federal employment are such that members of these groups cannot be considered as constituting a single bloc. With the exception of the relationship between blacks and Spanish-surnameds in GS levels 12-18, there is little evidence to indicate that what happens to one minority group, in terms of employment pattern, generally has substantial implications for what occurs with regard to others. Consequently, there appears to be no reason to treat minorities as a single unit in the administration of the Federal EEO Program.

The different employment patterns among the minority groups under consideration could be attributed to a number of factors, including subculture, geographic distribution, and different educational levels. However, from the perspective of federal EEO it is also important to determine whether they are

TABLE 13

Relationships Between Changes in Majority Representation
and Changes in Representation of Minority Groups, 1967-73

| GS Levels | Correlation Coefficients (r) Majority Changes and Those of | | | |
	Blacks	Spanish-Surnameds	Native Americans	Orientals
1-4	−.87*	−.08	.04	.04
5-8	−.98*	.01	.17	−.16
9-11	−.87*	−.14	.05	−.18
12-13	−.94*	−.75*	−.07	.27
14-15	−.83*	−.65*	−.07	−.24
16-18	−.94*	−.84*	−.11	−.24

N = 21 agencies
*P <.001
Note: Correlation coefficients below .36 are not significant at .05.
Source: Compiled by the author.

directly related to the size and growth of each minority group within the federal service itself. For instance, it may be that there is a kind of "critical mass" or takeoff-point effect which makes further employment gains for members of separate minority groups dependent upon the extent of their numbers already in the federal service.

An indication of the impact of different levels of proportional representation on changing employment patterns can be gained by correlating a measure of representation according to grade level for each minority group in 1967 with the change in its employment proportions between 1967 and 1973.* Table 14 reports the most important findings obtained and supports the conclusion that different minority groups manifest different employment patterns and therefore should be treated separately in terms of EEO policy. It indicates that in several instances the greatest minority group gains in proportional terms occurred where the representation of that minority group was *greatest* in 1967.

---

*The measure of representation was derived by subtracting the proportional strength (in percent) of a minority group in each agency and grade grouping from the minority group's percentage representation in the U.S. population. Negative values therefore reflect proportional overrepresentation, while positive values reflect underrepresentation.

This occurred throughout the lower grades in the cases of Spanish-surnameds and native Americans, and in grades GS 14-15 for Orientals and native Americans. The tendency of minority groups to make the greatest gains where they are already best represented can be interpreted in several ways. This is related, in part, to the "tipping" phenomenon. Furthermore, although this pattern was not found to exist with regard to blacks, a study of black employment in the private sector in major U.S. cities came to the conclusion that "the best single predictor of the rate at which blacks were applying for firms' professional and white collar jobs was clearly the proportion of blacks currently employed in the firms' white collar jobs at the time of the survey."[19] The major reason for this was believed to be that employers without inhibitions against the hiring of blacks were more capable of expanding their hiring efforts. Moreover, such employers were no doubt perceived in a more favorable light by prospective black job applicants. This gravitation towards a more welcome work setting greatly facilitated the hiring of blacks. Perhaps similar patterns occur within federal agencies; that is, those agencies employing the largest proportions of members of minority groups are most willing to recruit others and are considered more desirable as employers by members of these groups.

TABLE 14

Relationships Between Minority Group Employment, 1967, and Changes in Minority Group Representation, 1967-73 (r)

GS Levels	Blacks	Spanish-Surnameds	Native Americans	Orientals
1-4	.24	−.00	−.90 [b]	.34
5-6	−.31	−.63	−.94[b]	.55[a]
9-11	.19	−.57[a]	−.81[b]	.26
12-13	−.05	.03	−.21	.72[b]
14-15	.03	−.22	−.70[b]	−.78[b]
16-18	−.03	−.17	.32	.53[a]

N = 21 agencies
    a $P < .01$
    b $P < .001$
    Note: Correlation coefficients below .36 are not significant at .05. A negative coefficient suggests that those groups which were most strongly represented in 1967 made the greatest proportional gains during the period under investigation.
    Source: Compiled by the author.

In the context of the overall EEO problem, it is important to note that insofar as the greatest gains for Spanish-surnameds and native Americans are being made where their representation is already highest, special efforts might be appropriate to help them gain entry and promotion to grades where their representation is lowest. To the extent that a "multiplier" effect is present, entry becomes of greater significance. At the same time, it is evident that Orientals tended to make the greatest proportional gains where they were *least* represented in 1967; no consistent pattern, moreover, was found for blacks. This again points to the uniqueness of each racial or ethnic group.

SOCIAL CLASS

No analysis of the social composition of the federal service would be complete without a consideration of the social class background of its members. The social class composition of the federal service is not an element of much political concern nowadays, although this has not always been the case. There appear to be two major reasons for this state of affairs. First, whatever its genuine political significance, social class is not a politicized element in the United States today. Second—and more relevant to the concerns of this study—the federal service is generally considered to be among the most representative of national bureaucracies, in terms of social class, in the world; thus, this aspect of its composition is unlikely to be a matter of political contention.

Although at the outset the federal service was overwhelmingly staffed by members of the upper social class, Presidents Jefferson and Jackson strengthened social, political, and economic forces that destroyed its elite composition.[20] By the time of the Civil War, the federal service was no doubt highly representative of the social class origins of the citizenry as a whole. When civil service reform[21] was instituted in the 1880s, there was some concern that the system of examinations would provide unfair advantages for the wealthier segments of the population and that the federal service might consequently return to the control of upper-class "gentlemen." It was charged, for example, that civil service reform would create an "opening wedge" for aristocratic elements to reassert their dominant position in the federal service. The reformers scoffed at the notion of an American aristocracy of postal clerks and customs officials, and, of course, none arose.

Evaluations of the social class composition of the federal service in the 1940s and the 1960s demonstrate that it was largely middle class and highly representative in terms of social class background. V. Subramanian, for example, found that 81 percent of the federal service came from middle-class backgrounds, as did about 60 percent of the nation's total work force.[22] In terms of higher federal service officials only, Reinhard Bendix found that in 1940 they predominantly came from lower middle-class backgrounds.[23] In 1963 W. Lloyd Warner and his associates found that although career executives were disproportionately drawn from business executive and professional backgrounds, entrance for others was becoming easier:

> . . . there is strong evidence of the operation of rank and the effects of high birth in the selection of the American business and government elites. Men born to the top have more advantages and are more likely to succeed than those born further down. There is not full freedom of competition; the system is still sufficiently status-bound to work to the considerable advantage of men born to higher position. Fathers at the elite levels still find it possible to endow their sons with greater opportunity, but, in business and in all probability in government, they do so now in decreased numbers. The sons of men from the wrong side of the tracks are finding their way increasingly to the places of power and prestige. The values of competitive and open status are higher today than yesterday and those of inherited position and fixed position, while still powerful, are less potent now than they were a generation ago.[24]

It is difficult to obtain exact figures, but there is evidence that many foreign public services are far less representative in terms of social class. For instance, in India the middle class has about ten times greater representation in the civil service than in the society as a whole. In Sweden, which has sometimes been considered a model for social equality, as late as the 1950s, after 20 years of social democratic rule, 52 percent of all higher levels of civil servants came from the leading social class, which constituted only 5 percent of the population.[25] Furthermore, only 10 percent of all Swedish higher officials came from the working class.[26] In some branches of the public service, social class inequality of representation was even more pronounced. Thus, 30 percent of the diplomatic corps were members of the nobility.[27] In other European nations, levels of inequality are thought to be much closer to the Swedish case than to that of the United States. Finally, in terms of the occupational status of civil servants, the U.S. federal bureaucracy is far more representative of the society of which it is a part than are the national bureaucracies of several other democratic nations, including Turkey, France, Denmark and, to a lesser extent, the United Kingdom.[28]

CONCLUSIONS

The foregoing analysis of the social composition of the federal service has yielded several observations of great importance to the policy and structure of the Federal EEO Program. Foremost among these are:

1. The primary EEO problem today is not minority underrepresentation but rather minority concentration in the lower grades of the federal service.
2. The same is true with regard to the employment of women.
3. The social composition of the federal work force varies from agency to agency; the problem therefore has an uneven quality.

4. This variation is related to such structural factors as agency size and distribution of agency employees along the hierarchy of the general schedule. It is also related to the nature of agency missions.

5. The EEO problem is complicated by the phenomenon of "tipping," whereby increasing minority employment in an agency may lead to decreasing integration within the same agency.

6. The employment pattern for women is substantially different from that of men within both the majority and minority groups.

7. There is some competition among members of different minority groups for positions in the federal service, but more significant is a tendency for the employment patterns of different minority groups to be largely unrelated to one another.

8. The social class composition of the federal service has not been politicized in recent years and appears to be quite representative of the social class composition of the society as a whole.

In terms of policy, these findings suggest the following course of action:

1. Emphasis should be placed upon upward mobility for women and members of minority groups and upon their recruitment to the upper grades. Continuing stress upon minority and female entry to the federal service will increase the tendency for disproportionate numbers of these citizens to be employed in the lower levels.

2. The program and its policies must allow for a good deal of flexibility so that different agencies can meaningfully address the unique or special aspects of the social composition of their work forces.

3. As a result of "tipping," a policy choice will have to be made as to whether to stress the objective of increasing minority and female employment or seek an integrated and sexually balanced work force.

4. In view of the fact that members of minority groups do not constitute a single unit in terms of their employment patterns, and because the employment pattern for Orientals in some respects compares favorably with that of the majority group, it is questionable whether special efforts on their behalf can currently be justified as a rational course of action.

Subsequent discussions will demonstrate that the EEO program does, in fact, take many of these elements into account. The historical roots of the social composition of the federal service today will also be explored. Prior to assessing these matters, however, it is desirable to consider the competing political principles which have been utilized in the past—and are still being used—to determine how civil service positions should be distributed. Only then will it be possible to understand fully the political nature of the program.

NOTES

1. See Franklin P. Kilpatrick, Milton C. Cummings, Jr., and M. Kent Jennings, *The Image of the Federal Service* (Washington, D.C.: Brookings Institution, 1964).

2. For example, see Woodrow Wilson, "The Study of Administration," *Political Science Quarterly* 56 (December 1941): 481-506; F. Goodnow, *Politics and Administration* (New York: Macmillan, 1900).

3. See Luther Gulick, "Science, Values and Public Administration," in *Papers on the Science of Administration,* ed. L. Gulick and L. Urwick (New York: Institute of Public Administration, 1937), pp. 191-95.

4. This is true of Max Weber. See Max Weber, *From Max Weber: Essays in Sociology,* trans. and ed. H.H. Gerth and C.W. Mills (New York: Oxford University Press, 1958), especially Chapter 8. For example, he writes: "The individual bureaucrat cannot squirm out of the apparatus in which he is harnessed." (p. 228)

5. For instance, during the 1968 presidential campaign, when the war in Vietnam and urban disorder were among the major problems facing the nation, the New York *Times* (October 7, 1968, p. 1) reported: "Richard M. Nixon said yesterday that the chief revolt in America was against 'an increasingly impersonal' Federal bureaucracy that saps individual initiative."

6. Wallace S. Sayre, "Introduction: Dilemmas and Prospects of the Federal Government Service," *The Federal Government Service,* ed. W. Sayre (Englewood Cliffs, N.J.: Prentice-Hall, 1965), p. 2.

7. Herbert J. Storing, "Political Parties and the Bureaucracy," in *Political Parties, U.S.A.,* ed. Robert A. Goldwin (Chicago: Rand McNally, 1961), especially p. 152.

8. Seymour M. Lipset, "Bureaucracy and Social Change," in *Reader in Bureaucracy,* ed. Robert K. Merton et al. (New York: Free Press, 1952), p. 230.

9. Samuel Krislov, *Representative Bureaucracy* (Englewood Cliffs, N. J.: Prentice-Hall, 1974), p.40.

10. Ibid., pp. 7-8.

11. D. Hellriegel and L. Short, "Equal Employment Opportunity in the Federal Government: A Comparative Analysis," *Public Administration Review* 32 (November/December 1972): 851-58, make this attribution, but much of the change has been due to other factors.

12. Ibid, p. 854.

13. See D. Nachmias and D. Rosenbloom, "Measuring Bureaucratic Representation and Integration," *Public Administration Review* 33 (November/December 1973): 590-97. The measure of variation is symbolically expressed as follows:

$$MV = \frac{\sum f_i f_j}{n \frac{(n-1)}{2} (\frac{f}{n})^2}$$

$i \neq j$

n = number of social characteristics

f = group size

A simple example of computation is as follows. In a group consisting of 8 whites, 5 blacks, and 2 Orientals, the number of racial differences is (8 x 5) + (8 x 2) + (5 x 2) = 66. The maximum possible number of differences in a group of 15 in which three racial groups are represented is $\frac{3(3-1)}{2} \frac{(15)^2}{3} = 75$. Therefore the MV = .88. For a review of other measures of integration, see Karl Taeuber and Alma Taeuber, *Negroes in Cities* (Chicago: Aldine, 1965). Unlike the MV, these measures do not reflect aggregate heterogeneity where the number of social groups exceeds two. See, also, P. Grabosky and D. Rosenbloom, "Racial and Ethnic Integration in the Federal Service," *Social Science Quarterly* 56 (June 1975): 71-84.

14. For a discussion of size and its relationship to other organizational variables, see Richard Hall, *Organizations: Structure and Process* (Englewood Cliffs, N.J.: Prentice-Hall, 1972), Chapter 4.

15. The U.S. Civil Service Commission's *Federal Civilian Manpower Monthly Release* is the only regularly published source for data on accessions and separations in federal agencies. It does not, however, provide data concerning the general schedule component of agency work forces; in the context of this analysis, therefore, it is difficult to make much use of the data presented in this source. Some agencies experience substantial overall turnover rates, but the turnover in general schedule positions could be considerably lower.

16. Samuel Krislov, *The Negro in Federal Employment* (Minneapolis, Minn.: University of Minnesota Press, 1973).

17. U.S. Civil Service Commission, *Minority Group Employment in the Federal Government* (Washington, D.C.: Government Printing Office, 1973, 1975).

18. Samuel Lubell, *The Future of American Politics* (New York: Anchor, 1955), especially Chapter 4.

19. Peter H. Rossi et al., *The Roots of Urban Discontent* (New York: John Wiley, 1974), p. 316.

20. See the next chapter of this study for a more detailed examination of the subject. See also, D. Rosenbloom, *Federal Service and the Constitution* (Ithaca, N.Y.: Cornell University Press, 1971), Chapters 1 and 2.

21. Ibid., Chapter 3.

22. V. Subramanian, "Representative Bureaucracy: A Reassessment," *American Political Science Review* 61 (December 1967): 1010-19.

23. Reinhard Bendix, *Higher Civil Servants in American Society* (Boulder, Colo.: University of Colorado Press, 1949).

24. W. Lloyd Warner et al., *The American Federal Executive* (New Haven, Conn.: Yale University Press, 1963), pp. 22-23.

25. Brian Chapman, *The Profession of Government* (London: Unwin University Books, 1959), p. 315.

26. Ibid., p. 316.

27. Ibid.

28. Kenneth J. Meier, "Representative Bureaucracy: An Empirical Analysis," *American Political Science Review* 69 (June 1975): 537, Figure 6.

2

MERIT AND
REPRESENTATION

Despite the tendency on the part of political scientists and others to consider public personnel administration little more than a "specialty 'tool' . . . generally taught as a technical specialty, revolving around such topics as position classification . . . and methods of recruitment and selection for the civil service,"[1] in reality it involves much more. The nature of public personnel administration, considered in its broadest sense, is hardly less significant than the nature of electoral systems in determining the distribution of political power in modern, technological, and highly bureaucratic governments. Indeed, major changes in the nature of U.S. federal personnel administration have historically been directly related to fundamental transformations of the political system as a whole. It is important to examine this relationship in some detail because past practices and ideas continue to have a significant impact on present policy options: they illustrate the overall significance and sensitivity of the EEO policy area, and they continue to have an impact on the human composition of the federal bureaucracy. Moreover, the historical relationship existing between politics and public personnel administration provides contrasting answers to the fundamental question facing the Federal EEO Program: "What principle(s) shall govern how positions in the federal service are to be filled?"

From a political perspective, the development of public personnel administration in the United States is best viewed as a conflict between two competing values: merit and representation. Although there is no inherent logical contradiction between them, it has nevertheless been the case that merit-oriented public personnel administration has not yielded a degree of representation that has been deemed fully satisfactory. In fact, combining merit and representation is now the greatest challenge facing the Federal EEO Program. Because the arguments and assumptions supporting these separate values are not self-evident, some elaboration is necessary.

MERIT

The value of merit is less complex and easier to grasp than that of representation. Much of what public bureaucracies do involves technical functions: delivering mail, performing clerical tasks, budgeting and accounting, medical practices and research, employing scientists and lawyers, distributing social security checks, monitoring tax returns, and performing a host of similar functions. Moreover, they do all of this at the taxpayers' expense. It is evident, therefore, that much is gained by maximizing the efficiency of the federal bureaucracy, whereas much is lost through imcompetence. This is especially true with respect to a soaring federal budget, for even wasting a mere 1 percent through inefficiency entails a substantial sum. In the view of many, one of the prerequisites for achieving efficiency in the public sector is personnel administration based on merit: "Only the best shall serve the state" became the rallying cry of public personnel administrators[2] and "the process of selection by means of competitive examinations" has become "the cornerstone of the public personnel program. . . . "[3] Merit, however, not only requires an effort to select, retain, and promote the best qualified and most competent individuals, it also implies that this will be accomplished in a nonpartisan or apolitical fashion. The latter element brings us closer to comprehending fully the nature of merit.

It is of crucial importance to emphasize that merit systems were historically often introduced at least as much in connection with demands for a redistribution of political power, authority, and influence among members of political communities as they were to secure better efficiency and economy. For example, in Great Britain, as J.D. Kingsley observes, "the debate occasioned by the Northcote-Trevelyan recommendations [for civil service reform in the nineteenth century] ran clearly along class lines,"[4] and the overall issue was the relative position of the middle and upper classes rather than simply how to obtain more efficient administration. Similarly, in ancient China, "after several centuries of division, the Sui (589-618) and the T'ang (618-906) dynasties saw in the training and recruitment of a centralized civil service the best means of overcoming the powers of regionalism and of the hereditary aristocracy."[5] Although there is some doubt as to whether "the rise of this aristocracy of merit . . . definitely freed the dynasty from its dependence on an older hereditary aristocracy,"[6] there is general agreement that personnel reforms were introduced with this prospect in mind. Nor was the introduction of the merit system within the U.S. federal bureaucracy an exception to this general tendency.

In the United States, the development of the merit system was an outgrowth of the civil service reform movement of the 1870s and 1880s. Perhaps some sort of personnel reform was inevitable, for the federal government became more positive in its functions, public policy became more regulatory in nature, technology and business methods advanced, and the size of the federal service increased in conjunction with these factors. The civil service reformers believed that public personnel administration based on partisanship or other nonmerit factors was rapidly becoming anachronistic. Carl Schurz, a leading reformer, argued that

> there are certain propositions so self-evident and so easily under-
> stood that it would appear like discourtesy to argue them before
> persons of intelligence. Such a one it is, that as the functions of gov-
> ernment grow in extent, importance and complexity, the necessity
> grows of their being administered not only with honesty, but also
> with trained ability and knowledge.[7]

There was nothing inevitable, however, about the specific measures reform would entail, and these were related less to honesty, trained ability, and knowledge per se than to the reformers' political objectives. Reform, as the reformers understood it, was never intended simply to improve the civil service. In Schurz's words, "The question whether the Departments at Washington are managed well or badly is, in proportion to the whole problem, an insignificant question. . . . "[8] The overall goals of the reformers were related less to the condition of the federal service than to that of the nation as a whole and to the role of people like themselves in the political system.

The reformers were intellectual and social leaders; some had been active as abolitionists and later became antiimperialists. They included lawyers, editors, clergymen, professors, and mercantile and financial (rather than industrial) businessmen. They tended to be Protestant and usually came from urban areas. They were especially prominent in the northeastern part of the country; many were from well-known, established New England families. In general, the reformers were similar in their social makeup to a group which was important in political life before being largely displaced by the Jacksonian revolution and the era of the common man. Like Jackson before them, they advocated changes in the nature of federal personnel administration as a means of transforming several features of the political system rather than merely those of the federal service. Their overall objective was to "restore ability, high character, and true public spirit once more to their legitimate spheres in our public life, and to make active politics once more attractive to men of self-respect and high patriotic aspirations."[9]

The reformers hoped that their proposals for civil service reform would decrease the ability of professional politicians to control the federal service for partisan purposes and thereby relegate them to a relatively minor role in the political system. Dorman B. Eaton, another leading reformer, expressed the idea most concisely:

> We have seen a class of politicians become powerful in high
> places, who have not taken (and who by nature are not qualified to
> take) any large part in the social and educational life of the people.

> Politics have tended more and more to become a trade, or separate occupation. High character and capacity have become disassociated from public life in the popular mind.[10]

Their main vehicle for overcoming this state of affairs was the substitution of merit, ascertained by means of open, competitive examinations, for politics in the selection of federal servants. They believed that only through open, competitive examinations could political favoritism and patronage be eliminated, the most qualified federal servants be obtained, and justice prevail. The idea was not original; it had been tried elsewhere in one form or another (most notably in Great Britain, as mentioned earlier). It could be presented "not merely as a fine theory or as a high, ideal conception of purity and justice in politics, but as an embodiment of principles and methods matured during a century."[11] The British example pointed to the following conclusion:

> Open competition presents at once the most just and practicable means of supplying fit persons for appointment. It is proved to have given the best public servants; it makes an end of patronage; and, besides being based on equal rights and common justice, it has been found to be the surest safeguard against both partisan coercion and official favoritism.[12]

Unlike those in other countries, however, merit examinations in the United States were to be of a practical nature; this has had the effect of limiting the importance of higher education as a requirement for the federal employment and, consequently, of limiting the impact of social class background in gaining entrance and promotion in the federal service as well.

Thus, even a brief review of the origins of the merit system in the United States suggests that its chief proponents viewed it as a means of achieving fundamental political reform. Although the reformers favored nonpartisan public personnel administration, they did not argue that it could or should be apolitical or antipolitical in the larger sense of macro politics or system-politics. Nor did they believe that administration was not related to politics. On the contrary, they clearly believed that public personnel administration and administrative systems were extremely important in terms of their political consequences, and that, after all, is how they came to view civil service reform as a means of displacing a whole group of politicians. By taking partisan politics out of public personnel administration, they hoped to create a new national politics. Depoliticization of the federal service, therefore, was not so much a political objective in itself as one which was directly related to a systematic attempt to effect an all-encompassing political change. Merit must consequently be viewed as a political value adopted during a specific period of American political and economic development in an effort to restructure national politics and leadership. Although it later became an end in itself to many public personnel administrators, it was perhaps inevitable that merit would eventually come under attack by those seeking to maximize other political values.

REPRESENTATION

At the present time, the chief opposition to the dominance of merit as the primary value to be maximized through public personnel adminstration comes from those who advocate greater social and political representativeness in public bureaucracies. This line of reasoning is based upon wholly different premises. While realizing that at the broadest level there was a connection between the two, the civil service reformers and personnel administrators of an earlier day made clear distinction between politics and day-to-day administration. For example, in his classic essay, "The Study of Administration," Woodrow Wilson wrote, "Most important to be observed is the truth already so much and so fortunately insisted upon by our civil service reformers; namely, that administration lies outside the proper sphere of politics. Administrative questions are not political questions."[13] In a sense, the reformers were *forced* to make such a distinction. Merit is best suited for apolitical, technical functions; representation is appropriate for political functions. Herein lies a major difference between those who advocate merit and those who advocate representation as the primary value to be maximized in public personnel administration. Whereas the former tend to view public bureaucracies in a somewhat apolitical light, the latter consider them to be full-fledged political institutions.

Presidents Jefferson and Jackson were perhaps the first vaguely to conceive of the federal service as a political body with a representational role. Jefferson was the first president to be elected in opposition to an incumbent. Having inherited a federal service overwhelmingly staffed by Federalists, he sought to redress this situation by making the percentage of Federalists and Republicans in the government's employ roughly equal to the percentage of each party in the nation as a whole. He apparently intended to ignore partisanship once such a balance had been reached, but in practice he continued to appoint only Republicans even afterward. To a considerable extent, of course, his chief concern was patronage, but he nevertheless displayed an interest in establishing a public service that was politically representative of the nation's population.[14]

President Jackson went much further. In his view, both social and political representation were objectives to be maximized in the composition of the federal service. Jackson, like Jefferson before him, found himself at the head of a federal service whose human composition was not to his liking. From 1789 to 1829 it had taken on a distinctly upper-class flavor. In fact, office tended to be considered a form of property, as in aristocratically based administrative systems, and in some cases it was even informally "inherited."[15] Jackson, the nation's first successful counter-elite, or representative of the common man, set out to change this state of affairs by introducing the principle of rotation in office in the federal service. In his view, efficient performance of the technical functions of public administration was secondary to other considerations. He reasoned that "the duties of all public officers are, or at least admit of being, so plain and simple that men of intelligence may readily qualify themselves for their performance; and I cannot but believe that more is lost by the long continuance of men in office than is generally to be gained by their experience."[16] He apparently also believed that it was desirable to "fill the various offices at the disposal of the Executive with individuals uniting as far as possible the qualifications of the head and heart, always recollecting that in a free government the demand for moral qualities should be made superior to that of talents."[17] Finally, he sought to ensure that the "road to office" was "accessible alike to the rich and the poor, the farmer and the printer. . . ."[18] Although some changes in the social class composition of the federal service may have occurred at the highest levels under earlier presidents, historians agree that the upper social class was not displaced until the arrival of the Jackson administration. For instance, Leonard D. White, the foremost historian of the federal service, concluded that "certain it is that the year 1829 marked the end of an era, politically and administratively. The gentlemen who since 1789 had taken the responsibility of government were driven from the scene, to be replaced by a new type of public servant and by other ideals of official action."[19]

In the Jeffersonian and Jacksonian approaches, representation was related to patronage, and patronage was related to partisan advantage. Yet there was an inherent and more fundamental logic to these approaches. The government was designed to be representative and somewhat responsive to the electorate. Insofar as the federal service performed political functions, it stood to reason that its members should be politically appointed. Patronage in the hands of the chief executive established a connection, albeit not a very direct one, between the will of the electorate and the composition of the federal bureaucracy. But a patronage-oriented administration had other consequences as well, and some of these were undesirable. For example, administrative operations were highly corrupt and inefficient under the spoils system; federal servants were subjected to widespread partisan coercion and "taxation"; and administrative justice was often highly politicized.[20] It remained for a much later generation of politicians and social scientists to resurrect the value of representation in the federal service and to argue that it could be made operational without the partisan abuses of the past.

It is an interesting coincidence that the 1940s saw both the development of the first Federal Equal Employment Opportunity Program and the beginning of the formation of modern concepts of representative bureaucracy. Credit for the latter has usually been given to J. Donald Kingsley, who, according to Samuel Krislov, articulated "the concept for the first time in an even halfway systematic form."[21] Perhaps his chief contribution was to refocus attention upon the human composition of civil services by arguing that the social basis of a public bureaucracy is related to its political and administrative outlook. Referring specifically to the British public service, he wrote:

> There are obviously points beyond which a man cannot go in carrying out the will of another; and the fact that those limits have seldom been approached in the conduct of the Civil Service since 1870 bears witness to the unity of the middle class State. The convention of impartiality can be maintained only when the members of the directing grades of the Service are thoroughly committed to the larger purposes the State is attempting to serve; when, in other words, their views are identical with those of the dominant class as a whole.[22]

Since the appearance of *Representative Bureaucracy* in 1944, this concept has undergone considerable development. Krislov, for example, upon reviewing the literature published after 1944, found that it had "four intertwined meanings":

> The most obvious is the simple representational notion that all social groups have a right to political participation and to influence. The second can be labeled the functional aspect; the wider the range of talents, types, and regional and family contacts found in a bureaucracy, the more likely it is to be able to fulfill its functions, with respect to both internal efficiency and social setting. Bureaucracies also symbolize values and power realities and are thus representational in both a political and an analytic sense. Therefore, finally, social conduct and future behavior in a society may be channelized and encouraged through the mere constitution of the bureaucracy.[23]

It is important, at this point, to distinguish between two of these meanings. First, representative bureaucracy refers to the social composition of a civil service. This aspect has generally been labeled "passive," "descriptive," "social," or "sociological" representation. In and of itself, it is important mainly for symbolic reasons and from the perspective of distributive justice. Symbolically, the nature of a social group's representation in a public bureaucracy provides an indicator of the political community's attitude towards that group. Exclusion of a group by the government is likely to engender adverse social and economic treatment elsewhere as well. Krislov is again helpful here:

> More significant is the "multiplier" importance of public service—great changes in a wide arena are instigated by small alterations in governmental personnel policy. The symbolic role of public position should not be overlooked. In seeking to implement the goal of greater equality in society generally government has a special

responsibility to come to others with clean hands. If the elimination
of prejudice cannot be achieved in the public bureaucracy it is unlikely that it will be achieved anywhere.[24]

Certainly, the denial of positions of authority to members of specific groups can
have the effect of contributing to the low social status of those groups in general.
A striking example of the relationship, in the area of equality, between governmental practices and those of society in general reportedly occurred when some
federal agencies became racially segregated under Presidents Taft and Wilson:
"With the government setting the example for the community, Negroes lost
what rights they had previously enjoyed in Washington theaters and restaurants,
and were systematically segregated in housing and private employment."[25]

Although there has been considerable opposition to it, even token social
representation, despite its other effects, is symbolically important. This is true
with respect to both image and self-image, as Kenneth Clark explains:

Since every human being depends upon his cumulative experi-
ences with others for clues as to how he should view and value himself, children who are consistently rejected understandably begin to
question and doubt whether they, their family, and their group
really deserve no more respect from the larger society than they
receive. These doubts become the seeds of a pernicious self- and
group hatred. . . .[26]

Even a few highly visible models of acceptance and advancement, such as
Supreme Court justices and department heads, might go a long way toward
negating the more general tendency.

In addition, social representation in public employment directly affects
the economic status of groups to a varying degree. There are presently about
2.5 million federal service positions. About a fifth of all jobs in the nation are
in public employment. The fact that this segment of the nation's economy is
not fully open to one or more groups can decrease the ability of individual
members of those groups to compete economically with members of other
groups; moreover, it may have a negative effect on the groups' overall economic
standing. There is no doubt, for instance, that if blacks were denied the 390,000
full-time civilian federal jobs they currently hold, it would have a serious impact
on the nation's black community as a whole—particularly those individual
black communities in the Washington, D.C., area.

A second kind of bureaucratic representation is sometimes referred to as
"active representation." It consists of a situation in which, according to Frederick
Mosher's definition, "an individual (or administrator) is expected to press for the
interests and desires of those whom he is presumed to represent, whether they
be the whole people or some segment of the people."[27] There is considerable
agreement that active representation is a fundamental characteristic of the
federal bureaucracy. Indeed, as Norton Long has observed, the bureaucracy is

recognized by all interested groups as a major channel of representation to such an extent that Congress rightly feels the competition of a rival."[28] For instance, the Departments of Agriculture, Labor, and Commerce have relatively well-defined constituencies with whom they interact and whom they often represent. The Equal Employment Opportunity Commission, the Commission on Civil Rights, and the Cabinet Committee on Opportunities for Spanish-Speaking People are formally considered to be representatives of and advocates for members of minority groups. Similarly, there is a tendency for regulatory commissions, such as the ICC, the Federal Trade Commission (FTC), and the FCC, to become spokesmen for the interests that they were originally designed to regulate. In the most advanced case of this kind of active representation, writes Grant McConnell, "the function of policy-making is often turned over to the private group in what amounts to delegation."[29]

In recent years it has been repeatedly argued that the federal service can be made even more representative in an active sense by making it more socially representative of the nation's population as a whole. Implicit in this line of reasoning is the fact that there is a connection between passive and active representation, and that the latter can be based on social background as well as structural and functional elements (agencies, bureaus, departments, and programs). If this is true, the virtues of a socially representative bureaucracy are readily apparent. Indeed, since public bureaucracies are potentially the most socially representative branch of government,[30] they might also be most politically responsive to and reflective of the values of the general citizenry. The existence of such a connection, however, has been questioned by many, and it has yet to be demonstrated definitively; this issue will be raised at a later point. Having discussed the public personnel values of merit and representation, it is now necessary to consider their interrelationship.

MERIT VERSUS REPRESENTATION

There is no inherent reason why merit and representation must be competing values. In theory, a merit-based civil service could also be highly representative in a social, and perhaps active, sense. However, such a state of affairs would depend on a conjunction of several factors. Given the fact that most bureaucratic jobs are predominantly middle class in nature,[31] it appears that such representation is only possible in a middle-class society such as that found in the United States. Thus, Subramanian found that, although the middle-class occupational component of the Indian and U.S. civil services were roughly similar, the size of the middle class in the former nation was so small that it was greatly overrepresented in the bureaucracy, whereas the much larger American middle class was only slightly overrepresented in the federal service.[32] In addition, passive representation within a merit framework is likely to exist only if all major social groups are distributed equally, in proportional terms, along the social stratification system. This, of course, is decidedly not the case in the United States. Blacks, native Americans, and the Spanish-surnamed population are concentrated in the lower or poverty classes. For example, during the past several decades black unemployment has remained at about twice the rate of white unemployment; black income has remained in the neighborhood of about 60 percent of white income. Native Americans are even worse off economically. These economic realities and disadvantages inevitably have an impact on the nature of the employment patterns of minority group members in the federal service. In fact, a serious problem facing the Federal EEO Program today is finding ways in which the federal service can compensate for these economic inequalities in the society at large and thereby equalize the opportunities of members of disadvantaged minority groups to compete for positions in the bureaucracy.

As will be shown in Chapters 5 and 6, this is a point which has very important policy consequences. The basic problem is that poverty, like wealth, is often inherited and the poor have developed a relatively distinct culture of their own. As Michael Harrington observes, "There is, in short, a language of the poor, a psychology of the poor, a world view of the poor. To be impoverished is to be an internal alien, to grow up in a culture that is radically different from the one that dominates the society."[33] For example, the poor have a different family structure, there is less marriage, earlier pregnancy, less education, and the choice between delayed or current gratification is often a hypothetical one. It is still an open question as to whether, in the short run, the poor could take full advantage of greater opportunities when and if they were afforded. As Harrington writes:

> Even when the money finally trickles down, even when a school is built in a poor neighborhood, for instance, the poor are still deprived. Their entire environment, their life, their values, do not prepare them to take advantage of the new opportunity. The parents are anxious for the chldren to go to work; the pupils are pent up, waiting for the moment when their education has complied with the law.[34]

In sum, establishing a high level of passive representation in the federal bureaucracy through the merit system is difficult because the poor, who are disproportionately nonwhite, are not educated in a fashion which is bureaucratically useful. Moreover, their work habits, values, and discipline are ill-suited to career advancement or even steady employment. They cannot gain access to positions in the higher realms of the corporate world and they may not even be able to enter at the lowest levels. Hence, there are few avenues of training available to them, and when they are trained it is often for the lower positions which may have no counterpart in government. Their inadequate housing and diet make them more vulnerable to sickness and therefore less desirable as workers. Ultimately, there is a limit as to how much the poor can do for themselves to become attractive candidates for public employment. If greater social representation is to be achieved, therefore, the government itself must take the initiative.

Another constraint on social representation grows out of the nature of the distribution of political power. About 90 percent of all positions in the federal service are under the merit system. However, some of the most important positions are filled through political appointment. These include department secretaries, agency heads and commissioners, and a number of noncareer assignments within the general career structure. Because blacks, members of other minority groups, and women are severely underrepresented in the ranks of politicians throughout the political system,* they have not received much in the the way of patronage in the federal service and have not been frequently recruited by those at the top of the administrative structure. Significantly, when members of these groups are appointed to bureaucratic positions at the higher levels, they tend to be advisors rather than individuals with more direct administrative authority. There has also been a tendency to place them in positions dealing primarily with the interests of the groups to which they belong. Thus, high-level appointments of blacks are disproportionately found in the civil rights and urban areas. Native Americans are disproportionately found in positions dealing with the problems of their group. To a lesser extent, women in the higher ranks have tended to be involved in programs which are of special interest to women in general. This, of course, is not inconsequential, for it is an indication that members of these groups have been able to gain some entry into the power structure at points of great relevance to their social groups. But it has also had the effect of limiting the number of positions they receive and isolating them from other political areas of greater importance and power in terms of the nation as a whole.

An unequal distribution of political power among social groups affects passive representation in a more complex way as well. Recruitment to positions in public bureaucracies is necessarily a political affair. Personnel "needs" and the desired "skills," "talents," and "types," are seldom, if ever, determined without reference to political values. In Krislov's words, "A public office makes for public fuss. The process of preferring one or another set of criteria is one of policy making, of agenda setting, of preference ordering, of cue giving for the other sectors as well."[35] Moreover, despite the tendency of authors of public personnel textbooks to write in terms of techniques designed "to assure that

---

* Despite recent increases in the number of black elected officials, for example, they still constitute only about 0.0057 percent of all elected officials in the United States (New York *Times,* April 23, 1974, p. 20).

the government service attracts its proper share of the best qualified persons,"[36] in reality "qualification is a relative conception"[37] and "there is no natural dividing line between intrinsic and extrinsic criteria."[38] Thus, politics impinges upon recruitment by playing an instrumental role in determining who will be "selected in" and who will be "selected out." Indeed, the content of merit examinations varies widely from one political system to another. The British, for instance, tend to rely on "literary" exams which test knowledge of ancient history and other aspects of a traditional, classical education. This procedure contributes to "Establishment" dominance of the civil service. In the United States, on the other hand, merit exams tend to be practical in orientation. But even here they have sometimes displayed a white middle-class bias that has made it more difficult for members of minority groups to gain entrance into the federal service. In the words of a former high-ranking CSC official, "We have white middle class exams, damn it, because we have white middle class jobs!"*

A final reason why a merit system may not yield a high level of passive representation in a public bureaucracy is that patterns of social discrimination in the society as a whole are almost inevitably reflected in its operation. The history of direct discrimination against women and members of minority groups, especially blacks, in federal personnel procedures will be presented in the next chapter. It is therefore reasonable to concentrate here on the impact of a discriminatory *environment* upon these practices. During the 1960s, the CSC engaged in a series of policy evaluations, called community reviews, which provided a "first-hand lesson on how the mores of the local community can and do affect personnel operations of Federal field installations."[39] For example, the CSC was able to identify some of the more overt reasons why supervisors failed to appoint and promote members of minority groups; included among these were:

> Dissatisfaction and unrest is expected among the present force when minority goup members are employed in technical and clerical positions. . . . Currently whites and Negroes are not normally in competition for appointment . . . to the same types of jobs.
>
> When the first Negro is appointed to a clerical or professional position, the establishment will incur much resentment from the white citizens both on and off the station.
>
> Supervisors stated that they would prefer not to employ minority group members because such action would adversely affect the cooperative relationship which exists between the state and the Federal activities.

---

*Statement to the author, August 1970.

It is anticipated that minority group (employees) would face severe difficulties in securing housing in the small communities of the State.[40]

Role stereotyping with respect to women has had a similar effect; until recently, women were automatically excluded from consideration for many kinds of positions, including some managerial posts in the higher ranks.

Thus, although in theory it is possible to obtain a high level of passive representation within a merit-oriented public personnel system, in practice there may be several constraints present which make the simultaneous maximization of the values of merit and passive representation difficult. Several of these limitations are certainly present in the U.S. system and are reflected in the human composition of the federal service. Indeed, it appears that the merit system will have to undergo considerable change if representation is to be maximized. Consequently, in the current political context of the Federal EEO Program, merit and representation have been posited as somewhat contradictory goals, and the desirability of each has been increasingly questioned.

THE CRITIQUE OF MERIT

Contemporary criticism of the merit system is two-pronged. First, it is alleged that, since there is no convincing evidence to show that the merit system has produced the best federal servants or even anything above basically qualified employees, they might just as well have been recruited and trained in some other fashion. There is widespread agreement that, except during times of extreme economic hardship, the federal service has had great difficulty in attracting highly qualified personnel. For example, Senator Henry Jackson observed: "The fact is, we have encountered disturbing difficulties in securing first-rate talent at the very time when the national security calls for the country's 'best brains' to man key posts at home and abroad.[41] The CSC's *Annual Report* often contains statements such as the following: "The need of the Federal Government for career personnel of outstanding ability has never been greater."[42]

But the argument against the merit system in this regard goes far deeper. In order to serve their current objective, merit examinations must have predictive validity, that is, individuals' scores on the exams must be strongly related to their performance on the job. However, predicting human behavior is extremely difficult, and even more so when the environment is relatively fluid and the work process involves many highly qualitative and intangible aspects. Past performance, knowledge, and ability are generally related to future performance, but so are individual reactions to specific environments and forms of supervision. The latter factor is almost never taken into account adequately under merit procedures.

Some elements of organization theory are of interest in this respect. At least 12 types of "organization men" have been identified or hypothesized.[43] It has also been convincingly argued that the behavior of individuals in the environments of large and complex organizations is strongly related to their personality predispositions and to their *specific* positions in organizations, as opposed to their natural and learned abilities.* Yet it is the latter upon which merit examinations concentrate; there is consequently an inherent limitation in their ability to predict on-the-job performance.

In addition, because public personnel administrators have tended to assume that a strong relationship exists between test scores and on-the-job performance, not enough work has been done to empirically ascertain or improve the validity of the exams they administer. Kenneth Wentworth has concluded, for example, that "hundreds of public jurisdictions have probably never done a validity study."[44] Although some attempts have been made in the federal government to determine the validity of some merit exams, in general these efforts have provided little meaningful evidence of a relationship between test scores and job performance.

Sometimes "validity" is established by checking the items on a test against the criteria for validity suggested by professional associations concerned with testing. This approach, however, ignores a host of different environmental factors, as well as the broader differences in the nature of public, as opposed to private, employment. It could be convincingly argued that, given present-day technology in the social sciences, it is impossible to find a significant relationship between merit scores and job performance for most kinds of federal jobs, especially the politically more important positions. Thus, at the present time there is no universal or even acceptable way of measuring "job success" in most cases; this is true for virtually all positions involving the formulation of public policy. According to Glenn McClung, "A 'success rating' usually amounts to a kind of 'report card' which is made out by the employees' supervisor," and "such ratings are inevitably limited in reliability—particularly when different supervisors are rating different people,"[45] as is generally the case in the federal service and the vast majority of large jurisdictions.

Another barrier to ascertaining the validity of merit examinations, McClung suggests, is that "generally only a limited proportion of the test-taking group ever get the chance to perform on the job"[46]; nothing is therefore known concerning how those with lower scores who were not appointed would have actually performed if given the opportunity. Moreover, those appointed often have very similar scores, a fact which, given the relatively unsophisticated nature

---

*This is especially true of Anthony Downs' approach (*Inside Bureaucracy*, Chapter 9).

of the tests, consequently limits the amount of variation likely to be explained by the differences in their scores.

Finally, public jurisdictions are frequently politically coerced into giving examinations having "face validity"; that is, they must appear outwardly reasonable to laymen. It is generally agreed, however, that face validity and content validity do not necessarily coincide. As a result of these difficulties and a host of others, the validity coefficients of civil service examinations are characteristically at the .25 level and rarely, if ever, greater than .50.[47] In other words, performance on these exams usually explains only about 6 percent of the variance in on-the-job performance and rarely more than 25 percent. In general, the larger the percentage of variance explained, the less important the nature of the position.

To some extent, the low validity coefficients of merit exams might be due to a statistical artifact, that is, they result from the conditions under which their validity may be investigated; they might therefore be accepted despite their questionable predictive powers. However, this possibility is rejected in the minds of some because they attribute a harsh racial impact to the merit system. This constitutes the second, and increasingly more important, aspect of the challenge to the merit system. Many believe that some public personnel examinations manifest an undue amount of "cultural bias" and consequently are used as a device for "selecting out" minority group members from public employment. It has been charged, for example, that the merit examinations given by the federal government are "among the most discriminatory given by any employer."[48] Indeed, there have been a number of court cases challenging merit exams on the grounds that they are racially discriminatory. The inability of public personnel administrators to demonstrate their validity has led the courts to declare their use unconstitutional in several instances.[49] Significantly, in a number of such cases the judiciary has ordered that a representational principle (quota hiring) be substituted for merit in redressing past discrimination. In addition to the examinations, it has been alleged that more general qualifications often contain a considerable bias. Thus, it has been charged that

> unrealistic prerequisites and qualifications have been established by Federal agencies. Minority candidates are not heartened by the possibilities of employment mainly because of prohibitive prerequisites and because Federal recruitment personnel tend to seek only those candidates who satisfy the established qualifications. Federal recruiters also place great emphasis on the previous earnings of job candidates—rather than on their previous work experience and levels of responsibility. The result is that black candidates who have a history of low earnings get jobs which are less responsible and which pay salaries that are lower than the jobs received by their white counterparts. In addition, Federal recruiters often rule out many black candidates because of their inferior educational

preparation. They give little or no weight to the biases and discrimination that set in motion the inequities and injustices which limited
the educational preparation and work experience of minority candidates.[50]

It has consequently been charged that "application of the merit system without
regard to existing preferential practices and procedures is tantamount to ignoring
the most prevalent form of discrimination in employment."[51] In the view of
some, the incompatibility of merit and passive representation in the federal
service is perhaps best illustrated by the fact that "a number of EEO officers
say they constantly encountered opposition to their efforts on grounds their
proposals conflict with the merit system."[52]

In sum, the gravamen of the argument against merit as the primary value
of public personnel administration is that it has outlived its usefulness. For the
civil service reformers, public personnel administration and the merit system
were avenues for introducing fundamental political change. It is not too much
to say that they have today become processes for maintaining a particular
status quo. Public personnel administrators, whose profession largely grew out
of the reform movement, have become wedded to the merit system and are
hostile to proposals for modifying any of its essential characteristics. Hence,
the tool of the reformers has become an end in itself for their heirs. The chief
problem presently facing the federal service and the political systems is not the
spoils system and its attendant corruption; rather, it is a question of racial,
ethnic, and sexual inequality and discrimination. In the view of many, representation must once again be elevated to a level of importance greater than that
of merit if public personnel administration is to preserve its historic connection
with fundamental political change in the United States.

THE CRITIQUE OF REPRESENTATION

Matters of this nature, however, are seldom one-sided, and others are
wont to consider representation a false value. Although from the perspective
of distributive justice few individuals seriously question the desirability of a
high level of social representation in public bureaucracies, many reject the
notion that it yields active representation and express doubt as to the utility of the
latter. Arguments in favor of active representation are ultimately based on two
assumptions. First, it is believed that public bureaucracy is uncontrollable,
particularly in democratic regimes. This line of reasoning is perhaps best expressed
by Max Weber. In what remains the most important analysis of bureaucracy in
the literature of the social sciences, Weber wrote:

Under normal conditions, the power position of a fully developed
bureaucracy is always overpowering. The "political master" finds

himself in the position of the "dilettante" who stands opposite the "expert" facing the trained official who stands within the management of administration.[53]

Bureaucracy possesses the advantages of expertise, knowledge of the past and precedent, precision, specialization, continuity, secrecy and discretion. Given the fact that public bureaucracy in modern democratic nations has important political and policy-making roles, Weber argued that it must "inevitably" come into conflict with democracy itself.[54] Hence, the bureaucratization of democratic political systems raises some very fundamental questions. According to Frederick Mosher:

> The accretion of specialization and of technological and social complexity seems to be an irreversible trend, one that leads to increasing dependence on the protected, appointive public service, thrice removed from direct democracy. Herein lies [a] central and underlying problem . . .: how can a public service so constituted be made to operate in a manner compatible with democracy? How can we be assured that a highly differentiated body of public employees will act in the interests of all the people, will be an instrument of all the people?[55]

As we have already seen, one partial answer that has frequently been suggested is: "by insuring that such a civil service is also socially representative of the body politic."

The second underlying assumption of those who argue in favor of active representation is that there is a strong and direct link between passive and active representation. This approach has been most forcefully advanced by Norton Long, who views active bureaucratic representation as a counterweight to the unrepresentativeness of other political institutions:

> As it operates in the civil service, the recruitment process brings into federal employment and positions of national power, persons whose previous affiliations, training, and background cause them to conceive of themselves as representing constituencies that are relatively uninfluential in Congress. These constituencies, like that of the presidency, are in the aggregate numerically very large; and in speaking for them as self-appointed, or frequently actually appointed, representatives, the bureaucrats fill in the deficiencies of the process of representation in the legislature.[56]

Although Long's argument is not confined to racial or ethnic representation, it clearly applies in this context; others, including Lipset, Kingsley, and Krislov, have also viewed passive representation as a means of fostering active representation.

In recent years, both of these assumptions have come under considerable attack. On the one hand, it has been argued that traditional mechanisms for in-insuring bureaucratic responsibility and accountability, such as legislative over-sight, spending controls, and presidential direction, are effective and that the federal bureaucracy is therefore not "uncontrolled."[57] From this perspective active representation is unnecessary, if not actually dangerous, because the elective branches are able to direct the course of bureaucratic policy making and its implementation and, consequently, there is a powerful link between the people and their civil servants.

On the other hand, it has been argued that even if the bureaucracy were uncontrolled, social representation would not insure responsiveness because it is only very loosely connected, if at all, to active representation. Mosher, for example, writes:

> I lay stress on the distinction between active and passive representativeness because it seems to me there has been a good deal of confusion on the matter in the recent literature about public executives. The fact is that we know too little about the relationship between a man's background and pre-employment socialization on the one hand, and his orientation and behavior in office on the other. Undoubtedly, there are a good many other intervening variables: the length of time in the organization, or the time distance from his background; the nature and strength of the socialization process within the organization; the nature of the position . . . ; the length and content of preparatory education; the strength of associations beyond the job and beyond the agency; etc.[58]

In a related manner, Kenneth Meier argues that "socialization is a process which continues throughout the life of the bureaucrat, and the role the agency creates from [sic] him may be as important as his childhood training."[59] Moreover, ". . . civil servants, especially upper-level civil servants, differ significantly from a randomly selected group of people with the same family social characteristics; they are highly upwardly mobile."[60] Therefore, "the assumption . . . that socioeconomic characteristics determine values for upwardly mobile, adult bureaucrats is in need of revision; the degree of revision necessary is dependent on further empirical studies."[61]

Unfortunately, there has been no resolution of these conflicting points of view. Whether the federal bureaucracy is adequately responsive and is controlled by the other branches of government is debatable; it is obviously well controlled in some cases and almost totally uncontrolled in others. How one characterizes it as a whole is dependent upon one's expectations, perspectives, and values. Studies on the possible link(s) between passive and active representation yield contradictory conclusions,[62] and there are clearly insufficient grounds either for totally rejecting or accepting the existence of such a link at the present time. It is readily apparent that there are many constraints upon bureaucrats who would seek to represent the groups to which they belong. Yet it is equally evident that significant examples of such representation have occurred.[63]

Here, too, it appears that it is the specific context rather than the overall characterization which is of greatest importance. If one were looking for a balanced approach, one might well follow Krislov in arguing for, "above all else, responsiveness—but responsiveness through increased representativeness."[64] However rational such an approach might be, though, it is somewhat beside the point politically in that not only much of the history of public personnel administration in the United States, but also a good deal of the policy development of the Federal EEO Program is best explained in terms of a struggle between "meritists" and "representationists." A study of the early phases of this policy development is presented in the next chapter.

NOTES

1. Stephen Wasby, *Political Science—The Discipline and Its Dimensions* (New York: Scribner's, 1970), pp. 425-26.

2. See Norman Sharpless, Jr., "Public Personnel Selection—An Overview," in *Recruitment and Selection in the Public Service*, ed. J. Donovan (Chicago: Public Personnel Assoc., 1968), pp. 8-9.

3. O. Glenn Stahl, *Public Personnel Administration* (New York: Harper and Row, 1962), p. 67.

4. J. Donald Kingsley, *Representative Bureaucracy* (Yellow Springs, Ohio: Antioch Press, 1944), p. 63.

5. See *The Chinese Civil Service.* ed. Johanna Menzel (Boston: D.C. Heath, 1963), p. vii.

6. Ibid., p. viii.

7. Carl Schurz, *Congress and the Spoils System* (New York: George G. Peck, 1895), p. 4.

8. Carl Schurz, *Speeches, Correspondence, and Political Papers of Carl Schurz,* 6 vols. ed. Frederick Bancroft (New York: Putnam's, 1913), II, p. 123.

9. Carl Schurz, editorial in *Harper's Weekly,* July 1, 1893, p. 614.

10. Dorman B. Eaton, *The Civil Service in Great Britain* (New York: Harper and Bros., 1880), p. 392.

11. Ibid., p. 370-71.

12. Ibid., p. 365.

13. Woodrow Wilson, "The Study of Administration," *Political Science Quarterly* 56 (December 1941): 494. But Wilson did not consider public administration to be unconnected to politics. He wrote that "it is, at the same time, raised very far above the dull level of mere technical detail by the fact that through its greater principles it is directly connected with the lasting maxims of political wisdom, the permanent truths of political progress." (Ibid.)

14. See Nobel E. Cunningham, Jr., *The Jeffersonian Republicans in Power* (Chapel Hill, N.C.: University of North Carolina Press, 1963).

15. See David H. Rosenbloom, *Federal Service and the Constitution* (Ithaca, N.Y.: Cornell University Press, 1971), Chapter 1.

16. Andrew Jackson, "First Annual Message," in *A Compilation of the Messages and Papers of the Presidents of the United States, 1789-1897*, 10 vols., ed. James D. Richardson (Washington, D.C.: U.S. Government Printing Office, 1896-99), 2: 448-49.

17. Andrew Jackson, *The Correspondence of Andrew Jackson,* 7 vols., ed. J.S. Bassett (Washington, D.C.: Carnegie Institution, 1926), 4: 11-12.

18. Ibid., p. 32.

19. Leonard D. White, "Preface," *The Jeffersonians* (New York: Free Press, 1965), p. viii. This interpretation is disputed by Sidney Aronson in *Status and Kinship: Standards of Selection in the Administrations of John Adams, Thomas Jefferson, and Andrew Jackson* (Cambridge, Mass.: Harvard U.P., 1964). Aronson believes that the major change in the social composition of the federal service occurred under Jefferson. His analysis, however, does not support this conclusion. See David H. Rosenbloom, "A Note on the Social Class Composition of the Civil Service, 1789-1837," *Polity* 5 (Fall 1972): 136-38.

20. See Rosenbloom, *Federal Service and the Constitution,* Chapter 2.

21. Samuel Krislov, *The Negro in Federal Employment* (Minneapolis, Minn.: University of Minnesota Press, 1967), p. 48.

22. Kingsley, *Representative Bureaucracy,* p. 278.

23. Krislov, *The Negro in Federal Employment*, p. 64.

24. Ibid., p. 5.

25. National Committee on Segregation in the Nation's Capital, *Segration in Washington* (Chicago: National Committee on Segregation in the Nation's Capital, 1948), p. 62.

26. Kenneth Clark, *Dark Ghetto* (New York: Harper & Row, 1965), p. 64.

27. Frederick Mosher, *Democracy and the Public Service* (New York: Oxford University Press, 1968), pp. 11-12.

28. Norton Long, "Power and Administration," in *Bureaucratic Power in National Politics*, ed. F. Rourke (Boston: Little, Brown, 1965), pp. 17-18.

29. Grant McConnell, *Private Power and American Democracy* (New York: Knopf, 1966), p. 163.

30. Krislov, *Representative Bureaucracy,* (Englewood Cliffs, N.J.: Prentice-Hall, 1974), p. 63.

31. Ibid., Chapter 3; see also, V. Subramaniam, "Representative Bureaucracy: A Reassessment," *American Political Science Review* 61 (December 1967): 1010-19.

32. Subramaniam, "Representative Bureaucracy," p. 1015.

33. Michael Harrington, *The Other America* (Baltimore, Md.: Penguin, 1964), p. 25.

34. Ibid., p. 17.

35. Krislov, *Representative Bureaucracy,* p. 4.

36. Felix Nigro, *Public Personnel Administration* (New York: Henry Holt, 1959), p. 155.

37. E. Pendleton Herring, *Federal Commissioners* (Cambridge, Mass.: Harvard University Press, 1936), p. 5.

38. Krislov, *Representative Bureaucracy,* p. 4.

39. U.S., Civil Service Commission, Bureau of Recruiting and Examining, *Equal Opportunity in Federal Employment, May 15, 1963–June 30, 1964,* p. 89.

40. Ibid., p. 46; U.S., Civil Service Commission, *The Opening Door,* October 1962, p. 15.

41. Quoted by Franklin P. Kilpatrick, Milton C. Cummings, Jr., and M. Kent Jennings, *The Image of the Federal Service* (Washington, D.C.: The Brookings Institution, 1964), p. 4.

42. U.S., Civil Service Commission, *Annual Report* 80 (1963): 3.

43. See Leonard Reissman, "A Study of Role Conceptions in Bureaucracy," *Social Forces* 27 (March 1949): 305-10; Anthony Downs, *Inside Bureaucracy* (Boston: Little, Brown, 1967), Chapter 9; and Robert Presthus, *The Organizational Society* (New York: Random House, 1962), Chapters 4, 6, 7, and 8.

44. Kenneth Wentworth, "The Use of Commercial Tests," in *Recruitment and Selection,* p. 155.

45. Glenn McClung, "Statistical Techniques in Testing," in *Recruitment and Selection,* pp. 339-40.

46. Ibid., p. 340.

47. Ibid., Table 2.

48. U.S., Congress, Senate, Subcommittee on Labor, Committee on Labor and Public Welfare, "Equal Employment Opportunity Enforcement Act," 91st Cong., 2d sess., August 12, 1969, p. 156.

49. See, for example, *Vulcan Society v. CSC,* 360 F. Supp 1265 (1973); *Chance v. Board of Examiners,* 458 F2d 1167 (1972); *Bridgeport Guardians v. Bridgeport CSC,* 482 F2d 1333 (1973); *Western Addition Community Organization v. Alioto,* 330 F. Supp. 536 (1971); *Kirkland v. New York State Department of Correctional Services,* 374 F. Supp. 1361 (1974), reversed, 520 F2d 420 (1975); *Carter v. Gallagher,* 452 F2d 315 (1971). See also, *Washington v. Davis,* 48 L. Ed. 2d. 597 (1976).

50. "Equal Employment Opportunity Posture of the U.S. Federal Government," p. 1; mimeographed report (Washington, D.C., 1969), Roger Wilkins (former director, Community Relations Service, U.S. Department of Justice), James Frazier, Jr. (past director of the Office of Federal Equal Employment Opportunity, U.S. Civil Service Commission) et al. The report was widely circulated among EEO and civil rights officials in the late 1960s. It represents a candid statement of the thinking of several leading black officials at the time.

51. Ibid., p. 4.

52. Ibid.

53. Max Weber, "Bureaucracy," *From Max Weber: Essays in Sociology,* trans. and ed. H. H. Gerth and C. W. Mills (New York: Oxford University Press, 1958), p. 232.

54. Ibid., p. 226.

55. Mosher, *Democracy and the Public Service,* pp. 3-4.

56. Norton Long, *The Polity* (Chicago: Rand McNally, 1962), p. 70.

57. Kenneth J. Meier, "Representative Bureaucracy: An Empirical Analysis," *American Political Science Review* 69 (June 1975): 526-42, especially p. 528.

58. Mosher, *Democracy and the Public Service,* p. 13.

59. Meier, "Representative Bureaucracy," p. 529.

60. Ibid.

61. Ibid.

62. See Seymour M. Lipset, "Bureaucracy and Social Change," *Reader in Bureaucracy,* ed. Robert K. Merton et al. (New York: Free Press, 1952) pp. 221-232; Dennis L. Dresang, "Ethnic Politics, Representative Bureaucracy, and Development Administration: The Zambian Case," *American Political Science Review* 68 (December 1974): 1605-17; Kenneth J. Meier and Lloyd G. Nigro, "Representative Bureaucracy and Policy Preferences," *Public Administration Review* 36 (July/August 1976): 458-69.

63. See, for example, the protest by black attorneys in the Department of Justice to Congress concerning school segregation, as reported in the *International Herald Tribune,* April 27. 1972, p. 3.

64. Krislov, *Representative Bureaucracy,* p. 126.

3

THE POLITICS OF
DISCRIMINATION AND
EARLY EEO DEVELOPMENTS

The current Federal EEO Program, inaugurated in 1965, is the fifth such program to be established since 1941. It has inherited a considerable legacy from these earlier programs, and from a past in which racial and sexual discrimination were fundamental features of federal personnel administration and were even enforced by law. Some knowledge of the historical background of the present program and earlier policy evolution is necessary for a proper understanding of current policy options and development. In addition, this information will illustrate why merit is distrusted by representationists and how representationist objectives and approaches gradually began to work their way into contemporary EEO policy and administration.

DISCRIMINATION AGAINST BLACKS

Racial, religious, ethnic, and sexual discrimination have historically been widespread in the federal service. Blacks and women, however, have been subjected to the most far-reaching official and unofficial inequities. They consequently constitute two of the major groups at which EEO efforts are being currently aimed. An examination of the history of discrimination against these two groups will prove instructive in that it will clarify some of the inherited obstacles which the federal government has yet to overcome. An even more basic reason is the fact that past practices against blacks and women have largely been responsible for the institution of reforms.

Even as American colonists were fighting the British for the establishment of a new political order, it was reasonably clear that whatever improvements a successful struggle for independence might bring to whites in the new world, blacks were not very likely to receive a substantial share of the prospective benefits. This fact was symbolically demonstrated at the outset by

General Washington, who, although in need of increased manpower, was reluctant to utilize black troops.[1] This unwillingness to employ blacks in the government service outlasted the Revolution; in the view of some, it is still evident in the United States today. The first formal application of this attitude occurred in 1810, when Congress enacted a law providing that "no other than a free white person shall be employed in conveying the mail."[2] The law was a belated "answer" to a letter written in 1802 by Postmaster General Gideon Granger to a Senate committee. Granger warned against "everything which tends to increase their [the black people's] knowledge of natural rights, of men and things, or that affords them an opportunity of associating, acquiring and communicating sentiments, and of establishing a chain or line of intelligence."[3] He was especially opposed to blacks learning "that a man's rights do not depend on his color."[4] The law was reenacted in 1825 and modified by departmental order in 1828 to allow blacks to carry mailbags from stage coaches to post offices under white supervision.[5] It was finally repealed, after several efforts, in 1865,[6] but a person's rights still depended, to a great extent, on his or her color in most other respects.

Although the statute applied only to postal employees, it is believed that there were no blacks in the bureaucracy until 1867, the year when Solomon J. Johnson was appointed to serve in the Treasury as a first-grade clerk.[7] Blacks subsequently made slow, but generally steady, inroads and by 1928 they apparently achieved a proportional representation in the federal service roughly equal to their proportional representation in the nation as a whole.[8] These gains came about in two ways. First, following Reconstruction, Republicans began to make a number of significant black civil service appointments as a form of compensation to the black race as a whole. The party eventually established a tradition of appointing blacks to minor posts in the District of Columbia and to diplomatic posts in such black nations as Liberia and Haiti.[9] This route to bureaucratic representation, however, proved to be short-lived, blacks subsequently were disfranchised in the South, and the Republicans lost interest in their lot. In fact, the Republicans actually were reluctant to make black appointments for fear of further alienating Southern whites.

A second, more lasting, means used to increased black passive representation in the federal service has been the merit system, but, as was discussed in the previous chapter, this, too, has been problematical. When the Civil Service Act was passed in 1883, there were 620 persons identified as black in the federal service in Washington, D.C.[10] By 1892 their number had increased to 2,393,[11] probably as a result of merit procedures which made it more difficult to openly discriminate. In its eighth *Annual Report,* the CSC concluded that

> Another excellent feature of the examinations in the Southern States has been the elimination not only of the questions of politics and religion but of the question of race. A fair proportion of the men appointed from these States has been colored, these successful colored applicants being in many cases graduates of the colleges or

higher institutions of learning established especially for their race. They rarely belonged to the class of colored politicians which has hitherto been apt to monopolize such appointments as colored men receive at all. On the contrary they were for the most part well educated, self-respecting, intelligent young men and women who having graduated from their colored schools and colleges found but few avenues open for the employment of their talents. It is impossible to overestimate the boon to these colored men and women of being given the chance to enter the Government service on their own merits in fair competition with white and colored alike.[12]

The merit system, however, could not protect blacks from being discriminated against in removals. For example, in 1894 Civil Service Commissioner Theodore Roosevelt wrote: "In the War Department they have turned out about two-thirds of the young colored men who came through our examinations during the past three or four years."[13] Moreover, the merit system did not prevent segregation and other inequalities within the federal service.

The most important setbacks for blacks, after the establishment of the merit system, occurred during the Taft and Wilson administrations. In the words of W. E. B. DuBois, Taft "began his reactionary administration by promising the South that he would appoint no Federal official to whom the Southern people were opposed. . . ."[14] He believed that blacks should not hold office where whites complained about their presence and he accordingly reduced black appointments in the South. Furthermore, he initiated a policy of segregation in the federal service by segregating black and white census takers in Washington, D.C., thus restricting the activities of the latter to their own racial group.[15]

The Wilson administration played a crucial role in the area of racial inequality. During his campaign Wilson wrote to a black leader: "Should I become president of the United States they [the blacks] may count on me for absolute fair dealing and for everything by which I could assist in advancing the interests of their race in the United States."[16] He openly appealed to the black vote, which was largely Republican, and received more black support than had any other Democratic presidential hopeful before him. Indeed, he was supported by no less esteemed a personage than Booker T. Washington, who stated: "Mr. Wilson is in favor of the things which tend toward the uplift, improvement, and advancement of my people, and at his hands we have nothing to fear."[17]

There can be little doubt, however, that in terms of the federal service the Wilson administration held the worst record, with respect to blacks, in the history of the merit system. As Arthur Link expressed it, "To state the matter bluntly, the return of the Democrats to power had meant precisely what blacks feared most—control of the federal government by a party dominated by men determined to impose the caste system on the nation's capital."[18] The Wilson administration, Link continues, clearly "shared the southern view of race relations."[19] Segregation was introduced in the Postal and Treasury Department offices, shops, rest rooms, and lunchrooms.[20] In 1914 every black clerk in the auditors office and the Post Office, with two exceptions, was reduced in rank and photographs were (for the first time) required by the CSC before appointments could be made.[21] Due, in part, to Wilson's own attitudes and those of the Senate, presidential appointments of blacks also lagged.[22] Even the traditionally black posts of Minister to Haiti and Register of the Treasury went to whites, although blacks did remain in some other positions.[23] The dismissal or downgrading of blacks in the competitive service was sanctioned by some department heads.[24] In some cases, according to Laurence Hayes, "colored clerks in the central post office were transferred in groups of 10 or 15 at a time to branch offices which it had been decided to abolish. Upon the abolition of these branches the jobs of the colored employees would automatically end."[25]

Under the Wilson administration, then, the government not only condoned the racial discrimination which existed throughout American society, it openly encouraged discrimination and represented the vanguard of racism. Wilson himself argued:

> It is true that the segregation of the colored employees in the several departments was begun upon the initiative and at the suggestion of several of the heads of departments, but as much in the interest of the Negroes as for any other reason, with the approval of some of the most influential Negroes I know, and with the idea that the friction, or rather the discontent and uneasiness, which has prevailed in many of the departments would thereby be removed. It is as far as possible from being a movement *against* the Negroes. I sincerely believe it to be in their interest.[26]

The color of one's skin had become a test of fitness for federal employees and segregation had entered the federal service. This policy left a legacy of discrimination and distrust which has yet to be overcome entirely.

In general, the three Republican administrations which succeeded Wilson's administration continued the existing patterns of discrimination, although there were some improvements from the point of view of equality. According to Hayes, "the Negro Federal Government workers expected nothing from Mr. Coolidge, and they were not disappointed."[27] Hoover, as Secretary of Commerce in the 1920s, desegregated the Census Bureau and instituted some other measures to bring greater racial equality into government. As president, however, he echoed Taft in stating that "officials shall enjoy the confidence and respect of the people with whom they serve,"[28] and consequently would not appoint blacks to federal positions in the South. There is also evidence that the number of black clerks in the Washington, D.C., area had declined from the "thousands" to about 300 by 1930.[29]

On the other hand, in the late 1920s some offices in the Departments of Commerce, Interior, and Treasury were partially desegregated.[30] An analysis of racial relationships in the federal service in Washington, D.C., during the late 1920s was undertaken by W. T. Andrews and Walter White, two officials of the National Association for the Advancement of Colored People (NAACP).[31] Andrews' report documented

> the existence of the physical segregation of Negro from white employees in the following offices and under the following circumstances: (1) Negro workers occupied separate rooms from those occupied by white workers in the Registrar's Office of the Treasury Department, and in the Veterans Bureau, the General Accounting Office, the Division of Statistics, the Navy Department, the Department of the Interior, the main Post Office Building; (2) Negro and white workers occupied the same room, but manifest devices of physical separation existed in the Government Printing Office and generally in the Bureau of Printing and Engraving; (3) segregated cafeterias existed for workers in the Bureau of Printing and Engraving, the Navy Department, the Interior Department, the Post Office Department, and the General Accounting Office; (4) separate lockers existed in the Bureau of Printing and Engraving and in the Post Office Department; (5) separate toilet facilities (for [black] women) existed in the Government Printing Office and in the Bureau of Printing and Engraving.[32]

The report also indicated that there was a widespread belief that blacks were discriminated against in appointments and promotions. White, on the other hand, thought that perhaps "the sum total of discrimination has been somewhat exaggerated."[33] He thought that it was much more important that the merit system worked for blacks as well as for whites and that "qualified Negroes, when certified by the Civil Service Commission, are not refused appointment by prejudiced personnel officers or department chiefs."[34]

The CSC, which has been the central personnel agency of the federal government since 1883 and the administrator of the Federal EEO Program since 1965, was also somewhat ambiguous in its attitude towards discrimination. Its secretary, Dr. John T. Doyle, indicated that the CSC had no legal basis for preventing racial discrimination outside its own organization, but that it planned to "exert moral suasion" upon biased officials when discriminatory practices were obvious.[35] The CSC itself, however, encouraged racism by "not certifying Negroes to Bureaus where they would be turned down or made unhappy."[36] According to Doyle, moreover, as a general rule, the CSC "sent Negroes to Bureaus in such numbers where it was likely that they would have a separate section or Division."[37] Although Doyle believed that "on the score of efficiency Negroes made as good a showing as whites,"[38] he apparently supported the segregation which existed in the CSC and other agencies.

During the New Deal, racial relationships began to undergo a major, if somewhat haphazard, change. As Assistant Secretary of the Navy in Wilson's administration, Franklin D. Roosevelt had been associated with the introduction of far-reaching, officially sanctioned racist practices, but there is no doubt that his administrations afforded significant new opportunities to black Americans. F.D.R.'s personal contribution to the reduction of racism in the federal service was not quantitative. Rather, it was in terms of the nature of the positions to which they could now hope to be appointed. Blacks were now hired as consultants, special assistants, or advisors in various departments. Moreover, despite the fact that discriminatory practices continued in some agencies or organizations, there were also important instances of desegregation.[39]

Far more important than its record, which, by current standards, may not appear very impressive, was the fact that the "basic New Deal programs of social amelioration created a logic and a moral dimension of their own,"[40] which, in Krislov's words, encouraged the adoption of a long series of positive measures to prevent discrimination on the basis of race, religion, color, national origin and, eventually, sex. The legislative history of these measures will be examined in the following pages. Jumping ahead for a moment, however, one can state that by 1941 the relationship between the government and blacks with regard to federal service employment had been fundamentally altered. Race was no longer considered a legitimate basis for personnel actions. In theory, the government, which had previously been profoundly racist, had now become "color-blind."

DISCRIMINATION AGAINST WOMEN

Although the employment of women in the government service in America actually predates the formation of the Union, historically women have not generally been treated as equals in the federal service and there have been periods during which there were no female federal employees. As in the case of blacks, discrimination against women was once formally sanctioned by law and official directive. The most important formal piece of legislation to discriminate on the basis of sex was derived from an 1870 statute which, paradoxically, had been intended to give women greater equality: "Women may, in the discretion of the head of any department, be appointed to any of the clerkships therein authorized by law, upon the same requisites and conditions, and with the same compensations as are prescribed for men."[41] The law was interpreted to allow an appointing officer to exclude women for reasons unrelated to their qualifications or the efficiency of the service, and until 1919 women were excluded from about 60 percent of all civil service examinations.[42] Unequal compensation had originally been provided for by law,[43] and despite the 1870 statute it remained in effect in some agencies until 1923, when the Classification Act provided that in determining the rate of compensation which an employee would receive the principle of equal compensation for equal work irrespective of sex would be followed.[44]

Equality was sometimes abridged with regard to married women rather than women in general. In 1913 Section 157 of the postal regulations stated that no married woman could "be appointed to a classified position"[45] and that women in such positions would not be reappointed after marrying. The Economy Act of June 30, 1932, provided that in instances involving reductions in force, an employee whose spouse was also in the service should be dismissed before other civil servants. The provision led to three times more dismissals of women than of men.[46] In 1937 marital status was declared to be an illegal basis for infringing upon equality.[47] According to Lucille F. McMillin, the second female Civil Service Commissioner, there were, technically speaking, no longer any "provisions discriminating against women in the laws and rules governing the Federal service."[48] At the same time, however, there was little official basis for action to *prevent* sexual discrimination. Moreover, veteran preference, which has existed in various forms throughout the history of the federal service, continued to be a major obstacle for obtaining sexual equality. The 1870 statute was still being used to discriminate against women in hiring and promotion. According to Evelyn Harrison:

> A study made by the Civil Service Commission in 1960 of all agency referral requests to the Commission's Washington office during a six-month period showed that in all job categories, 29 percent specified men only, 34 percent specified women only, and 37 percent did not specify sex. The significance of these figures was revealed when broken down by grade level: more than half the requests to fill positions above the lowest four grades were for men only, and 94 percent to fill positions at the three highest regular grades (GS-13, 14 and 15) were restricted to men.[49]

Although women as a group made major advances during World War II and gained access to new positions, it was not until the 1960s that important steps, including the repeal of the 1870 law, were taken to ensure a greater degree of sexual equality.

In some ways, the experience of women in the federal service has roughly paralleled that of blacks. In the words of Commissioner McMillin:

> In the Federal Government . . . women entered the lower-grade work long before they were admitted to the higher ranks. The factory-type occupations at the Philadelphia mint were opened to women at an early date. Later, the arsenals, the Bureau of Engraving and Printing, and the Government Printing Office employed women in certain types of light shop work. Women exclusively were recruited as printer's assistants in the early days of the Civil Service Commission, and even as late as 1910 these formed by far the bulk of the

jobs to which women were appointed. In the case of clerical work,
the lower grades, such as copyist positions, were opened to women
about 1850, at a lower salary than that paid to men.[50]

Paradoxically, although in a sense women were worse off than blacks, they
nevertheless secured more advanced positions in a shorter period of time. Women could not vote until well after the enactment of the Civil Service Act, and
they were never politically important enough, or effectively organized for political action, to receive much in the way of patronage. Moreover, the introduction of the merit system had less of an impact on women than blacks because
women were formally excluded from most positions for many years. By 1897,
however, women had attained impressive positions in several categories, including
agrostologist, botanist, ethnologist, technical artist, librarian, translator, and
teacher.[51]

As in the case of blacks, the attitudes of the CSC have at various times,
encouraged sexual discrimination. At the outset, however, CSC was ideologically
opposed to sexual inequality:

> Nowhere on the part of the Commission or its subordinates
> is there any favor or disadvantage allowed by reason of sex. Only
> under free, open, competitive examinations have the worthiest
> women the opportunities, and the Government the protection,
> which arise from allowing character and capacity to win the prece-
> dence and the places their due.[52]

The CSC, however, eventually developed a rationale for accepting, and, in fact,
encouraging sexual discrimination that was similar in many ways to its rationale
for allowing and fostering racial discrimination. In the words of Commissioner
McMillin:

> Because the public service must by its nature be responsive
> to public opinion, and because the public does not yet accept with
> the same readiness a woman in authority, it is not astonishing
> that the proportion of women executives is small as compared with
> the total number of women in the Federal Service, nor that a depart-
> ment hesitates to give such positions to any but very outstanding
> women of proven ability.[53]

The CSC's lack of leadership in the quest for sexual equality has instilled a
sense of distrust against the CSC among women, minority group members, and
representationists in general, one which still affects its current operations.

THE MOVE TOWARDS EEO

The history of federal efforts to prevent discrimination and promote EEO in the federal service is complex yet instructive. It is impossible to view the present Federal EEO Program in its proper political and administrative contexts or to understand its policy development without entering into a consideration of past developments.

In a sense, the gradual development of the current program might be traced back to the enactment of the Civil Service Act, or even to the framing of Article VI of the Constitution. It was not until the late 1930s and early 1940s, however, that a continuing, systematic effort to ensure equal opportunity in the public service became a major feature of federal personnel administration. The Hatch Act of 1939[54] was the first significant link in the chain of laws and executive orders leading to the present program. Section 4 provided that:

> It shall be unlawful for any person to deprive, attempt to deprive, or threaten to deprive, by any means, any person of any employment, position, work, compensation, or other benefit provided for or made possible by any Act of Congress appropriating funds for work relief purposes, on account of race, creed, [or] color. . . .

Although the provision applied only to a peripheral kind of public employee, it did establish the principle that public employment or public funds should not be denied to individuals for reasons of race, color, or religion. Although this principle has been repeatedly reinforced, its realization remains somewhat elusive.

The next piece of important legislation to combat discrimination based upon race, creed, or color in the civil service was the Extension of Civil Service Act, or, as it is also known, the Ramspeck Act of 1940.[55] Section 3(e) prohibited "discrimination against any person, or with respect to the position held by any person, on account of race, creed, or color" in the fixing of salaries, allocation of positions to grades, and transferring of employees, as well as in promotions and other personnel actions. This section was added to the original bill without significant debate. The Senate also adopted an amendment which would have had more far-reaching consequences, namely, "*provided*, that the Civil Service Commission shall not require the submission with examination papers on examinations ordered or conducted by said Commission the photograph of the applicant. . . . ' [56] There was significant opposition to this provision in the House, however, and it was not included in the final bill. One congressman proclaimed, "I want to call your attention to the fact that there is a vast difference between racial distinction and racial discrimination. Under this amendment, the employer who wanted to secure a colored stenographer might secure a white one instead, and vice versa."[57] He went on to relate the experience of one office manager in the federal service who received an eligible list from the CSC and found, apparently to his dismay, that "all three eligibles on this list were Negro girls."[58] This led him to exclaim "O merit, merit, what crimes are committed in thy name"[59]—a refrain frequently echoed by present-day civil rights and minority group organizations. On the other hand, the provision was supported by some government officials on the following grounds:

> It is to the good fortune of America and the glory of the Negro race that as yet Negroes reply to overt and obvious discrimination with good humor, even if wryly. They deserve for all their long suffering [all] the forms of fairness until they can appreciate the very fact of fairness. This provision . . . would initiate a policy of at least fairness in form. Some of you will not let us do more than this. Many of us, under heaven, cannot do less than this and keep our own self-respect.[60]

The requirement of photographs was finally dropped by the CSC in 1942, but the reaction in the House was indicative of a pattern which was to characterize efforts to eliminate discrimination for several years to come. At the precise moment that a policy of nondiscrimination was being formulated and adopted, even the most rudimentary regulatory tools required to enforce it were being denied.

The Ramspeck Act was important because it represented the first major piece of legislation to outlaw discrimination in the federal service based on race, creed, or color. It also acted as a catalyst in encouraging similar actions undertaken by the executive branch. Shortly before the act was passed, but after its prospects for enactment were favorable, President Roosevelt issued Executive Order 8587, which amended the civil service rules to prohibit discrimination on the basis of race.[61] Roosevelt apparently did not want the primary impetus for such a policy to come from another branch of the government. The history of the development of these early regulations demonstrates the fact that the government only reluctantly formulated a policy of nondiscrimination in the federal service and basically lacked a strong commitment to equality.

The Fair Employment Practice Committee

In 1941 pressure for further reform began to mount. This pressure was, in part, due to the philosophical impact of the New Deal and to the increasing likelihood that the United States would become involved in the war. It was deemed desirable by many to promote racial harmony and unity in the face of a racist foe, and to expand war production through the utilization of manpower without regard to factors unrelated to output and efficiency. Perhaps the most dramatic and visible gesture in support of government action in the area of racial equality was A. Philip Randolph's threat to lead a mass march on Washington to protest discrimination against blacks. This strategy was developed in January 1941, and the march was scheduled for June. Roosevelt wanted to prevent this kind of direct action by blacks and tried to convince Randolph to cancel the march.[62] He failed, and in June these various forces came to a head and positive action was taken to create fair employment practices in the federal service and defense industries. Although Vito Marcantonio, an American Labor Party representative from New York, introduced the nation's first bill to this end,[63] it was the executive branch that finally led the way. On June 25, shortly before Randolph's proposed march, Roosevelt issued Executive Order 8802.[64] It declared:

> *Whereas*, it is the policy of the United States to encourage full participation in the national defense program by all citizens of the United States, regardless of race, creed, color, or national origin, in the firm belief that the democratic way of life within the Nation can be defended successfully only with the help and support of all groups within its borders; and
>
> *Whereas*, there is evidence that available and needed workers have been barred from employment in industries engaged in defense production solely because of consideration of race, creed, color, or national origin, to the detriment of workers' morale and of national unity:
>
> *Now, Therefore*, by virtue of the authority vested in me by the Constitution and the statutes, and as a prerequisite to the successful conduct of our national defense production effort, I do hereby reaffirm the policy of the United States that there shall be no discrimination in the employment of workers in defense industries or Government because of race, creed, color, or national origin.

The order also established a Fair Employment Practice Committee (FEPC) consisting of five persons in the Office of Production Management (OPM). The FEPC's function was to receive and investigate complaints of discrimination and to "take appropriate steps to redress grievances." It was also to make recommendations to governmental departments and agencies to effectuate the order. The initial draft of the order failed to include government agencies; it was changed only after requests for inclusion of the latter were made by A. Philip Randolph and Walter White.[65] The government had once again more or less backed into a policy of nondiscrimination in the federal service, but this time, significantly, it was at the behest of black leaders.

The FEPC's experience in counteracting discrimination within the federal government was varied. There is evidence that government officials did not take the order seriously; the FEPC, moreover, had no enforcement powers.[66] Acts of discrimination and segregation continued to occur. The FEPC was almost entirely complaint-oriented, that is, it addressed itself almost exclusively to individuals' claims that they were subject to discrimination, and it was unable to initiate large-scale programs to counteract discrimination. The FEPC was more concerned with equality in defense production; this fact explains why, throughout its five-year existence, it held only three hearings on discrimination in the government.[67] On the other hand, during the same period the representation of black civil servants in the Washington, D.C., area apparently increased significantly, although this was probably due to the laws of supply and demand rather than the committee's activities.[68] Even more significant, however, was the fact that for the first time the CSC had become actively involved in combatting discrimination.

Shortly after the order was issued, the FEPC and the CSC reached an agreement whereby the CSC would investigate and resolve complaints which had come to its attention. It was required to inform the FEPC of each complaint and of the action taken. The FEPC retained the right to criticize, request additional action, or assume jurisdiction in particular cases.[69] Although the CSC was effective in decreasing discrimination, it was nevertheless criticized for its weak handling of cases. Between October 1941 and March 1946 the CSC acted on 1,871 cases and found discrimination to exist in only 58.[70] In its *Final Report,* the FEPC reasoned that "the Commission found discrimination only when one of its rules had been violated. A conclusion may therefore be reached that some unrecorded discrimination was practiced within the field of discretionary action allowed a personnel officer by civil service rules."[71] It also concluded that although "the Civil Service Commission has an important role in the prosecution of nondiscrimination policy in Government, it is not logically the main enforcement agency."[72] This belief, still widely held even though the CSC is now the primary EEO agency, largely stems from the CSC's questionable record in the EEO field, its emphasis on merit, and its consequent lack of administrative credibility in the eyes of representationists.

Viewing the FEPC and CSC activities in retrospect, it should be noted that the shortcomings they possessed were not entirely of their own making. Fair employment practices, of course, were considerably less important than many other wartime activities. It was also somewhat difficult to be serious about nondiscrimination at a time when American citizens of Japanese descent were being interned in camps solely because of their national origin and racial characteristics. Moreover, Congressional hostility toward the FEPC was always evident. In addition, the committee had an unstable membership. In May 1943 it was moved from the OPM to the Office of Emergency Management(OEM).[73]

Congress refused to make the FEPC a permanent fixture. In 1946 it was discontinued by virtue of an amendment to an appropriations bill. In analyzing this development Will Maslow, a former director of the FEPC's Division of Field Operations, concluded: "Unquestionably the failure of FEPC was not solely due to antiquated rules of parliamentary procedure. The opposition to the FEPC was reflected not only in the well-organized Southern bloc but also in the apathy and uncertainty which characterized those who claimed to be supporters of the legislation."[74] Martin Luther King, Jr.'s contention that sympathetic but timid white liberals have been a major stumbling block to improved racial relationships seems to have been borne out at a relatively early date.

The Fair Employment Board

After the FEPC was dissolved, the CSC became responsible for the remains of the government's Fair Employment Program (FEP). It investigated complaints and prepared recommendations for resolving them. The CSC lacked adequate enforcement powers and could compel action only when it clearly demonstrated that an agency had actually violated CSC regulations. Paul H. Norgen and Samuel Hill have concluded that "proof of such violations was so difficult that little was accomplished."[75] From the point of view of effectiveness, the CSC's sacrosanct attitude (vis-a-vis its own regulations and its failure to recognize that discrimination was not only possible but inevitable within merit regulations) left much to be desired.

In 1948 the CSC's role was strengthened by Executive Order 9980.[76] The order declared that "the principles upon which our Government is based require a policy of fair employment throughout the Federal establishment, without discrimination because of race, color, religion, or national origin." It required that "all personnel actions taken by Federal appointing officers shall be based solely on merit and fitness." These officials were also "authorized and directed to take appropriate steps" to ensure nondiscrimination. Moreover, the department heads were made responsible for an effective program for fair employment within their organizations. The order also established a Fair Employment Board (FEB) within the CSC. The FEB had final authority in cases involving complaints of discrimination and theoretically could direct agencies to comply with its determinations.

The FEB continued to operate until 1955. During this period, it developed a substantial administrative apparatus to carry out the executive order. The FEB consisted of a chairman plus six members, all of whom supposedly were "persons who had had long experience in the public service and in community, business, or professional affairs."[77] At least one board member, however, was charged by the United Public Workers of America with being "an open advocate of discrimination against Negroes."[78] The FEB did not operate on a full-time basis; its day-to-day functions were carried forward by an executive secretary, an examiner, and a clerk-secretray. The program was administered in the various agencies by members of the agencies' central administrative staffs acting as fair employment officers (FEO). There were also deputy FEO's in several agencies' principal divisions, branches, and units.[79] The patterns for the current EEO bureaucracy were already beginning to develop more fully at this stage.

The FEB divided its work into two parts, of which the most highly developed part was the complaint-oriented corrective action program. In the FEB's

own words, it was "the first line of advance in the combat against discrimination."[80] Complaints had to be initiated by the agencies involved and at least
one hearing had to be held before an appeal could be made to the FEB. Initially,
only individual complaints could be heard, but by March 1949 third-party
complaints, which permitted the participation of civil rights and other groups,
were allowed under certain circumstances. The FEB's objectives with regard to
the corrective program were fourfold:

1. to insure full ascertainment of facts as a basis for action
2. to further good relations between complainants and administrative officers concerned, by means of informal discussion and
   negotiations
3. to give complainants easy access to officials specially designated to deal with discriminatory acts
4. to expedite the adjustment of complaints without unreasonable
   delay or expense.[81]

In assessing the validity of complaints, the FEB stressed the need to appraise
the "general employment patterns of Government units";[82] it therefore was
not solely confined to the specific facts involved in a particular case. The FEB
also reached the conclusion that "when confronted with charges of discrimination, appointing officers should be able to demonstrate affirmatively that their
selections were made solely on the basis of merit and fitness,"[83] thereby placing
a large share of the burden of proof upon these officials. Out of a total of
62 appeals during its first three years, the FEB found 13 cases of discrimination.[84]

The second part of the FEB's work was centered on the constructive
program, which was rather ill-defined and ineffective. It consisted of confer-
ences with fair employment officers and outside organizations, periodic surveys
and appraisals, and the adoption of some new recruitment techniques, better
training programs, and steps toward further integration. The FEB believed that
the impetus for direct action aimed at specific minority groups was strictly
guided by the need for "color-blindness" and merit:

> The fair employment policy does not mean that any fixed
> proportion of persons of different races, religions, or national
> origins must be given Federal employment. . . . No applicant or
> employee having merit and fitness shall be refused or deprived of
> employment or earned promotion by reason of his or her race, color,
> religion, or national origin. On the same principle, no one lacking
> merit or fitness shall receive preferment for the same reasons. The
> fair employment policy is a double-edged tool. . . . [85]

This conception of EEO was held by the CSC (and the government as a whole)
until 1971.

The FEB was far from effective for several reasons. Aside from its one questionable member, the FEB occasionally expressed a patronizing attitude — which was probably indicative of its overall outlook—and failed to consider the question of whether the merit system created a barrier to social representativeness. For example, after noting that blacks were making gains in federal employment, the FEB concluded that "there can be no doubt that this fact can be credited in part to a higher degree of merit and fitness among employees of the Negro race, based on longer experience, greater confidence, and improved standards of education and business training."[86] Equally significant is the fact that the FEB's directives frequently met with opposition in various agencies and were often ignored entirely.[87] There was also a genuine question concerning the government's desire to establish racial equality in the federal service. During this period, for instance, the United Public Workers of America observed that "the Panama Canal Zone is the one place under complete control of the executive branch of the Government of the United States . . . [and] racial bias is the official policy of the government."[88] A system of almost total segregation, including lower wage scales for nonwhites, was maintained there. De facto segregation, moreover, continued to be practiced in a few agencies.[89]

More importantly, however, the nation had entered the McCarthy era. The fact that racial equality had always been an official doctrine of communist ideology in the United States and elsewhere was sometimes distorted to serve as demonstrative evidence that *anyone*, including blacks, who believed in racial equality was a communist or communist sympathizer and was therefore disloyal to the nation, not to its officially condoned policy of racism. It was revealed, for example, that "scores of Negro and white Government employees who have been active in combatting discrimination have been brought up on charges of disloyalty under President Truman's Executive Order on employee loyalty."[90] The following were among the questions asked of employees and their acquaintances under the loyalty-security program:[91]

- What were your feelings at that time concerning race equality?
- Have you ever had Negroes in your home?
- Did you ever write a letter to the Red Cross about the segregation of blood?
- Have any of the neighbors made complaints about having Negroes in your home?
- Do you think the employee might have been an extremist about civil rights—race discrimination—questions of that nature?
- Would you say that the accused employee's feelings about racial matters were of such a nature as to indicate that he was a member of the Communist Party?

Of course, the fact that a person believes in racial equality doesn't prove that he's a Communist, but it certainly makes you look twice,

doesn't it? You can't get away from the fact that racial equality
is part of the Communist line.[92]

Given this kind of atmosphere, further efforts towards racial equality were not
likely to be forthcoming. Despite the FEB's own shortcomings and the climate
it had to cope with, it managed to establish a longevity record for the government program—about six years and five months—that has only recently been
surpassed.

The President's Committee on Government Employment Policy

In January 1955, as a result of Executive Order 10590, issued by President
Eisenhower, FEB was replaced by the President's Committee on Government
Employment Policy (PCGEP). The order represented a limited yet significant
break with the past. It reaffirmed the policy of nondiscrimination and proclaimed that "it is the policy of the United States Government that equal opportunity be afforded all qualified persons, consistent with law, for employment
in the Federal Government."[93] This was interpreted to mean that the government was obliged to take whatever action it deemed necessary to overcome
societal inequities and to equalize opportunity—not just the treatment received
by individuals.

The conflict between merit and representation in American society was
gradually beginning to have an impact on EEO policy. Under this policy, special
efforts in recruitment, training, and other areas of personnel administration
were directed towards those minority groups thought to be proportionally
underrepresented in the federal service as a result of societal inequalities. In
a limited sense, government employment policy became compensatory, although
there was no concerted effort to make representation a full-fledged objective.
At the same time, however, the desire to end individual acts of discrimination
was promoted.

The PCGEP was established to oversee the administration of new and
continuing EEO policies. It consisted of one representative from the Department of Labor, the CSC, and the Office of Defense Mobilization (ODM), and
two public members appointed by the president; in 1957 a representative from
the DOD and another public member were added. Specifically, the PCGEP
was required to report to the president, consult with departments and agencies
(especially the CSC), review cases of alleged discrimination brought to   its
attention, render advisory opinions, and carry out investigations. The order
also gave the department and agency heads significant authority. For example,
they were responsible for the effectuation of the order in their respective
agencies. In this capacity, they were instructed to establish complaint and
appeals procedures as well as to designate employment policy officers to advise

them, receive and investigate complaints, and make recommendations. The CSC's major function was to issue regulations necessary to implement the policy of the order.

The new system achieved mixed results. The PCGEP was always seriously underbudgeted and was further weakened by a lack of central authority.[94] It found that a complaint-oriented system was inherently of limited utility because there was "no doubt that many" complaints were "withheld because of reluctance" on the part of the complainants "to become identifed as trouble makers or risk reprisal," and because "even with complaints at hand descrimination is often elusive and difficult to pin down."[95] At the end of its existence, the PCGEP concluded that "the objective of attaining a Federal civil service unimpaired by discrimination has not been reached, that racial and religious descrimination yet remain, and that many of the problems which have confronted the Committee have not yet been solved."[96]

Despite this conclusion, the PCGEP did make some important contributions. The Employment Policy Officer (EPO) was made independent of the personnel officer at an early date, and although the two functions can again be combined under current regulations, it established a greater sensitivity to the problem of conflict of interest within the EEO realm. The PCGEP engaged in statistical surveys that have now become a standard measure of rate of progress. Finally, in a general sense the PCGEP succeeded in further sensitizing officials to the advisability of attaining EEO and making them aware of the needs of minorities and the importance of a successful program. The PCGEP found discrimination to exist in 33 out of a total of 225 cases it had reviewed.[97]

The President's Committee on EEO

Despite earlier progress, it was not until the 1960s that programs of non-discrimination and EEO began to have a major impact upon federal personnel administration. Between 1961 and 1965 the civil rights movement attained a position of prominence in the political arena; civil rights became the dominant national issue. It was a sign of the times when President John F. Kennedy stated, "I have dedicated my administration to the cause of equal opportunity in employment by the Government."[98] Accordingly, he issued Executive Order 10925,[99] which revamped the EEO program once again. The order reaffirmed the policies established by the Eisenhower Order, but was even more positive in its emphasis: it reunited the governmental and private programs; abolished the PCGEP; and established the President's Committee on Equal Employment Opportunity (PCEEO). The new committee was composed of: the vice-president, in the role of chairman (a fact which enhanced its prestige); the Secretary of Labor as vice-chairman; the chairman of the Atomic Energy Commission (AEC);

the Secretary of Commerce; the Attorney General; the Secretary of Defense; the Secretaries of the Army, Navy, and Air Force; the Administrator of General Services; the chairman of the CSC; and the head of NASA. There was also an ex officio executive vice-president who could act for the committee between its meetings. The PCEEO was to provide procedures and policies to implement the order, make reports to the president, and act in an advisory capacity. The order also required all executive departments to initiate studies of their employment practices.

The PCEEO implemented a program that was much more aggressive and positive than previous programs had been. Its activities were primarily divided into three categories. First, it adopted a more representationist approach. The PCEEO aided agencies and departments in implementing the affirmative action required of them by the executive order. This included adopting special measures to increase the number of blacks and Spanish-speaking individuals on the federal service registers; this might consist of making recruitment drives at high schools and colleges heavily attended by these groups. The PCEEO also encouraged various agencies to provide better training both for their employees and for the unemployed and unskilled outside the government. It made special efforts to identify and promote underutilized employees. It also took action to counteract the general societal tendency to deny minority group members access to those skills which might lead to better employment. For example, the PCEEO found that in the field of data processing blacks were often denied entry into training schools in the South. The committee counteracted this situation by encouraging the CSC to forbid "government agencies to deal with employment agencies, trade schools and similar recruitment sources that discriminate because of race, creed, color or national origin."[100] This situation provided a clear example of how public personnel policy could reach beyond the government and, moreover, it demonstrated why a strict merit approach could not yield a high level of passive representation. The PCEEO also initiated programs for training officials to carry out the executive order and held a series of regional meetings to implement the program.

Second, with the help of the CSC the PCEEO took an annual census of minority employment, thus making monitoring and appraisal possible. The categories identified were Negro, Mexican-American and Puerto Rican, Oriental, American Indian, and other. The initial surveys showed that only a few blacks had broken "invisible, but substantial" barriers to middle- and upper-grade employment and, in addition, that there was considerable proportional underrepresentation of other groups at these levels.[101] Later surveys showed limited improvements. The surveys were also used to encourage agencies to discover and promote persons who had been passed over unfairly in the past.

Third, the PCEEO was engaged in reviewing agency actions in response to complaints. Unlike earlier committees or boards created for this purpose, however, the PCEEO deemphasized the importance of complaints and noted that their usefulness in combatting discrimination was limited because of the possibility—perhaps probability—of reprisals against complainants. By November 1963, the PCEEO had processed 2,242 cases out of a total of 2,699 filed complaints; moreover, it took corrective action—such as promotion or reassignment—in over one-third of these cases.

The PCEEO, however, rarely decreed discrimination to exist because it believed that such a finding would needlessly encourage hostility.[102] This belief, still very much alive in the current program, has created a sense of disillusionment on the part of some individuals who feel that those guilty of discrimination should be disciplined or, at the very least, exposed. Moreover, this tendency to pass over instances of discrimination has made hearing sessions appear management-oriented; this, in turn, has considerably reduced the administrative credibility of complaint systems.

In general, it may be said that the Kennedy program was more effective than any of the earlier programs primarily because its approach was more positive, the PCEEO was more forceful, and the time for advances in the area of EEO was ripe. For example, when areas on noncompliance were discovered, it was required that all appointments and promotions be pre-audited for a given period in order that corrective action might be instituted. The PCEEO also took the position that "it is apparent that full equality of employment opportunity requires that we face up to the whole problem of equality itself,"[103] and accordingly was not reluctant to explore the possibility of adopting more representationist measures. Moreover, the PCEEO tried to develop close ties with "local community leadership," wherever possible, and with civil rights groups in general.

The Kennedy program was continued by President Johnson up until 1965, when a major change occurred. Shortly after Kennedy's death, the outlook of the civil rights movement altered significantly. "Black Power" loomed on the horizon. The Civil Rights Act of 1964 established the Equal Employment Opportunity Commission (EEOC),[104] which is authorized to attempt to prevent discrimination in most areas of private employment. The act made the problems of coordination among the various agencies—about 18 of which were actively engaged in civil rights—acute. The act also stated: "It shall be policy of the United States to ensure equal employment opportunities for Federal employees without discrimination because of race, color, religion, sex or national origin and the President shall utilize his existing authority to effectuate this policy." However, the PCEEO, which was indirectly financed through various agency budgets, ran into serious funding difficulties in Congress. Vice-President Humphrey, who was the committee chairman, initially sided with Congressional opponents either to phase the committee out of existence or to seek direct appropriations.[105] He eventually decided, however, that the government program should be managed by the CSC, which gave the appearance of being "eager to set up a tough new program to promote equal opportunity within the federal establishment."[106] This move was accomplished by Executive Order 11246.[107] The program has remained under CSC supervision ever since. The development of the "women's" part of the program, however, requires further explanation.

In December 1961 President Kennedy issued Executive Order 10980, which established a Presidential Commission on the Status of Women (PCSW). The preamble stated that "prejudices and outmoded customs act as barriers to the full realization of women's basic rights, which should be respected and fostered as part of our Nation's commitment to human dignity, freedom, and democracy." The PCSW's task was to develop recommendations for "overcoming discriminations in government and private employment on the basis of sex and for . . . services which will enable women to continue their role as wives and mothers while making a maximum contibution to the world around them."[108]

With regard to the federal service, the PCSW was to suggest action regarding "the employment policies and practices of the Government of the United States, with reference to additional affirmative steps which should be taken through legislation, executive or administrative action to assure non-discrimination on the basis of sex and to enhance constructive employment opportunities for women." The PCSW exerted pressure for a reinterpretation of the 1870 law, which had been interpreted as allowing officials to discriminate on the basis of sex. A ruling by Attorney General Kennedy in June 1962 declared that this interpretation was invalid and that the law did not prohibit the president or the CSC from prescribing the conditions under which federal service officials could consider only males or females in personnel actions.[109] In July, after receiving a memorandum from the president, the CSC amended the civil service regulations to read that appointments and promotions in the career service should be made without regard to sex except in highly unusual circumstances in which it finds sexual differentiation to be justified.[110] As in the case of minority groups, outlawing discrimination against women did not prevent instances of the latter from occurring. Further action was therefore taken.

The CSC played a limited role in combatting sexual discrimination under the revised regulations because it had to make determinations as to when the division of labor on the basis of sex was legitimate. In general, the CSC has permitted such discrimination in certain "law enforcement positions requiring the bearing of firearms," and positions of a "custodial or institutional nature where duties can be properly performed only by a member of the same sex as the individuals under his or her care."[111] The CSC was also involved in conducting inspections to determine the extent of discrimination. In the course of the inspections it was found that overt discrimination was rare, and that only in less than 10 percent of the establishments inspected was there a reluctrance to hire or promote women as a result of hazardous job conditions, unpleasant surroundings, arduous activities, "moral dangers," or simply a lack of general acceptance.[112] On the other hand, it was also found that women were almost universally confined to the lower-level positions. Although this was attributed to "cultural factors" rather than to overt discrimination, it was undoubtedly also the result of a prior policy of exclusion of women from upper-level positions. No important developments concerning sexual discrimination occurred until 1967, when the women's program was incorporated into the overall Federal EEO Program as a result of Executive Order 11375.[113] This development will be discussed at greater length in the next chapter, where the organization of the current program will be considered.

CONCLUSIONS

Several aspects of the history of discrimination in the federal service and efforts to institute greater EEO in the federal service prior to the establishment of the current program have been stressed in the preceding pages. First, and in some ways foremost, it is very clear that merit practices were not as socially neutral as has often been claimed. The merit system permitted, and in some instances, created direct discrimination against minority group members and women. To a certain extent, such discrimination was the result of a deviation from merit principles in the strictest sense; but it was a type of deviation which was officially sanctioned and fostered by CSC, department and agency heads, and other high-ranking governmental officials. The merit system did not simply aim at obtaining the best federal servants; rather, it was directed toward recruiting and promoting to positions of importance the "best" white males.

Past instances of discrimination under the merit system have created a political force of considerable importance today. Support for a strict interpretation and application of merit principles has weakened considerably, especially among minority group federal servants who have largely come to regard support for the merit system as a form of covert support for continued inequality. It has also become increasingly difficult to argue against "diluting" the merit system by including representationist objectives in federal personnel policy. Moreover, the CSC, which is the strongest supporter of merit, has encountered great difficulty in justifying its activities and winning its pro-merit points in recent years precisely because of its official support for discrimination in the past and its consequent traditional deviation from strict merit principles.

A second point which should be emphasized is the fact that the history of efforts to establish greater EEO is, to a considerable extent, a history of unwillingness to bring about genuine reform. The federal government only reluctantly adopted a policy of nondiscrimination. The organizations with responsibility for overseeing EEO have, until just recently, been weak and only marginally effective at best. They have generally been underbudgeted, understaffed, and have lacked real authority. The initial pattern of placing much of the responsibility for achieving EEO in the hands of the agencies and departments and of appointing a board or committee to offer them guidance has militated against change. In general, it may be said that discrimination was rife because the departments and agencies favored or at least condoned it. The expectation—if it ever truly existed—that they would adopt a different policy in response to executive orders asking them to do so has still not been met. Moreover, the authority, prestige, image, and budget of agencies is primarily a function of their operational activities, as opposed to their personnel activities. Agencies were not willing, until recently, to divert their energies from operations to EEO, or to run the risk of disharmony, low morale, decreased efficiency, and so forth, all of which might result if a strong and progressive EEO program were instituted.

A third point to bear in mind is the fact that considerable difficulties have been encountered in establishing a satisfactory complaint system. There has been a general sense of reluctance, and perhaps even an inablility, to uncover instances of discrimination and to effectively punish those officials who engage in outright discrimination. The early belief that discrimination was solely a matter of violation of the laws or civil service rules proved to be far too short-sighted. The substitution of another standard, however, has not been easy. Discrimination has been viewed as a matter of intent, but CSC officials who discriminate can almost always develop some other rationale for their actions. One solution has simply been not to uncover acts of discrimination, but rather to take "corrective action" in the absence of such a finding if it is clear that illegal, unfair treatment existed. This course of action, however, has probably decreased the credibility of the complaint system in the eyes of those who not only want to be treated fairly but also want it known that they have been treated unjustly. Handling complaints promptly, protecting employees against reprisals, and overcoming the latter group's fear of filing such complaints have also proved to be significant problems.

Fourth, if there has been a question of conflict of interest involved in vesting considerable authority in the various departments and agencies, a much greater controversy surrounds the role of the CSC itself. On the one hand, making the government's central personnel agency responsible for EEO is logical. EEO is primarily a personnel function which should probably be integrated with other personnel functions. On the other hand, however, the CSC is largely responsible for the development of a personnel system that permitted and fostered a good deal of discrimination; to some extent, therefore, it has had a vested interest in the maintenance of past practices. The CSC also strongly supports merit concepts and has mainly opposed and obstructed representationist practices. When the CSC serves as the main EEO agency, there is no independent check on the fairness of personnel activities. When, conversely another agency is put in charge, EEO tends to be superimposed upon, rather than integrated into, public personnel administrative activities. This dilemma, which has yet to be resolved, is of considerable political importance at the present time; the truth of this statement will become clear in the remainder of this study.

Another point to be noted is the fact that there has been a slow yet steady drift towards a public personnel policy which favors modification of "color-blind" merit procedures in favor of a more representationist approach. At the outset, the objective of the Federal EEO Program was to implement simple nondiscriminatory measures. It was thought that the eradiction of discriminatory treatment in the federal service would clear the way for the entrance and advancement of members of minority groups. As federal personnel practices became less discriminatory, however, it became apparent that there were other important barriers preventing greater passive representation of minority group members. The concept of directing special efforts to specific groups began to gain importance during the second half of the 1950s, and by the 1960s a fuller recognition of the interrelationship between societal inequalities and EEO in the federal service had developed. It was not until the 1970s, however, that significant support for goals or quotas materialized. In addition, the history of the EEO program well illustrates that

> reorganization has become almost a religion in Washington. It has its symbol in the organization chart, Old Testament in the Hoover Commission Reports, high priesthood in the Bureau of the Budget, and society for the propagation of the faith in sundry groups such as the Citizens Committee for the Hoover Report.
>
> Reorganization is deemed synonymous with reform and reform with progress. Periodic reorganizations are prescribed if for no other purpose than to purify the bureaucratic blood and to prevent stagnation. Opposition to reorganization is evil and attributable, according to Mr. Hoover, to the "gang up, log-rolling tactics of the bureaus and their organized pressure groups."
>
> For the true believer, reorganization can produce miracles: eliminate waste and save billions of dollars; restore to health and economic vigor a chronically ill maritime industry; abate noise at airports; control crime in the streets, to name but [a] few. The myth persists that we can resolve deep-seated and intractable issues of substance by reorganization.[114]

Yet in an "alliance" somewhat reminiscent of that existing between church, temperence group, and bootlegger, there is no doubt that many have sought to benefit from, in Seidman's words, "the tactical and strategic uses of organization structure as an instrument of politics, position, and power."[115] The Federal EEO Program has been a major victim of the propensity to reorganize. It has been subject to reorganization seven times since its inception in 1941. It has been shifted into the CSC twice and removed from it once. Two president's committees dealing with EEO were established and disbanded. By 1965, the average life of the Federal EEO Program in any one organizational form was less than five years; the shortest period was about two years; and the longest about six-and-a-half years. Some of the reorganizational maneuvers were clearly intended to kill or weaken the program, while others were meant to demonstrate a presidential commitment to civil rights and increased EEO. Whatever the reason, however, reorganizations have undoubtedly delayed progress in the EEO area. If we assume that it takes about 1 year, given the bureaucratic environment, to get a program such as EEO moving again after a reorganization, then 6 years out of the program's first 24 were largely wasted. Moreover, it is naive at best, and damaging at worst, to expect a great deal of visible progress to take place in so short a time and in an area as complex as this one. Yet the tendency toward reorganization is not a thing of the past, and in recent years there has been considerable support for the transferral of the program from the CSC to the EEOC.

NOTES

1. Samuel Krislov, *The Negro in Federal Employment* (Minneapolis, Minn.: University of Minnesota Press, 1967), p. 8.

2. U.S., *Statutes At Large,* vol. 2, 594 (April 30, 1810). This provision applied to contractors as well as postal employees.

3. Quoted by Krislov, *The Negro in Federal Employment,* p. 9.

4. Leon F. Litwack, *North of Slavery* (Chicago: University of Chicago Press, 1961), p. 57.

5. U. S., *Statutes At Large,* vol. 4, 104 (March 3, 1825); Litwack, op. cit., p. 58.

6. U.S., *Statutes at Large,* vol. 13, 515 (March 3, 1865). Repeal was attempted in 1862 and was successful in the Senate but tabled in the House. In 1863 reenactment of general mail statutes neither repeated not repealed it. U.S., *Statutes At Large* vol. 12, 701 (March 3, 1863). See Litwack, *North of Slavery,* pp. 58-59; see also, Krislov, *The Negro in Federal Employment,* p. 10.

7. See Laurence J. W. Hayes, *The Negro Federal Government Worker,* (Washington, D.C.: Howard University Press, 1941), p. 21. Krislov, p. 12, cites Ebenezer Basset, Minister to Haiti, as the first black to serve in the bureaucracy.

8. See Hayes, *The Negro Federal Government Worker,* p. 153, Appendix K. He estimates that 51,882 out of a total of 540,867 (9.59 percent) federal employees in the Washington, D.C., area were black.

9. Krislov, *The Negro in Federal Government,* p. 14.

10. Hayes, *The Negro Federal Government Worker,* p. 19.

11. Ibid., p. 153, Appendix K.

12. U.S. Civil Service Commission [CSC], *Annual Report* 8 (1891): 6; cited by Hayes, *The Negro Federal Government Worker,* p. 24.

13. Quoted by Leonard D. White, *The Republican Era* (New York: Free Press, 1965), p. 342.

14. W.E.B. DuBois, *Dusk of Dawn* (New York: Harcourt, Brace, 1940), p. 233.

15. National Committee on Segregation in the Nation's Capital, *Segregation in Washington* (Chicago: National Committee on Segregation in the Nation's Capital, 1948), p. 60.

16. Quoted by Kathleen Long Wolgemuth, "Woodrow Wilson's Appointment Policy and the Negro," *Journal of Southern History* 24 (November 1958): 457.

17. Quoted by Arthur S. Link, *Wilson: The New Freedom* (Princeton, N.J.: Princeton University Press., 1965), p. 244.

18. Ibid., p. 246.

19. Ibid.

20. Ibid., p. 247; Krislov, *The Negro in Federal Government*, p. 20.

21. National Committee on Segregation in the Nation's Capital, *Segregation in Washington*, p. 61; Krislov, *The Negro in Federal Government*, p. 21. Photographs may have legitimate uses, but in the context of the Wilson administration they were undoubtedly used to facilitate discrimination.

22. Wilson was under constant pressure, with respect to blacks in the civil service, from Southern members of Congress; the latter organized the "National Democratic Fair Play Association," which, according to Link (*Wilson: The New Freedom*, p. 246), was made up of demagogic "rabid white supremacists."

23. See Wolgemuth, "Woodrow Wilson's Appointment Policy and the Negro," for a detailed study of this question. It should be remembered that at the time most blacks were Republicans.

24. According to Link, *Wilson: The New Freedom*, p. 248, "Burleson and McAdoo made a clean sweep of Negro political appointees in the South and allowed local postmasters and collectors of internal revenue either to downgrade or to dismiss Negro workers with civil service status." Louis Ruchames, *Race, Jobs and Politics: The Story of FEPC* (New York: Columbia University Press, 1953), p. 6, states that between 1912 and 1918 blacks in the Departments of the Navy, Interior, Commerce, Agriculture, and the Post Office were demoted, dismissed, denied positions, and forced to resign.

25. Hayes, *The Negro Federal Government Worker*, p. 41.

26. Quoted by Link, *Wilson: The New Freedom*, p. 251.

27. Hayes, *The Negro Federal Government Worker*. p. 65.

28. Quoted by Hayes, ibid., p. 66.

29. Ibid.

30. See Krislov, *The Negro in Federal Government*, p. 22.

31. See Herbert Aptheker, "Segregation in Federal Government Departments: 1928," *Science and Society* 28 (Winter 1964): 86-91.

32. Ibid., p. 88

33. Ibid., pp. 88-89.

34. Ibid., p. 89.

35. Ibid., pp. 90-91.

36. Ibid., p. 91.

37. Ibid.

38. Ibid.

39. See Krislov, *The Negro in Federal Government*, pp. 22ff, for specific examples.

40. Ibid., p. 23.

41. U.S., *Revised Statutes*, no. 165, U.S. Code (1964 ed.), vol. 5,33 (July 12,1870); originally U.S., *Statutes at Large*, vol. 16, 250.

42. Paul P. Van Riper, *History of the United States Civil Service* (Evanston, Ill.: Row, Peterson, 1958), p. 261.

43. U.S. Civil Service Commission, *History of the Federal Civil Service, 1789 to the Present* (Washington, D.C.: U.S. Government Printing Office, 1941), p. 35.

44. U.S., *Statutes At Large*, vol. 42, 1488 (March 4, 1923). Reaffirmed by the Classification Act of 1949, U.S., *Statutes at Large*, vol. 63, part 1, 954.

45. Quoted by Lucille Foster McMillin, *Women in the Federal Service* (Washington, D.C.: U.S. Government Printing Office, 1941), p. 26. The provision, amended in 1918 to allow the appointment of women whose husbands or sons were in the armed forces, was revoked in 1921.

46. Ibid., pp. 21-22.

47. U.S., *Statutes At Large*, vol. 50. part 1, 534 (July 26, 1937).

48. McMillin, *Women in the Federal Service*, p. 21.

49. Evelyn Harrison, "The Working Woman: Barriers in Employment," *Public Administration Review* 24 (June 1964): 80.

50. McMillin, *Women in the Federal Service*, p. 3.

51. Ibid., p. 15.

52. U.S. Civil Service Commission, *Annual Report* 1; quoted by McMillin, *Women in the Federal Service*, p. 11.

53. McMillin, *Women in the Federal Service*, p. 42.

54. U.S., *Statutes At Large*, vol. 53, part 2, 1147 (August 2, 1939).

55. Ibid., vol. 54, part 1, 1211 (November 26, 1940).

56. U.S., Congress, Senate, *Congressional Record*, 76th Cong., 3d. sess., September 26, 1940, 86, pt. 11: 12640.

57. Ibid., October 7, 1940, pt. 12: 13331.

58. Ibid.

59. Ibid.

60. Ibid., p. 13333.

61. U.S., *Federal Register*, November 7, 1940, 5, pt. 4: 4445. The rules had previously prohibited discrimination on the basis of religion and politics.

62. See Krislov, *The Negro in Federal Government*, pp. 29-30; Ruchames, *Race, Jobs and Politics*, p. 15ff.

63. See Ruchames, *Race, Jobs and Politics*, p. 15.

64. U.S., *Federal Register*, June 25, 1941, 6, pt. 2: 3109.

65. Ruchames, *Race, Jobs and Politics*, pp. 20-21.

66. Ibid., p. 24.

67. See Krislov, *The Negro in the Federal Government*, pp. 33-34. These hearings involved the Department of Commerce, the Office of Education, and the Newport News Post Office.

68. Ibid., p. 30.

69. U.S. Fair Employment Practice Committee [FEPC], *Final Report* (Washington, D.C.: U.S. Government Printing Office, 1947), p. 31.

70. Ibid., pp. 31-32.

71. Ibid., p. 32.

72. Ibid.

73. The move was the result of Executive Order 9346, May 27, 1943. It represented a setback for the committee; see Louis C. Kesselman, *The Social Politics of FEPC* (Chapel Hill, N.C.: University of North Carolina Press, 1948), p. 20.

74. Will Maslow, "FEPC—A Case History in Parliamentary Maneuver," *University of Chicago Law Review* 13 (June 1946): 442. During this period, according to the United Public Workers of America (UPWA), as wartime agencies were being liquidated, efforts were being made to transfer their own personnel to permanent agencies. The following agencies refused to accept nonwhites: Patent Office, GAO, Bureau of Internal Revenue, Federal Security Agency (FSA), Alien Property Custodian, Navy, Government Printing Office, War Department, State Department, and Bureau of the Budget. UPWA, *The Story of Discrimination in Government* (n.p., [1948]), pp. 6-7.

75. Paul H. Norgen and Samuel Hill, *Toward Fair Employment* (New York: Columbia University Press, 1964), p. 194.

76. U.S., *Federal Register*, July 26, 1948, 13, pt. 4: 4311.

77. U.S., CSC Fair Employment Board [FEB], *Fair Employment in the Federal Service*, Pamphlet 44 (December 1951), p. 2.

78. UPWA, *The Story of Discrimination*, p. 12.

79. FEB, *Fair Employment in the Federal Service*, p. 2.

80. Ibid.

81. Ibid., p. 3.

82. Ibid.

83. Ibid., p. 5.

84. Ibid., p. 3.

85. Ibid., p. 1.

86. Ibid., p. 10.

87. See Norgen and Hill, *Toward Fair Employment,* p. 194.

88. UPWA, *Jim Crow Discrimination Against U.S. Employees in the Canal Zone* (n.p., n.d.). p. 2.

89. See John A. Davis, "Nondiscrimination in the Federal Services," *Annals of the American Academy of Political and Social Science* 244 (March 1946): 73.

90. UPWA, *The Story of Discrimination,* pp. 12-13.

91. See D. Rosenbloom, *Federal Service and the Constitution* (Ithaca, N.Y.: Cornell University Press, 1971), Chapter 6, for a discussion of this program.

92. Adam Yarmolinsky, *Case Studies in Personnel Security* (Washington, D.C.: Bureau of National Affairs, 1955), p. 89; L.A. Nikoloric, "The Government Loyalty Program," *American Scholar* 19 (Summer 1950): 294; *Bailey v. Richardson,* 182 F2d 46, 73 (1950); UPWA, *The Story of Discrimination,* pp. 13-14; Walter Gellhorn, *Security, Loyalty, and Science* (Ithaca, N.Y.: Cornell University Press, 1950), p. 152.

93. U.S., *Federal Register,* January 18, 1955, 20, pt. 1: 409.

94. According to the PCGEP, however, "to have given the Committee authority to make mandatory decisions on cases would have removed from department and agency heads the authority to dispose completely of matters of discrimination within their jurisdiction. There is no evidence that such infringement on the power of agencies would make the nondiscrimination program more effective. Second, the Committee has secured complete cooperation from all the departments and agencies in which cases involving the Committee arose." U.S., President's Committee on Government Employment Policy [PCGEP], *Fourth Report* (Washington, D.C.: U.S. Government Printing Office, 1961), p. 12. According to Norgren and Hill, *Toward Fair Employment,* p. 194, the PCGEP never had a budget larger than $40,000 per annum.

95. PCGEP, *Fourth Report,* p. 30.

96. Ibid., p. 43.

97. Ibid., p. 29.

98. U.S. Civil Service Commission, *The Opening Door,* October 1962, p. 1.

99. U.S., *Federal Register,* March 6, 1961, 26, pt. 2: 1977.

100. U.S., President's Committee on Equal Employment Opportunity [PCEEO], *Report to the President* (Washington, D.C.: U.S. Government Printing Office, 1963), p. 31.

101. Ibid., p. 3. See Chapter 6.

102. See Krislov, *The Negro in the Federal Government,* p. 40.

103. PCEEO, *Report to the President,* p. 134.

104. P.L. 88-352, U.S., *Statutes at Large,* vol. 78, part 1, p. 241 (July 2, 1964).

105. See Krislov, *The Negro in the Federal Government,* pp. 42-45; Christopher Pyle and Richard Morgan, "Johnson's Civil Rights Shake-Up," *New Leader,* October 11, 1965, pp. 3-6.

106. Krislov, *The Negro in the Federal Government,* p. 45; Pyle and Morgan, "Johnson's Civil Rights Shake-Up, p. 5.

107. U.S., *Federal Register,* 30, pt. 10: 12319.

108. U.S., *Federal Register,* December 14, 1961, 26, pt. 12: 12059.

109. U.S. Civil Service Commission, *Study of Employment of Women in the Federal Government, 1968* (Washington, D.C.: U.S. Government Printing Office, 1969), pp. 1-2. The 1870 statute was subsequently repealed by Congress in 1965.

110. Memorandum to heads of departments and agencies, dated July 24, 1962, cited in U.S., President's Commission on the Status of Women [PCSW], *Report* (Washington, D.C.: U.S. Government Printing Office, 1963), p. 15.

111. U.S. Civil Service Commission, *Consolidated Report of Inspection Findings on the Status of Women in the Federal Service, April 30, 1962–April 30, 1964* (Washington, D.C.: CSC, 1964), p. 1. The PCSW noted: "Even before the issuance of the new regulations, the Civil Service Commission began to require agencies to give reasons for specifying sex. The requirement had prompt effect. Comparison of the requests from Washington agencies for eligibles from the Federal Service Entrance Examination . . . during the two periods November 13–December 8, 1961, and February 4–March 3, 1962, shows that in the earlier period there were 33 requests for women, 205 requests for men, 216 requests with no sex specified; in the latter, 1 request for women, 11 for men, and 682 with no sex specified." See *American Women,* ed. Margaret Mead and F. B. Kaplan (New York: Scribner's, 1965), p. 51.

112. Civil Service Commission, *Consolidated Report of Inspection Findings,* p. 13.

113. U.S., *Federal Register,* October 13, 1967, 32, pt. 10: 14303.

114. Harold Seidman, *Politics, Position, and Power* (New York: Oxford University Press, 1970), pp. 3-4.

115. Ibid., p. 13.

4

THE POLITICS
OF ORGANIZATION

The historical background of the Federal EEO Program demonstrates that in this area, at least, organizational choices are often political choices.[1] An analysis of the organization of the current program only strengthens this conclusion. The nature of bureaucratic politics in the federal government demands that agencies have ideologies and "cultures," that is, well-patterned ways of behaving. These elements contribute to a program's internal cohesiveness and provide a defense against possible encroachments by outsiders. In addition, they also may have a profound effect upon policy development and the nature of its implementation. Thus, the current organization of the Federal EEO Program within the CSC has been intertwined with the content of its policy and the style of its administration.

AUTHORITY FOR THE CURRENT PROGRAM

The CSC has been the central personnel agency of the federal government since 1883, the year in which the Civil Service (or Pendleton) Act was passed. As such, it seemed a reasonable choice for assuming primary responsibility for the maintenance of a government-wide EEO program. The CSC, however, partly as a result of the almost reflexive propensity toward reorganization typical of the federal government, only played a major role in EEO affairs from 1948 to 1955 and from 1965 to the present. The current program for EEO in the federal service was inaugurated in September 1965 with the issuance of Executive Order 11246. The order, which reaffirmed the long-standing policy against discrimination in federal employment on the basis of race, color, creed, and national origin, also stressed the desire to "promote the full realization of equal employment opportunity through a positive, continuing program in each executive department and agency." The CSC was given authority to supervise and advise in the EEO realm, and to "provide for the prompt, fair, and impartial consideration of all complaints of discrimination."[2] The order specified that these procedures should include at least one review within the executive department or agency involved and a right to appeal to the CSC. The latter was also given authority to issue binding orders, regulations, and instructions to the department and agency heads. These heads, in turn, were responsible for the development and implementation of EEO programs within their own organizations. The order reflected an outlook which had previously been developed by the CSC. As was noted earlier, in 1967 equality on the basis of sex was incorporated in the Federal EEO Program by Executive Order 11375; thus, EEO included women for the first time.

Under the CSC's direction, the Federal EEO Program experienced considerable development. With the close of the Johnson administration, however, the CSC sought the issuance of a new executive order. There were two major reasons behind its action. First, it was politically advisable to operate under an executive order issued by an incumbent president. This was especially true in the case of EEO and the Nixon administration, which did not appear to be strongly committed to promoting civil rights. Without some type of formal support from the administration, the CSC's EEO position vis-a-vis other agencies might have been untenable. Second, the CSC wanted to legitimate the approaches it had adopted under the Johnson executive orders.

The CSC drew up a draft of an executive order for consideration by the White House. It contained provisions aimed at consolidating the previously adopted approaches and reinforcing the authority necessary for the continuation of its activities in the EEO realm. In addition, it could also serve as an indicator of the Nixon administration's support for its activities. The CSC was highly successful in its endeavor, and on August 8, 1969, President Nixon issued Executive Order 11478, which differed only slightly from the CSC's draft. The new order, while it did not represent a significant break with the past in any philosophical or policy-oriented sense, was stronger than previous orders in its verbal commitment to a program of more than just nondiscrimination, and its issuance coincided with the development of a somewhat more positive outlook within the CSC itself. Executive Order 11478 proclaimed:

> It is the policy of the Government of the United States to provide equal opportunity in Federal employment for all persons, to prohibit discrimination in employment because of race, color, religion, sex, or national origin, and to promote the full realization of equal employment opportunity through a continuing affirmative program in each executive department and agency. This policy of equal opportunity applies to and must be an integral part of every aspect of personnel policy and practice in the employment, development, advancement, and treatment of civilian employees of the Federal Government.

The agency heads were required to "establish and maintain an affirmative program of equal employment opportunity." Unlike earlier orders, however, specific techniques were outlined:

> It is the responsibility of each department and agency head, to the maximum extent possible, to provide sufficient resources to administer such a program in a positive and effective manner; assure that recruitment activities reach all sources of job candidates; utilize to the fullest extent the present skills of each employee; provide the maximum feasible opportunity to employees to enhance their skills so they may perform at their highest potential and advance in accordance with their abilities; provide training and advice to managers and supervisors to assure their understanding and implementation of the policy expressed in this Order; assure participation at the local level with other employers, schools, and public or private groups in cooperative efforts to improve community conditions which affect employability; and provide for a system within the department or agency for periodically evaluating the effectiveness with which the policy of this Order is being carried out.[3]

The CSC's overall role in EEO affairs and its responsibility for maintaining a complaint system were, of course, retained.

The CSC's role in EEO affairs was considerably strengthened by the Equal Employment Opportunity Act of 1972. For the first time ever, the act placed the program and the CSC's responsibility for it on a statutory basis. It reaffirmed the traditional policy of nondiscrimination and empowered the CSC to enforce its provisions "through appropriate remedies, including [the] reinstatement or hiring of employees with or without back pay . . . [and the issuance of] such rules, regulations, orders and instructions as it deems necessary and appropriate. . . ."[4] It also made the CSC responsible for the annual review and approval of agency EEO plans and for evaluating agency EEO activities. In terms of policy, the act stressed an affirmative rather than simply a corrective approach.

THE CSC

In the words of one recent critic: "Each agency has its own culture and internal set of loyalties and values which are likely to guide its actions and influence its policies."[5] It is therefore necessary to gain some understanding of the culture of the CSC before one can interpret developments in the current Federal EEO Program.

The CSC is an independent agency headed by three presidentially appointed commissioners, one of whom is designated as chairman. It is at the head of what might be called a "personnel complex" in the federal government.

Organizationally, the CSC shares its dominant role with the House and Senate Committees on Post Office and Civil Service. These three units interact on a regular basis with a host of other groups, including the National Civil Service League (NCSL), the National Federation of Federal Employees (NFFE), the American Federation of Government Employees (AFGE), and the postal unions, whose strength is considerable. These participants in the personnel complex have worked together over the years in such a way as to create a personnel system which lays heavy stress upon security and stability.

Although the federal personnel system revolves, to a very large extent, around positions rather than people, in some respects it also tends to place the individual's rights on a par with, or even above those of, the organization, and occasionally even above the rights of the public at large. A major result of this personnel philosophy has been to divorce public personnel administration from organizational goal attainment. Indeed, one might rightly argue that Brian Chapman's observation on this point, although aimed at Western Europe, is basically applicable to the United States as well: "The truth is that people employed in government service are tending to become not only self-governing but also self-employed. All the evidence . . . points in this direction. This drift towards the syndical state machine is one of the unnoticed oddities of the last 50 years."[6] Thus, organizations of federal employees have gained the right to participate in grievance proceedings, in the formulation and implementation of personnel policies and practices, and in matters affecting working conditions in general. On the whole, according to Louis C. Gawthrop, participants in the personnel complex

> seek to maximize individual security and protection against arbitrary personnel decisions. They agree that effective and efficient administrative actions can only be realized within a relatively stable organizational environment in which individual anxieties and tensions generated by feelings of occupational insecurity have been significantly eliminated. If one can remove the causes of such anxiety— threatened dismissals, reductions in rank, arbitrary reward allocations—then personnel security can be realized, administrative continuity develops, and operating efficiency increases.[7]

In terms of the CSC, these objectives are viewed as necessary features of a successful merit system.

This type of public personnel administrative philosophy, now largely written into law, has affected EEO in several general ways. To begin with, it has had a considerable impact on the prestige and image of the CSC both in the eyes of other agencies, and those of congressional committees and interest groups outside the personnel complex. The resulting state of affairs and the CSC's reaction to it have militated against EEO. The CSC, which, according to Gawthrop, "has consistently resisted major innovations in the federal career process,"[8] has also consistently suffered from a rather low level of prestige and respect. Opposition to the agency has come from many sources; a study of federal executives found that some of the antipathy arises from the fact that the agency "is charged with the responsibility of administering a myriad of statutes that prescribe in detail how the federal personnel system should operate in order to keep rascals and unfit persons out of government jobs."[9] As such, its role has historically consisted of policing and enforcing a basically negative set of requirements which, have had the effect of "hemming in the line operator with restrictive rules governing job classification, appointment, promotion, transfer, salary change, and dismissal of employees."[10] Federal executives, managers, and other employees charged with responsibility for production or "hard" output programs often consider it necessary to circumvent the restrictions governing their handling of personnel; they occasionally come to view the CSC as an antagonist in the struggle for results in what is often a high-pressure environment.

A second source of opposition to the CSC stems from the fact that "the Commission's role with respect to veterans' preference and similar provisions is not merely that of policeman; it is also an agency at the service of a clientele group. This is probably one of the least understood aspects of the Washington environment for new executives."[11] It is one thing to be severely restricted in dealing with personnel if this is deemed the only alternative to a highly politicized or inefficient bureaucracy. It is quite another to be limited and forced to conform to the desires of special interests groups. In this regard the observations of one executive are instructive:

> About a decade or more ago, we used to ask around Washington, "For whom does the Civil Service Commission work?" We used to reply, "Well, we think it works first for its congressional committees, second for the status of employees, third for the American Legion in support of veterans' preference laws, fourth for the civil service employees unions, and possibly fifth for the President." Since the end of World War II, the President has moved up in this list but it is difficult to tell just how far.[12]

Although changes in the order in which groups or individuals are listed are important, more significant is the fact that no mention is made of other agencies or of agency management in general.

A third source of opposition to the CSC stems, somewhat surprisingly, from the fact that despite its conservatism, the CSC has managed to develop an image as something of a troublemaker. This has largely been the result of its inspection activities, aimed at determining whether agencies are conforming to the requirements of personnel regulations. These activities, writes Bernstein, "have been attacked as unwarranted interference with agency administration."[13] As one federal executive expressed it:

Some of the Commission's staff have told local managers of our field offices that they have poor personnel programs, inadequate employee training, no coffee break, insufficient emphasis on incentive awards, and so on. The Commission can stir up a lot of employee criticism this way and interfere with administration.

Civil service inspectors have interviewed field personnel at lower salary levels, asking about the administration of personnel programs. They raise questions in the minds of employees. If there is an effective union, soon it is charging that we are treating the employees unfairly and not complying with some civil service law. If we are violating a personnel statute, the Commission should so inform the head of the agency, but it should not be stirring up trouble between the agency and its field staffs.[14]

In addition, the complexity of civil service law and its imprecision in many cases make it unlikely that nonpersonnel officials—and even many personnel officials—will be aware of the CSC's and the courts' most recent lines of interpretation.

In some ways, low prestige feeds upon itself. Perhaps as a form of compensation for what they and the general public consider to be the low prestige of working for the government, federal employees often tend to be acutely aware of prestige differentials within and among agencies. Even potential recruits, it seems, "are concerned not so much with the prestige of the government as a whole but rather with the standing of a particular agency. They want to be part of an organization that is accomplishing something useful."[15] It is generally conceded, both within and without the CSC, that CSC employees are not the best of the federal crop; many of them are inclined to leave the CSC when the opportunity arises. During 1971-72, for example, several high-ranking members of the Office of Federal Equal Employment Opportunity (OFEEO) voluntarily left the CSC. The exodus of its better employees is also facilitated by the relative ease with which many of them can acquire knowledge of vacancies and develop contacts in other agencies through the CSC's central personnel functions.

Low prestige also tends to be self-fulfilling in another way. Because the CSC suffers from a relatively poor image—as does the personnel function itself,[16]—and because many federal executives consider the agency to be something of a stumbling block which must be overcome if progress is to be achieved in their specific programs, there has been a definite, although unmeasurable, tendency to ignore the CSC or otherwise refuse to take it seriously. In the area of EEO, this has been most noticeable with regard to the attitudes some agencies display with regard to the submission of their action plans on time and in the proper form, and agency unwillingness to handle complaints according to the letter, and occasionally the spirit, of the law. Thus, low prestige and a poor image contribute to ineffectiveness, and ineffectiveness, in turn, reinforces low prestige and a poor image.

The CSC is aware of its image and prestige problems, as well as of some of the very real shortcomings in the nature of federal personnel administration, and has sought to make some improvements. Interestingly enough, however, the course of action it has chosen to adopt also tends to militate against the effective handling of the Federal EEO Program in several ways. According to most observers, a major change in the CSC occurred under the chairmanship of John Macy, Jr., which lasted from 1959 to 1968. Macy, ". . . directed many efforts at altering the uninspiring, negatively oriented personnel structure of the federal government."[17] In part, the change has involved greater decentralization of the personnel function and deemphasis of the CSC's traditional role of policeman. As John Presthus and Robert Pfiffner have observed:

> The Commission still has primary responsibility to ensure that such personnel activities as examining, classifying, and training are properly carried out. But now, instead of performing these activities itself, it serves as catalyst, mentor, and friendly counselor to help the agencies develop and administer their own personnel programs. To be sure, the Commission still administers such programs as retirement, security, investigations, and appeals, and it also handles various tests. . . . But, by and large, its operating philosophy has changed from "we must do it ourselves or it will not be well done" to one of helping the agencies carry on their own personnel programs.[18]

Despite this trend toward decentralization, however, a good deal of the traditional negativism still exists in the current personnel philosophy. Elaborate and highly restrictive job descriptions, hiring procedures, pay scales, methods of position classification, and appeal processes continue to exist. The major difference is that today individual agencies have a greater voice in the formulation, application, and revision of regulations in these areas; they therefore also have a better opportunity to make better use of public personnel administration as a tool for enhancing program administration.

In this regard, it is unfortunate, in the eyes of many, that the CSC was given primary responsibility for the Federal EEO Program after its general operational philosophy underwent such a change. The agency, for example, has consistently viewed its role in the Federal EEO Program as one of "stewardship" rather than leadership. It has consequently favored the delegation of a considerable amount of direct EEO responsibility and authority to individual agencies and departments. Many observers, however, feel that the policeman role is the most appropriate one for EEO. Thus, after his staff had completed a study of the CSC's performance in the EEO area, Ralph Nader observed: "Unlike some other Federal programs, there is no doubt whatsoever about the adequacy of the Commission's authority to do its job. It has ample authority, leverage, and disciplinary power vis-a-vis other Federal agencies, but it has been reluctant to use these tools."[19] Nor does it seem possible to act as policeman in one area of authority and not do so in others, especially given the CSC's belief that EEO must be integrated with other aspects of federal personnel administration. In many ways, therefore, the CSC—and the Federal EEO Program—suffer from the worst of all possible worlds in terms of agency culture, prestige, image, and effectiveness. Despite the changes in the CSC's overall operational philosophy, the output of the personnel complex is still basically "protectionist" and negative, although other agencies and employee organizations now have more to say about it. The prestige and image problems of the CSC continue to leave a good deal to be desired, and there is a significant tendency for EEO to be underenforced. These factors have permeated the whole structure of the current Federal EEO Program.

ORGANIZATION

The major role which politics plays in federal organization has already been examined. That politics can also play an important role in organization and reorganization within agencies is illustrated by organizational developments within the CSC. The commission participated in the drafting of Executive Order 11246 (issued by President Johnson) and engaged in extensive planning for its implementation both before and immediately after its issuance. The agency as a whole, however, including many of its bureau chiefs, has always tended to view EEO as representing a latent yet significant threat to the public personnel system, complex, and philosophy which have developed over the years. As was discussed in Chapter 3, traditional public personnel practices did little to create equal opportunity; minority group leaders and other interested in greater EEO have never been reluctant to point this fact out or to demand that major reforms be instituted.

The choice between traditional public personnel administration (which stresses merit, efficiency, economy, and order) and a new personnel administration (which would stress representation, equality, and would encompass forceful compensatory techniques) has been lingering in the minds of some observers for some time now. In the opinion of the CSC's leadership, the worst possible development in EEO would be to have responsibility for the program shifted to another agency with the authority and will to engage in far-reaching revisions of traditional personnel procedures in an effort to enhance equal opportunity. Such a state of affairs would divest the CSC of much of its mission and control over federal personnel administration. The best possible outcome, in the opinion of CSC officials, would be an almost complete "integration of equal employment opportunity with the personnel management function."[20] If the latter ever occurred, it would not only defuse the general threat that EEO poses to the traditional personnel system, it would also lead to the virtual disappearance of EEO as a special personnel function and would thereby lessen the possibility that EEO affairs might be shifted to another agency. This general attitude was incorporated into the Nixon EEO order. Moreover, it has had important organizational consequences.

The CSC's desire to thoroughly integrate EEO with other personnel procedures led to the establishment of an organizational scheme which fragmented authority and lacked a central focal point. It was decided that EEO policy would not be implemented by a single unit; rather, the CSC's various operating bureaus and offices would be utilized because this was formal integration per se. At the start of the current program, the various functions were assigned in the following fashion:

Bureau of Programs and Standards: To develop, modify, and strengthen regulations and prepare proposals for legislation and executive orders. Review job designs, occupational entrance levels, and written tests to facilitate the employment of minority group members with substantial potential. To conduct a follow-up study on the performance of disadvantaged persons. To develop a system for minority identification.

Bureau of Recruiting and Examining (subsequently reorganized into the Bureau of Personnel Management Evaluation): To develop a plan for recruiting minority group members. To evaluate minority participation and success in merit examinations and to provide information concerning the results of the federal recruiting and examining process. Currently enforces EEO requirements and evaluates agency EEO activities.

Bureau of Management Services: Responsibility for establishing a system of statistics on minority distribution and an automatic data-processing system for this purpose.

Bureau of Personnel Investigations: Provide investigations for complaints of discrimination: and take over investigations for other agencies under certain circumstances.

Board of Appeals and Review (Subsequently renamed Appeals Review Board): To review and act for the Commission on complaints, to prepare final decisions, monitor agency complaint processing.

Office of Career Development (Subsequently renamed Bureau of Training): To develop, revise, and provide training programs for federal managers, supervisors, and personnel officials that provide a solid EEO background and motivation. To promote private foundation support for special training courses to aid culturally deprived individuals and those lacking formal education or technical training.

Public Information Office: To provide publicity and public relations.

Regional Offices: To administer EEO and to provide publicity in the field.[21]

Further diffusion of authority and responsibility was created by the establishment of three extremely weak organizational elements to deal specifically and solely with EEO. First, primary responsibility for program operation (excluding policy formulation) was placed in the hands of an Office of the Project Manager—EEO. The office was located in the Bureau of Inspections (now subsumed in the Bureau of Personnel Management Evaluation [BPME]) and was subject to the authority of its head. The project manager held a relatively low-ranking position. The basic rationale behind this particular placement was that the Bureau of Inspections was the CSC's chief enforcement bureau; since it had inspection and evaluation functions, but virtually no policy-making functions, it therefore posed little threat to the other bureaus. Second, an Inter-Bureau Committee on EEO was established to aid in coordinating the activities and proposals of the various CSC bureaus. The committee had virtually no authority of its own. Finally, the position of Special Assistant to the Commission Chairman for EEO was created and filled. The individual appointed was to advise on policy matters, serve as the primary liason with minority groups and other organizations interested in greater EEO, and fill the political need of having someone at a high level who could give speeches, deal with congressmen, newsmen, and so forth. The special assistant had no significant authority of his own, and although it is undeniable that his high-ranking position enhanced his formal prestige, it also meant that the position was not integrated into the career and administrative structure of the agency.

This organizational scheme lasted until the fall of 1968, a period of roughly three years. Little tangible progress had been made towards greater EEO or further passive representation of minority group members. Other agencies and minority group organizations were beginning to become increasingly critical of the lack of centralization and coordination in the program. Agencies encountered difficulties in obtaining specific and timely answers to their questions and found that they were not receiving meaningful direction or advice. The CSC's initial reaction to the demands for some kind of reform was to shift the Office of the Project Manager out of the Bureau of Inspections and into the Bureau of Recruiting and Examining (BRE). In several respects this appeared to be yet another illustration of the tendency to try and solve fundamental problems by means of "organizational cosmetics," but there was also a legitimate rationale behind the move.

Recruiting and examining are, of course, crucial to EEO, and the BRE had primary responsibility for the operation of several other programs relevant to social change, including the women's program, the youth program, college recruiting, and worker-trainee examinations. Had there been a genuine interest in greater EEO in the BRE, important reforms and progress might have come about. By all accounts, however, the transfer placed the EEO in an even worse position because the BRE turned out to be highly committed to maintaining the status quo (which it had, in the past, done much to develop). Besides demonstrating a lesser commitment to EEO than had the Bureau of Inspections, the reorganization in the BRE had the effect of removing the Office of the Project Manager even further from the influence of the chairman and his special assistant. This was due to the fact that the BRE and its head were extremely powerful within the CSC and could afford to be somewhat unresponsive to the politically appointed (and therefore frequently temporary) commissioners and their staffs, and even to the agency's executive director, who remains the CSC's highest ranking career official.

It soon became clear to critics of the Federal EEO Program and the CSC in general that the transfer of authority to the BRE did not represent a solution to the problems that the program was encountering. One group of critics, for example, argued that "the diffusion of the EEO responsibility within the CSC does not provide the strong coordinated support needed by EEO offices in Federal agencies. . . . As a result, they do not utilize the services of CSC as fully as many would like and their contact with CSC personnel with EEO responsibilities is limited and impersonal."[22] Some prominent individuals within the CSC itself thought that the time had come to establish a stronger program with a considerable degree of centralization. Virtually everyone was aware of the possibility that the CSC might well lose the program altogether in the near future if it failed to obtain more impressive, tangible results. Nevertheless, the belief that the program should be fully integrated with other personnel functions remained strong and continued to provide the dominant rationale behind the CSC's EEO activities.

After some deliberation, it was finally decided to increase the degree of centralization by creating an Office of Federal EEO (OFEEO) within the CSC. This was accomplished in November 1969. The main purpose of the OFEEO was twofold: first, to combine all of the coordination and supervisory responsibilities into one organizational unit and, second, to provide a greater degree of centralization and focus in answer to the demands of other agencies and clientele groups. It was thought that the OFEEO would generate greater influence with respect to the latter two groups and thus be better able to formulate and implement EEO functions. (The OFEEO also incorporated the position of Program Manager for the Federal Women's Program (FWP)—subsequently renamed Director of the Federal Women's Program—and was therefore more rationally organized from this perspective as well.)

The OFEEO was headed by two directors of federal EEO, one for operations (at the GS-16 level) and the other for communications (GS-15). Although these positions were established at a relatively high rank, they were nevertheless below those of almost all other bureau directors. The primary rationale behind dual leadership was that it would foster the rapid development of the newly reorganized program. In reality, however, it appears to have been a device for keeping control of the program largely in the hands of those who had been highly loyal to the organization. The central problem appears to have been political: although it was necessary to put a black in charge of a significant portion of EEO activities, the agency had no blacks of suitable rank whom they could appoint to such a position. While it was possible to get a black from the outside, it was thought that no outsider would be sufficiently acquainted with the agency and federal personnel administration to serve the CSC's primary needs. In the end, a black from the outside was appointed Director of Communications and a well-trusted white (from the inside) was appointed Director of Operations. The former was largely without significant authority. The arrangement, however, was inherently irrational; it led to problems of coordination, created a general feeling that the Director of Communications was essentially a powerless front man, and strengthened the belief on the part of critics that the CSC was engaging in "tokenism."

In July 1970 the two directorships were consolidated and the position of Director of Federal EEO (GS-16) was created; the latter was filled by the former Director of Communications. The formal scheme, however, was at considerable variance from actual practice. The former Director of Operations became the Assistant Executive Director of the CSC. The latter kept his foot in the door by retaining responsibility for the Appeals Examiner Program, which is a part of the complaint system. Moreover, this same official had been most fully integrated into the agency's power structure; having held chief responsibility for the operational side of the program, he obviously possessed the greatest in-depth knowledge of the latter and had formed the strongest ties with several key members of the staff of the OFEEO.* Eventually this official was made agency EEO Coordinator and was given broad responsibilities for overseeing the CSC's EEO activities.

Although both of the officials who originally held these positions have left the agency, the organizational pattern remains the same. The extent to which the Director of Federal EEO is dominated by the Assistant Executive Director depends, of course, on a host of political and personal factors. But it is fair to say that to date no forceful EEO director has emerged. In addition, it should be stated that during all the organizational changes the various CSC bureaus retained their EEO responsibilities. Thus, although there now exists a greater degree of centralization in some respects, power and authority are, on the whole, still highly diffused.

The tendency toward decentralization and diffusion of authority has been enhanced by the relative separateness of the Federal Women's Program (FWP) and the Spanish-Speaking Program (SSP). As was discussed in Chapter 1, the special nature of the employment patterns of these groups makes separate EEO efforts on their behalf both rational and desirable. The origins of the EEO's program for women have already been examined. The director of the program

---

*Influence was maintained through a variety of techniques, including holding out the possibility of promotion and allocating much desired overtime work.

heads a relatively independent organizational unit with a different clientele group and a somewhat different set of general objectives and needs. In the words of the former director of the FWP, the latter has as its aims:

1. creating the legal, regulatory, and administrative framework for achieving equality of opportunity without regard to sex;
2. bringing practice in closer accord with merit principles through the elimination of attitudes, customs, and habits that have previously denied women entry into certain occupations, as well as high level positions through the career service; and
3. encouraging qualified women to compete in examinations for federal employment and to participate in training programs leading to advancement.[23]

The FWP is carried to the agencies through their EEO staffs and through FWP coordinators. The latter are supposed to advise agency and EEO officials on "the special concerns regarding women and to assure that equal opportunity for women is an integral part of the agency's overall equal opportunity program."[24] Moreover, it is "required" that the coordinators "have empathy with and understanding of the special problems and concerns of women in the employment situation."[25] An integral part of the coordinator's job is to use material supplied by the director of the FWP and other sources to dispel myths about women as employees and to raise sensitivity and consciousness in the area of equality for women. The coordinators are also supposed to help women employees with such matters as day-care centers and to monitor complaints of discrimination based on sex.

As was suggested in our analysis of the social composition of the federal service, the FWP has not been highly successful in attaining its objectives. This is due, in part, to the complexity of the problem, but it is also the result of organizational arrangements within the CSC. The director of the FWP is outranked by the director of Federal EEO, the assistant executive director, and several other CSC officials concerned with EEO. Nor have these officials—who tend to view EEO for members of racial minority groups as more important—been highly receptive to EEO for women. On several occasions the efforts and activities of Helene Markoff, former director of the FWP, were stymied by higher ranking officials. Indeed, at one time she was forbidden to meet with representatives of certain women's groups during working hours! Hence, although the relative separation of the FWP from other EEO activities may be desirable for several reasons, in the context of the organizational politics within the CSC it has had the effect of deemphasizing equal opportunity for women and frustrating the subsequent development of this aspect of the overall Federal EEO Program.

Although the Spanish-Speaking Program (SSP) reflects a similar organizational scheme, it has been somewhat more effective because of its political backing elsewhere in the government. The SSP originated on November 5, 1970, when President Nixon issued a 16-point program designed to insure equal opportunity for Spanish-speaking American citizens who choose to compete for federal positions.* The 16 points included the following recommendations:

1. Appoint a full-time official in the Civil Service Commission to provide advice and assistance on matters relating to the Spanish-surnamed population and to assure full application to this group [of] the EEO programs in all Federal agencies.

2. Begin an intensified drive to recruit Spanish-surnamed persons (particularly for identified public-contact positions) in areas having large Spanish-speaking populations, including the Southwestern States, Chicago, Detroit, New York and certain other major metropolitan areas.

3. Use specialized recruitment teams, to include Spanish-speaking persons, for college recruitment at campuses with heavy Spanish-speaking enrollments.

4. Begin work immediately with the Departments of Health, Education, and Welfare, Housing and Urban Development, and Labor to find ways to enhance opportunities, at all levels, for Spanish-surnamed Americans in programs dealing with the Spanish-speaking population, as well as in other programs and in other key occupations.

5. Step up recruitment for cooperative education programs at colleges with significant numbers of Spanish-speaking students— to permit entry from FSEE [Federal Service Entrance Examination] registers without the necessity of written examinations.

6. Emphasize to Federal agencies the availablility of selective placement on a bilingual basis, so that Spanish-speaking persons may be reached for appointment to positions dealing with the Spanish-speaking population.

7. Hold an EEO conference of Federal managers and equal opportunity officials in the Southwest—to assure equal opportunity for Spanish-speaking persons in employment and upward mobility in Federal agencies.

8. Develop plans for federal agencies, under CSC Area Official leadership, to work with high schools in Spanish-speaking areas—to make known job opportunities in the Federal Government and to counsel and encourage students to stay in school.

9. Hire, for summer employment in Federal agencies, high school and college teachers from schools serving Spanish-speaking

---

*Nixon's action was undoubtedly primarily motivated by the importance of Chicano voters, in Texas and California, to the building of a normal Republican majority in presidential elections. He also created a Cabinet Committee on Opportunities for Spanish-Speaking People to strengthen his election strategy; it has thus far provided the SSP with considerable external support.

students—to give them an understanding of the Federal Government which they can relate to students.

10. Make a special effort to inform Spanish-surnamed veterans of availability of non-competitive appointments for Vietnam era veterans, including appointments at the GS-5 level.

11. Require Federal agencies to review their EEO action plans and minority employment figures and make any necessary revisions to assure the full applicability of those plans to the Spanish-surnamed population.

12. Review with agencies the staffing of their EEO program offices, to make sure there is an understanding in those offices of the special problems of the Spanish-speaking.

13. Provide additional training, on EEO and personnel management, for Federal managers in areas of large Spanish-speaking populations.

14. With the Department of Labor, explore the feasibility of establishing an Intergovernmental Training Facility for upward mobility and skills training—for Federal, State and local government employees in the Southwestern U.S.

15. Collect necessary data and broaden the analysis of minority statistics to bring out special information relating to employment and upward mobility of Spanish-surnamed persons in the Federal Government.

16. Require that the EEO reports from agencies reflect special information on Spanish-surnamed persons, and include in the CSC agenda for EEO evaluation questions directed at particular problems relating to employment and upward mobility of Spanish-surnamed persons.[26]

The first official to oversee the SSP was appointed in December 1970. His role was largely advisory. In 1972 the nature and title of the position were changed. A director was appointed at the same level as the Director of Federal EEO, a change largely due to pressure exerted on the CSC by Spanish-speaking groups both within and without the government. The director took on a more operational role and was charged with implementing the 16 points. The director of the SSP currently heads a small staff, located in the CSC's headquarters, whose task consists of aiding this official and publicizing the SSP. There are also a number of SSP coordinators in other agencies whose functions are outwardly similar to those of the FWP's coordinators.

It should be noted, in passing, that although these special-emphasis programs are advisable in view of the employment patterns of women and Spanish-speaking citizens, they tax the organizational efficacy of the program as a whole. Specifically, the program has had difficulty in coordinating EEO activity. More importantly, however, the general Federal EEO Program has tended to focus attention almost exclusively on EEO for blacks. This policy has reinforced the need for the FWP and the SSP and has created a tension between these two groups and the OFEEO. As a further consequence of these arrangements, moreover, native Americans and Orientals are effectively denied organizational representation.

Another organizational arrangement in the EEO administrative hierarchy bears mention. The CSC's regional directors are also the regional coordinators of the Federal EEO Program. There is, in addition, at least one EEO representative in each of the ten civil service regions. These positions were established in 1970 in order to deal with EEO problems in the field. The EEO representatives are under the immediate authority of the regional directors and are charged with a diversity of functions: developing contacts with organized groups expressing an interest in EEO; working with various agencies to promote EEO; advising the regional directors; analyzing specific problems and proposals; taking part in inspections; lecturing to various groups; and, in general, finding and correcting serious breaches in EEO rules. Headquarters/field relationships tend to follow the typical EEO pattern of decentralization and diffusion of authority and responsibility. The formal line of communication between the director of the Federal EEO Program and CSC EEO officials in the field is as follows: from the director of the Federal EEO Program up to the executive director of the CSC; down to the deputy executive director; further down to the regional directors; and ultimately way down to the regional EEO representatives. There is no direct link between the director of the Federal EEO Program and either the regional directors or the representatives. Two important consequences of this arrangement are uneven performance in the field and lack of coordination. This organizational scheme, however, supports the CSC's objective of fully integrating EEO with other personnel activities.

EEO Organization Within Individual Agencies

The organization of the Federal EEO Program does not end with the CSC. There is also a general pattern of organization for EEO within other agencies. Each federal department and agency is required to designate a director of EEO to assist the agency head in administering the program. It is required that the EEO director be under the agency head's immediate supervision. The director's functions include advising, evaluating, and improving the agency's EEO program; providing for a counseling system; overseeing the complaint system; resolving individual complaints when authorized to do so; and making recommendations concerning disciplinary actions. The director is the agency's highest EEO official and is responsible for providing EEO for all members of minority groups and women; this is done in conjunction with FWP and SSP coordinators.

Departments and agencies also appoint EEO officers; they can either be bureau or field office managers or someone under their immediate supervision. EEO officers report directly to the office or installation head and are required to assist in providing overall leadership for the EEO program and in overseeing the complaint system. Since July 1969, agencies have also had EEO counselors. Counselors should have "empathy with empoyees who bring problems to his attention . . . and be able to work effectively with agency management in attempting to resolve problems."[27] Their chief purpose is to provide an informal means whereby employees can raise EEO-related issues. Employee organizations are sometimes consulted on the selection and appointment of counselors, and there has been considerable discussion concerning the desirability of allowing employees to elect them. Agencies are not required to appoint a specific number of counselors, but it is suggested that they appoint at least one counselor for every 500 employees in situations involving large concentrations of federal employees, and at least one councelor in all installations having 50 or more employees. The vast majority of counselors only perform part-time duties in the latter role, as do many EEO directors and officers.

OPPOSITION TO THE CSC

A good deal of dissatisfaction has arisen with respect to the CSC's organization and administration of the Federal EEO Program; many have pointed to significant deficiencies in its operations. The CSC has been criticized for its role vis-a-vis Executive Order 11246, which "was characterized more by passivity than by 'leadership' more by neutrality than by 'guidance.'"[28] Its early record was far from impressive. In addition to its inefficient, weak, virtually nonexistent organizational structure, its own EEO record was extremely poor:

> As of June 1966, 818 black classified employees were working at the Civil Service Commission itself and 73 per cent or 600 of these were in grades GS-4 and below. Some 21 or 2.6 per cent were in grades above GS-11.
> The Commission's new study shows that by November 1967, 70 per cent were still in grades GS-4 and below. The new study showed 23 black employees in grades above GS-11, an increase of only one-half of one per cent over 1966.[29]

Although the CSC's record has improved somewhat in recent years, as of 1974 it had only one minority group member in its 62 super grade positions—the director of the Federal EEO Program. Furthermore, 81 percent of all its minority group members were in grades GS-8 and below, whereas only 49 percent of its other employees were in these positions. The CSC's record appears to be less excusable than those of other agencies because many of its upper-level positions do not require extensive technical training or knowledge.

The CSC has also been criticized for the attitudes of its officials concerning EEO. There can be little doubt that, at least until the early 1970s, many of the bureau chiefs and their assistants were overly complacent and unable or unwilling to grasp the social and political implications of EEO; they failed to conceive of the program, in any sense, as an attempt at implementing political and social reform. The CSC's officials often utilized a racist and sexist language, thereby demonstrating a remarkable degree of insensitivity and an acute lack of understanding of the more general problems of equality. A former executive director, for example, was in the habit of referring to the director of the FWP as the "Virgin Mary" and used to freely reminisce about some of his "fine colored friends" before large groups of EEO agency officials, minority group members, and women. Other important officials within the Federal EEO Program often referred to black women as "girls" and employed such terms as "white hats" to characterize righteous individuals.

The CSC's Appeals Review Board (formerly the Board of Appeals and Review) has decidedly given the appearance of being unsympathetic to EEO and to those who are challenging management in general. Moreover, the Bureau of Personnel Investigations (BPI), whose primary function is to conduct investigations regarding employee suitability, has, over the years, demonstrated a significant lack of sensitivity to EEO and, in fact, was at the center of the development of a pattern of discrimination within the CSC itself. In the past, the majority of officials who attained high-level positions within the agency had been investigators at one time or another in their careers; service in the BPI was the CSC official's traditional means of advancement into high-level posts. The BPI, however, was not conducive to hiring and promoting members of minority groups and women, and the prevailing attitudes within it made the Bureau unattractive to members of these groups. Over the years, consequently, access to a major channel for advancement within the CSC has been denied to women and minority group members.

During 1970-71, much of the dissatisfaction with the CSC's administration of the Federal EEO Program culminated in congressional action aimed at transferring the program to the EEOC. The latter agency possesses jurisdiction over EEO in the private sphere; transfer of the program to it would therefore have represented an extreme threat to the CSC. Two bills introduced for this purpose, S. 2453 and H.R. 17555,[30] were mainly concerned with granting cease and desist powers to the EEOC, but the threat to the CSC was not merely a scare tactic. Support for the proposed transfer had been building for a number of years, fueled by the fact that the CSC appeared to be making little headway. During the hearings on these bills, several of the common criticisms of the CSC were repeated. For example, an official of the EEOC stated that "the Civil Service Commission has done less than an adequate job in overseeing discrimination in the Federal Government or in hiring minorities within its own Commission."[31] An official of the Urban League accused the CSC of being primarily concerned with complaints and of "giving little or no attention to the more positive concept of affirmative action."[32] An official representing the NAACP criticized the program thusly: "The Government of the United States is one of the leading discriminators in the world. . . ."[33] His greatest objection to the program was that "the Government of the United States acting through the Civil Service Commission and through the constituent agencies sits in judgment of its own conduct and in 99 percent of the cases it gives an unfair and prejudiced judgment which results in a finding that the complainant is not entitled to any kind of redress."[34] Finally, yet another critic of the CSC argued that the merit exams were highly discriminatory.[35]

A far-reaching indictment of the CSC also appeared in the *Federal Times* in an editorial supporting the proposed transfer of the Federal EEO Program to the EEOC. It reported that an earlier editorial:

> Brought a long letter from CSC Chairman Robert Hampton in which he claimed history and statistics showed control of EEO logically belonged in the commission.
>
> His arguments were sincere, but they left questions unanswered—or even unraised.
>
> The Commission is the government's counterpart of corporation personnel management. As a personnel manager, CSC has to rate an "A" for effort and about a "C" for achievement.
>
> Many programs have been tried and stacks of figures have been compiled to show the programs have worked. But, minority group members and women still suffer a lack of real promotion opportunities. This will continue to be true until officialdom stops worrying about who has responsibility for what program; and what statistics can be produced to make existing programs look good.
>
> We doubt that this can be changed under the present setup. Having CSC do its own enforcement is like having the management of a major corporation decide whether that firm is complying with anti-discrimination statutes.
>
> The basic question is whether the laws and regulations are being enforced. Secondary, but also important, is the question of whether moral and ethical obligations are being met.
>
> If these questions are to be answered affirmatively, then the CSC needs to forget about slogans and slick phrases and start thinking about its responsibility to the federal workforce and the nation.
>
> We marvel at some of the language used to explain the equal opportunity policy.
>
> Try this statement: "Since we (the commission) received prime responsibility in 1965, we have made a concerted effort to blend EEO concepts and practices into every aspect of good personnel management."
>
> EEO Concepts: What are they? Does the CSC mean Presidential Executive Orders? Is it talking about the 1964 Civil Rights Act which established the EEOC? One does not "blend" laws into "good personnel management." One obeys laws.
>
> There are many questions left unanswered. One of the first ones is why the commission is so worried about losing responsibility for the EEO program.[36]

The CSC, of course, opposed the proposed reorganization and argued that it could perform EEO functions more satisfactorily than the EEOC or any other agency. The heart of the CSC's defense has been that "true equal opportunity can result only from the closest integration"[37] of EEO and personnel administration in general, and that EEO "must be built into the everyday actions taken by managers on the job."[38] The CSC has claimed that it received authority for the program precisely because, in the words of the assistant executive director, "it was clear that to be effective equal opportunity needed to be moved closer to internal Government operations. It was evident that a program which was operating outside the normal channel of decision making could have only a limited impact in assuring equal employment opportunity in every aspect of personnel management."[39] Positing this assumption, the director's statement continued: "[Since] The Commission as the Government's central personnel agency has legal authority to prescribe employment practices, it is in the best position to assure that there is in fact equal opportunity in all employment processes and that an affirmative action program to assure equal employment is carried out at all levels of Government."[40] The CSC's assistant executive director also argued that the EEOC would not perform as well because it was poorly managed and complaint-oriented, whereas the CSC stressed less remedial, more positive concepts. Even with respect to complaints, the CSC spokesman argued that his commission was in a better position to be more effective in handling EEO affairs:

> [W]hen a discrimination complaint is lodged, it is in connection with other aspects of the work relationship, such as promotion, work assignments or as a defense in an adverse action taken by an agency against an employee. To separate the handling of appeals on discrimination grounds from appeals on these other grounds which are heard by the Civil Service Commission would create diffusion rather than coherence in the complaint process.[41]

Although the CSC's arguments are not simply rationalizations, there is no doubt that its opposition to external reorganization primarily stems from its fear that such a change could lead to a very significant loss of control by the CSC over the federal personnel system. Indeed, it even views the existence of a highly visible program within its own organization as a potential threat to traditional merit concepts.

There is a good deal of logic on both sides. The CSC lost the initial battles in congressional committees. The Senate Committee on Labor and Public Welfare reported: "The record conclusively demonstrates that minorities and women continue to be shut out of a large number of government jobs, particularly at the higher grade levels."[42] It also stated that CSC practices "are replete with artificial selection and promotion requirements that place a premium on 'paper' credentials that are highly questionable as predictors of job performance."[43] Furthermore, it concluded that the exams were administered "without any consideration that such a correlation might be appropriate."[44] The selection process, therefore, placed an unnecessarily heavy burden on culturally and educationally disadvantaged individuals. The committee voiced the common criticism that the current EEO system "creates a built-in conflict of interest in examining into that system to ascertain the structural defects causing the discrimination."[45] The report concluded that EEO could only be effectively handled by "an agency outside the regular personnel 'chain of command.'"[46]

The House Labor and Education Committee's report essentially agreed with the findings of the Senate committee. It reasoned that "the Civil Service Commission's own statistics show that there has been no major advances [sic] toward the solution of the problem."[47] The report continued:

> One of the most damaging and degrading forms of discrimination in the federal sector is the denial of promotions to minority groups and women. This is damaging not only to the civil servant who must suffer the consequence of his supervisor's prejudice, but also to the government at whose expense talent is wasted and to every member of a minority group who bitterly learns that the merit system does not apply to him.[48]

The committee report concluded that the government should be "willing to have its action reviewed by an impartial tribunal in a forum where all parties have equal rights to a fair hearing and meaningful redress."[49] Among other criticisms of the Federal EEO Program was the fact that back pay and promotion were not awarded to employees who had proven that they were subjected to prohibited discrimination, and that the hearing process was expensive for employees. The CSC won its case, however, when S. 2453 was passed without containing a provision to transfer responsibility for the Federal EEO Program to the EEOC. The possibility of EEO reorganization was made even more remote after the passage of the Equal Employment program within the CSC.

Why was the proposed transfer defeated? There are basically two reasons for this turn of events. First, many supporters of the program thought that administration under the EEOC, which has always had an unmanageable backlog of cases in the private sphere, would be even less satisfactory. More importantly, the possibility of reorganization was used as a means of forcing the CSC to adopt a more rigorous policy of affirmative action. This issue will preoccupy us in the next chapter. However, it is appropriate here to stress the fact that despite major policy changes, the CSC's pattern of organization continues to have important political and administrative consequences. The CSC's pattern of decentralization deprives the Federal EEO Program of a truly organizational focal point. It also gives agencies a considerable degree of autonomy in dealing with EEO. Moreover, as will emerge from subsequent discussion, it has militated against the gathering of necessary information on the program's operation by those organizational units in the CSC which are most concerned with the formulation and implementation of EEO policy. Although its organizational scheme is rational in many respects, the CSC's administration of the Federal EEO Program over the past decade suggests that organizational approaches have been used to protect the agency's larger mission and culture.

One is forced to conclude, therefore, that the CSC's organizational approaches have been adopted to foster its "meritist" outlook and to provide a defense against "representationist" demands. For several years the Federal EEO Program was virtually invisible. Even after the creation of the OFEEO, the CSC clung to its desire to integrate EEO fully with other aspects of federal personnel administration. The more EEO is intertwined with other personel activities, the more difficult it becomes to transfer authority for its operation to another agency and the harder it becomes for representationists to gather information and evaluate the Federal EEO Program. By "blending" EEO and merit through organization in this fashion, the strength of merit is enhanced and the likelihood of the disappearance of EEO as a separate program element is increased. Indeed, its most visible aspects—the FWP, the SSP, and the OFEEO— were created as a result of political pressure (partly from the White House) upon the CSC. Hence, the CSC's organizational development must ultimately be viewed as a reaction by a conservative agency to significant political threats aimed at its mission and culture.

NOTES

1. For a general discussion of this question, see Harold Seidman, *Politics, Position, and Power* (New York: Oxford University Press, 1970).

2. U.S., *Federal Register*, September 24, 1965, 30, part 10: 12319. The political implications of the transfer of the Federal EEO Program to the CSC have already been examined in Chapter 3.

3. U.S., August 8, 1969, *Federal Register*, 34, part 8: 12985.

4. P.L. 92-261, U.S., *Statutes at Large*, (March 24, 1972) vol. 86; part 1, 103.

5. Seidman, *Politics, Position, and Power*, p. 18.

6. Brian Chapman, *The Profession of Government* (London: Allen and Unwin, 1959)., p. 297.

7. Louis C. Gawthrop, *Bureaucratic Behavior in the Executive Branch* (New York: Free Press, 1969), p. 147.

8. Ibid., p. 146 n.

9. Marver Bernstein, *The Job of the Federal Executive* (Washington, D.C.: Brookings Institution, 1958), p. 75.

10. Ibid.

11. Ibid.

12. Ibid., p. 76.

13. Ibid., p. 77.

14. Ibid.

15. Ibid., pp. 163-64.

16. See Roger Wilkins, James Frazier, Jr., et al., "The Equal Employment Opportunity Posture of the U.S. Federal Government" (unpublished report transmitted to the CSC

on January 14, 1969) p. 1, which states that "a large number of personnel managers and administrators are the dregs of the Federal Government, lacking commitment and imagination to do the personnel jobs they are hired to do."

17. Gawthrop, *Bureaucratic Behavior in the Executive Branch,* p. 196.

18. John Pfiffner and Robert Presthus, *Public Administration* (New York: Ronald Press, 1967), p. 266.

19. Quoted in New York *Times,* June 25, 1972, p. 28.

20. Statement made by the assistant executive director of the CSC, on H.R. 6288 (April 7, 1970), p. 3 (CSC document).

21. "Implementation of the Commission's Responsibilities Under Executive Order 11246 in Equal Employment Opportunity." Memorandum from the executive director of the CSC to the Commission (November 2, 1955) (paraphrased and updated).

22. Wilkins, "The EEO Posture of the U.S. Federal Government," p. 6.

23. Helene Markoff, "The Federal Women's Program," *Public Administration Review* 32 (March/April 1972): 144.

24. CSC Federal Personnel Manual System, Installment for Basic Manual, 135, Chapter 713, 2-6-c (May 29, 1970).

25. Ibid.

26. CSC News Release, Office of the White House Press Secretary, November 5, 1970.

27. Federal Personnel Manual System 135, Chapter 713, 2-6-e (May 29, 1970).

28. U.S., Commission on Civil Rights, *Federal Civil Rights Enforcement Effort* (Washington, D.C.: U.S. Government Printing Office, 1970), p. 65.

29. Baltimore *Afro-American,* June 15, 1968.

30. 91st Cong., 2d sess.

31. U.S., Congress, Senate, Subcommittee on Labor, Committee on Labor and Public Welfare, "Equal Employment Opportunity Enforcement Act," 91st Cong., 1st sess., August 12, 1969, p. 61.

32. Ibid., p. 67.

33. Ibid., p. 83.

34. Ibid., p. 84.

35. Ibid., p. 156.

36. *Federal Times,* September 9, 1970, p. 8.

37. Statement of the assistant executive director of the CSC on H.R. 6288 (April 7, 1970), p. 3.

38. Memorandum of the CSC chairman, May 20, 1970.

39. Statement of the assistant executive director of the CSC on H.R. 6288, pp. 2-3.

40. Ibid., p. 3.

41. Ibid., p. 9.

42. See the *Federal Times,* September 9, 1970, pp. 1, 25.

43. Ibid., p. 25.

44. Ibid.

45. Ibid.

46. Ibid.

47. Ibid.

48. Ibid.

49. Ibid.

5

POLICY FORMULATION
AND IMPLEMENTATION:
AFFIRMATIVE ACTION

Organizational politics and the contest between meritists and representationists[1] have played a major role in the formulation and implementation of EEO policy. This has been most dramatic in the area of "goals and timetables" for the hiring and promotion of women and members of minority groups in the federal bureaucracy. This approach continues to be, in a political sense, the most controversial aspect of the Federal EEO Program. An analysis of its development shows that the politics of threatened reorganization and the political strength of representationists virtually forced upon the CSC a policy of discrimination in favor of women and members of minority groups to which the agency was and, to a lesser extent, remains opposed. Analysis of this facet of EEO illustrates, first, that bureaucratic agencies are often able to avoid doing what they do not want to do and, second, that they can be highly resistant to change. Thus, despite its defeat on the policy front, the CSC has been able to use organizational tactics to frustrate the effective implementation of the newer approach. Such an analysis provides further knowledge about the Federal EEO Program and its inner workings and also yields an interesting case study of public policy making in the national bureaucratic arena.

TOWARDS A SYSTEM OF GOALS AND TIMETABLES

On May 11, 1971, after several months of stalled deliberation, the CSC issued a memorandum to the heads of departments and agencies concerning the "use of employment goals and timetables in equal employment opportunity programs."* The memo defined a new strategy for achieving further EEO: "The establishment of goals and timetables is a useful management concept and should be used where they will contribute to the resolution of equal employment opportunity problems." On its face, the memo was somewhat revolutionary. It compromised the principle of nondiscrimination in terms of "color-blindness," an approach which had dominated the Federal EEO Program since its inception. The new policy also militated against the meritist principle of open competition which has been fundamental to federal personnel administration since 1883, the year in which the merit system and the CSC were established. In retrospect, it is apparent that the new policy foreshadowed a significant change in the general federal policy vis-a-vis civil rights, a policy which is now more favorably disposed towards the use of benevolent or compensatory (that is, reverse) discrimination. The CSC's decision to adopt the new policy, however, was not so much determined by its interest in greater EEO and civil rights than by its desire to preserve and protect its role in the formulation and implementation of federal personnel policy. In fact, the agency embraced the new strategy only after it became convinced that not to do so would be considerably more costly in terms of organizational authority and prestige.

Prior to the issuance of the "May Memo," the Federal EEO Program, as we have seen, was grounded on two fundamental principles: the first held that there was to be no discrimination on the basis of race, color, religion, sex, or national origin in federal personnel actions; the second, which was formulated during the Eisenhower administration and continued to develop under the Kennedy EEO Programs, was that affirmative action should be taken to "make it possible for all groups of persons, including those who are disadvantaged educationally or otherwise, regardless of their race, sex, or national origin, to compete for Federal employment on an equal footing with other citizens."[2] Today the term "affirmative action" is virtually synonymous with the goals-and-timetables approach, but it had previously meant taking positive action to enhance the competitive *ability*, rather than the *position*, of disadvantaged groups and individuals. One policy statement explained the original meaning of affirmative action as follows:

> . . .we must, through positive action, make it possible for our citizens to compete on a truly equal and fair basis for employment and to qualify for advancement within the Federal service. We must search for new ways to provide the necessary encouragement,

---

*Robert Hampton, Chairman, CSC, "Memorandum for Heads of Departments and Agencies," May 11, 1971. Here after "May Memo".

assistance, and training opportunities, where appropriate, so that all employees may utilize their capabilities to the fullest extent in meeting the manpower needs of Federal agencies.

Those who have potential to serve at the supervisory level and above should be identified and given the opportunity to develop to their fullest capability.

Special efforts must be made to assure that opportunities in the Federal Government at the professional levels are made known to men and women of all races, religions, and ethnic backgrounds, so that positions of leadership in the future can be assumed by persons from all segments of our population.

In addition to assuring equal employment opportunity for all persons, the Government, as a responsible employer, must do its part along with other employers to provide special employment and training programs to those who are economically or educationally disadvantaged.[3]

It is important to stress the fact that although, from a policy angle, affirmative action of this type might be applied most appropriately to such groups as women, blacks, and other minorities, in theory it was not until the use of goals and timetables was introduced that affirmative action could be taken seriously solely on the basis of race, ethnicity, sex, or religion. In the words of the CSC,

> Equal employment opportunity under our merit system is not a program to offer special privilege to any one group of persons because of their particular race, religion, sex, or national origin. Equal employment opportunity applies to all persons including those of different races, women, handicapped persons, veterans, rehabilitated offenders, and others.[4]

Prior to the issuance of the "May Memo," it was deemed that benevolent discrimination or compensatory treatment would violate the principle of non-discrimination and, consequently, that special opportunities, such as training, could not properly be allocated solely to members of specific racial or ethnic groups. Rather, these opportunities had to be made available to a wider range of people, such as disadvantaged or underprivileged citizens.

As was discussed in Chapter 2, there exists in the United States an incompatability or tension between the merit system and a high level of social representation in the federal service. If the merit system reflected proportional representation of all major population groups, there would be no need for a Federal EEO Program. Similarly, if the use of goals and timetables yielded the highest degree of merit, there would be no threat to the current system and both these elements could readily be incorporated into it. Yet it appears that

neither the merit system nor the use of goals and timetables is capable of pro-
ducing this end result, at least as things stand now. The stage has consequently
been set for an ongoing political struggle between representationists and
meritists.

THE REPRESENTATIONIST INITIATIVE

During the late 1960s and early 1970s, representationist approaches had
begun to crystallize. Those individuals advocating such approaches suddenly
emerged as an important political force in the civil rights policy arena. With
reference to the Federal EEO Program, representationists were able to seize
hold of and develop three factors which encouraged a fundamental policy
change. First, by 1970 it had become increasingly evident, from a theoretical
and practical standpoint, that the older EEO approaches had more or less run
their courses and that different strategies would be necessary to deal effectively
with the changing nature of the EEO problem. As was discussed in Chapter 1,
the initial stage of the EEO problem concerning the entrance of women and
members of minority groups into the federal service has virtually been resolved.
Consequently, since the late 1960s more attention has been focused upon the
second stage of the problem, namely, that of achieving a greater degree of
representation for women and members of minority groups in the upper half
of the GS. However, neither the principle of nondiscrimination nor the early
affirmative action approach was best suited to accomplish this task. For the
most part, overt or conspicuous discrimination had become far less of a barrier
to greater representation in the upper grades than the unavailability of minority
group and female applicants who could meet the formal (occasionally indirectly
discriminatory) requirements for appointment and promotion to these levels.
Hence, the complaint process,* which is the administrative answer to the principle of nondiscrimination, has been of limited utility in this area.

At the same time, earlier affirmative action techniques were not being
effectively utilized to overcome this problem because the background requirements pertaining to high-level positions were generally related to formal education and it was usually considered either impractical or too expensive for agencies to provide disadvantaged individuals with an opportunity to improve their
training in this area. While some in-house and external training could be allocated, providing women and members of minority groups with professional
skills in such areas as accounting and law, for example, or with sufficient managerial experience to move rapidly up the career ladder was, for the most part,

---

*The workings of this system will be examined in Chapter 6.

out of the question. By the same token, efforts to enhance the upward mobility*
of women and members of minority groups were not calculated to enable
disadvantaged individuals to rise much above the GS-9 level, if indeed that
far. Consequently, in the view of representationists and others concerned individuals, new strategies were clearly necessary.

A second factor which tended to encourage policy change along the lines
desired by representationists was the more general emergence of compensatory
treatment in public policy. Just when the Federal EEO Program seemed to have
reached the limit of its usefulness (a result of a lack of the development of new
approaches), the strategy of using goals and timetables for minority hiring and
promotion was being more forcefully urged. This change was directly related
to the shifting objectives of civil rights and minority group organizations; the
latter were beginning to stress direct, substantive equality as opposed to the
more traditional aim of equal opportunity solely on the basis of nondiscrimination. In 1967 the use of goals and timetables was embraced by the federal
government with the issuance by the Office of Federal Contract Compliance of
the Department of Labor of the then controversial "Philadelphia Plan." The
latter, as will be recalled, stated that those individuals bidding on contracts for
federal and federally funded projects in the Philadelphia area be required to
submit EEO plans, including specific goals for the employment of members
of minority groups.

By 1970, the Office of Management and Budget (OMB), the Department
of the Army, and other federal agencies had expressed a desire to use numerical
goals and timetables in their EEO action plans. In addition, the White House
issued the 16-point program for Spanish-speaking citizens which was somewhat
compensatory in nature. The Commission on Civil Rights (CCR), after completing a massive study of federal civil rights activities, made the following recommendations:

> The Civil Service Commission . . . should clarify its current
> policy, emphasizing specific goals in the Federal equal employment
> opportunity effort and develop a Government-wide plan designed
> to achieve equitable minority group representation at all wage and
> grade levels within each department and agency. This plan should
> include minimum numerical and percentage goals, coupled with
> specific target dates for their attainment, and should be developed
> jointly by CSC and each Department or agency.[5]

Early in 1971 it appeared that the OMB and the Department of the Army
were determined to use goals and timetables regardless of the CSC's policy.

---

*See Chapter 6.

At this point the CSC concluded that it would have very little to gain and much to lose by attempting to prohibit them from doing so. (It should be remembered that, if one does not consider the DOD as a single element, the Department of the Army represents the government's largest organizational unit.) Perhaps even more significant, the OMB's strategic position with regard to matters of policy, budget, executive orders, and legislation made its support for goals and timetables a fact of great importance.

Thirdly, representationists were able to capitalize on the widespread opposition to the CSC and demands for transferring the program to the EEOC, points which were discussed at length in the previous chapter. The CSC opposed both the proposed transfer and the use of goals and timetables. However, if forced to make a choice, it greatly preferred the latter option. Transfer posed a severe threat because any agency having responsibility for EEO in the federal service potentially also had a great deal of control over the federal personnel system. Recruitment, promotion, dismissal, and so forth, have a direct bearing upon the possibility of achieving an acceptable degree of EEO. An EEO agency could, for example, find that specific procedures relating to testing or promotion were discriminatory and might be able to compel widespread revisions. The loss of EEO might therefore mean the loss to the CSC of a good deal of its authority to formulate and implement major features of the personnel system. Thus, the agency could find itself in the unconventional position of having to justify its regulations to another organization far less interested in those goals which the CSC values most, namely, orderly, standardized, "non-political," and efficient public personnel administration grounded upon the concepts and values implicit in the term "merit system." On the other hand, the adoption and full-fledged implementation of a goals-and-timetables approach might also entail a substantial compromise in the values of the merit system and could, in a sense, be viewed as an admission that both merit and the CSC had contributed to patterns of discrimination and inequality.

In 1971 the choice between loss of the Federal EEO Program or adoption of the new goals-and-timetables approach was concretely presented to the CSC by representationists when the CCR gave the CSC tentative support before a congressional subcommittee holding hearings on a new version of the house bill proposing transfer of the Federal EEO Program to the EEOC. The CCR, however, made its support explicitly contingent upon the CSC's acceptance of the goals-and-timetables approach in addition to less significant changes.[6]

THE CSC'S GAMBIT

The CSC, of course, was not oblivious to the factors which were giving representationists the upper hand. It developed programmatic approaches, such as an emphasis on upward mobility, in an effort to counter the charge that a radical policy change was necessary for the achievement of further EEO. As we have seen, the CSC was ultimately successful in blocking transfer of the Federal EEO Program to another agency, although this was achieved at considerable cost. The CSC also rebutted its critics, insofar as this was possible, and strengthened the internal organization of the program. Nevertheless, the combination of forces demanding change presented the agency with a considerable organizational dilemma. The CSC had traditionally opposed the use of goals, timetables and other compensatory techniques because it viewed them as seriously weakening the open, competitive system. A commitment to the latter system still ranks at the top of the CSC's institutionalized scale of values and was its original raison d'être. It is constantly reflected in the decisions of the CSC's top officials as well as in their public statements; many of these officials have risen to their high positions largely by virtue of their loyalty to the organization and as a result of their ability to accept its values as their own. Very few problems of significance confronting the CSC are approached from a frame of reference other than that of open competition and merit.

Given the political climate existing at the time, the CSC reasoned that if it tried to "save" the merit system by refusing to dilute it, by setting goals and timetables for minority hiring and promotion, this might well lead to either a Pyrrhic victory or an out-and-out loss, both possibilities representing a much greater compromise of this system. Yet the CSC did not want to adopt the use of goals and timetables as a strategy for achieving EEO until it was convinced that there was no reasonable alternative. This point would be reached when it sensed that the likelihood of transfer of the Federal EEO Program to the EEOC was too risky. The CSC, however, did not want to create the impression that it was tied exclusively to the old EEO principles; it therefore reasoned that it could reduce the likelihood of losing the Federal EEO Program by outwardly appearing to entertain new concepts. The CSC consequently began issuing ambiguous policy statements which enabled it to avoid *adopting* a new policy, while nevertheless creating an aura of change.

On July 24, 1970, the CSC responded to a report prepared by the CCR. The report suggested that the success or failure of the Federal EEO Program was directly related to the extent of minority group representation in all grade levels and that the use of goals and timetables for the hiring and promotion of minority group members would be of help in achieving an increase in this regard. The CSC's reply is indicative of its traditional philosophy:

> The report presumes that the only manifestation of a successful equal employment program is immediate proportional representation of minorities at all grade levels, in every occupation, in all regions of the country. *This is tantamount to a quota system and is inconsistent with the Executive Orders on equal employment . . . as well as with the concept of the merit system itself. . . .* [T]he establishment of numerical minority quotas is not the answer, as

implied in your report. This concept would result in employment on
the basis of race or national origin, rather than merit and fitness.[7]

In effect, the CSC was arguing that there is no practical distinction between
goals and quotas, that the test of the Federal EEO Program should not depend
solely upon the degree of minority representation, and that merit and fitness are
the only legitimate criteria for public employment.

On August 6, 1970, in a well-publicized letter to Roger Kelly, Assistant
Secretary of Defense, the CSC embraced the representational argument and
seemingly moved towards acceptance of the policy of setting goals for the hiring
and promotion of minority group members:

> We believe that to the extent practicable organizations of the
> Federal Government should, in their employment mix, broadly
> reflect, racially and otherwise, the varied characteristics of our popu-
> lation. This is a desirable goal to achieve within the context of
> employment on the basis of merit. The imposition of numerical
> quotas for the employment of a particular group of persons is con-
> trary to Executive Order . . . and Civil Service Commission regu-
> lations and is violative of merit principles. While quotas are not per-
> missible, Federal agencies may use numerical guidelines to assess
> progress toward equal employment opportunity and as one means of
> determining the need for additional affirmative action regarding
> minority employment.[8]

In February 1971 the CSC accepted the distinction between goals and
quotas but appeared to reverse itself on the desirability of greater bureaucratic
representativeness:

> We see no incompatability between the open competitive system
> which assures a fair opportunity for all persons and the establish-
> ment of reasonable goals in connection with minority employment
> as an aid to managerial action in recognized problem areas. However,
> we oppose any dilution of the open competitive system . . . to
> achieve an artificial homogeneity of racial and ethnic backgrounds at
> every level of Federal employment. . . . We disagree with the basic
> assumption that this is a desirable and realistic objective.[9]

The CSC's policy statements during this period clearly reflected its desire
to give the appearance of readily adopting new EEO concepts while at the same
time avoiding the establishment of a government-wide policy of setting goals and
timetables for hiring and promoting members of minority groups. These statements consequently tended to be ambiguous, both in isolation and when considered together. Initially the CSC had not accepted a distinction between goals
and quotas and had rejected minority group representation as the overriding

objective of the Federal EEO Program. It took an intermediate position which consisted of accepting the representational concept while only very vaguely suggesting a means for its attainment. The CSC subsequently accepted the use of goals and timetables but continued to deny the validity of the representational objective which the utilization of these devices was meant to achieve. It is important to note that these shifting policy stances were neither the result of an internal conflict within the CSC nor a sign of vacillation and indecision. They were, rather, the direct result of a well-defined strategy to avoid endorsing the use of goals and timetables on a government-wide basis for as long as possible while at the same time appearing to be open to considerable change.*

Finally, in May 1971, after new congressional hearings on the proposed transfer of the Federal EEO Program to the EEOC, the CSC concluded that further avoidance of policy changes would prove too costly and accordingly issued a policy statement encouraging the use of goals and timetables:

> Employment goals and timetables should be established in problem areas where progress is recognized as necessary and where such goals and timetables will contribute to progress, i.e., in those organizations and localities and in those occupations and grade levels where minority employment is not what should reasonably be expected in view of the potential supply of qualified members of minority groups in the work force and in the recruiting area and available opportunities within the organization. The skills composition of the minority group population in the recruiting area used by the organization and the occupational nature of the jobs in the organization must be considered.

This statement differed from earlier pronouncements in that it represented a genuine change in policy. It controverted the principle of nondiscrimination in the sense that it permitted discrimination in favor of minority group members. The new policy also made it possible to legitimately consider affirmative action on the basis of race or ethnicity. Although the memo did not deal with women per se, subsequent regulations have authorized the use of goals and timetables to increase their employment opportunities.[10] However, despite the CSC's inability to forestall the adoption of the new policy, it has nevertheless been able to limit its importance in the process of overseeing its application.

---

*This interpretation has been confirmed by the former assistant executive director of the CSC, the former director of EEO, the former director of the FWP, as well as several other individuals associated with the CSC's OFEEO.

IMPLEMENTATION: DEFENSE IN DEPTH

Given the CSC's initial strong opposition to the use of goals and time-tables and the political circumstances surrounding the agency's final acceptance of this approach, it should come as no surprise that the CSC developed an administrative framework for implementation of the policy which militated against its effectiveness. Nor is it surprising that the agency qualified the policy in such a fashion as to make it difficult to apply. This, after all, is the nature of bureaucratic politics; an agency's ultimate defense of its values, mission, and culture is often obscurantist implementation. In keeping with most of the organizational arrangements concerning the Federal EEO Program, the administration of goals and timetables is highly decentralized. Here, as elsewhere, decentralization may be viewed as a kind of defense: it prevents the effective communication of knowledge as to how well a given policy is functioning and tends to assure that it will not be performing with the optimum results its supporters had hoped for.

Under the Equal Employment Opportunity Act of 1972, the CSC is responsible for an annual review and approval of other agencies' national and regional EEO action plans. In implementing this provision, the CSC's OFEEO requires that agency action plans include a statement on the use of goals and timetables. While the latter might not be established or even endorsed, there is little likelihood that a plan ignoring them entirely would be approved in the absence of further discussion with EEO agency officials. The OFEEO, however, deals exclusively with agency-wide national EEO action plans. Ignoring, for the moment, problems arising from the fact that some agencies are not organized on a regional basis, (which is contrary to one of several assumptions made in the 1972 EEO Act), there can be no doubt that much of the real EEO action is in the field. Only about 10 percent of all federal employees are employed in their agencies' Washington, D.C., headquarters. Goals and timetables established at the regional and installation levels are supposed to be compatible with those set by an agency's headquarters in its national affirmative action plan. A great deal of flexibility, however, is permitted in this area. The plans covering employees in the field are reviewed, not by the CSC's OFEEO, but rather by the CSC's regional offices. Whatever the formal requirements, the OFEEO does not systematically obtain, analyze, or review the contents of agency regional and installation action plans. Matters are complicated by the fact that there is little if any exchange of information, standards, or judgments among the CSC's regional offices and, as noted earlier, there is no direct formal communication between these offices and the OFEEO. Furthermore, agency headquarters often do not know what kinds of goals have been set by their own regions and installations.

The CSC also requires that agencies file a progress report along with their action plans so that the nonachievement or nonimplementation of goals can be ascertained and investigated. To date, only a few agencies have been able to do this in a meaningful (that is, statistical) fashion. These reports, covering most employees, are sent to the CSC's regional offices rather than to the OFEEO. Under this administrative framework, therefore, policy formulation, implementation, and feedback are all decentralized, both within the CSC and within individual agencies.

One of the major consequences of this administrative arrangement is that any systematic evaluation of the impact of the new policy becomes extremely difficult, if not impossible. Given the political controversy surrounding affirmative action with reference to the Federal EEO Program specifically and society in general, it is reasonable to attempt to determine its efficacy as a technique for securing further EEO. The best way to go about this (in the federal context) would be: 1) to ascertain the goals that have been set by various agencies; 2) to see how well these have been met; and 3) to gauge their impact on the social composition of the Federal service. Unfortunately, obtaining this information is not simple—either for the individual researcher or the OFEEO. Neither the OFEEO nor the EEO staffs in agency headquarters necessarily know what goals, if any, have been set, much less whether they are being met. Until a far greater degree of data centralization occurs, it will be impossible to determine precisely how much change in the racial, ethnic, and sexual composition of the federal work force can be attributed to the use of goals and timetables.[11] Moreover, both the decentralization of authority and the absence of data serve as a protective shield for the initiators the CSC has placed on the application of the new approach.

The first step the CSC took in establishing a complete policy framework for the implementation of goals and timetables was to draw a clear distinction between the latter and quotas. The "May Memo" had stated:

> A "goal" is a realistic objective which an agency endeavors to achieve on a timely basis within the context of the merit system of employment. A "quota," on the other hand, would restrict employment or development opportunities to members of particular groups by establishing a required number or proportionate representation which agency managers are obligated to attain without regard to merit system requirements. "Quotas" are incompatible with merit principles.

The difference, it would appear, is not in the objective but rather in the degree of flexibility required. Quotas require that if a black leaves a post another black be placed in his or her stead. If there are no blacks available who have established their eligibility under the merit system, then one without merit prerequisites will have to be found. Goals, on the other hand, permit either a nonblack to fill the post or a black to be given training so that he or she will subsequently qualify under merit standards. Moreover, whereas a quota should not be surpassed, exceeding a goal might be considered desirable.

Whether this is actually the way the system works, however, is another matter. The CSC has warned: "Goals and timetables must not be interpreted by managers and supervisors as quotas. Agency action plans and instructions involving goals and timetables must state that all actions to achieve goals must be in full compliance with merit system requirements."[12] Yet several agency EEO functionaries believe that in practice there is a tendency for goals to be treated as quotas and for the merit system to be circumvented when practicable. Once goals are met, little concern may be paid to EEO. For the agency manager, supervisor, and personnel specialist it is often easier to meet a goal than to explain why it could not be attained with strict adherence to the merit system. Indeed, the latter tactic makes one wonder why a "reasonable" goal was not established in the first place:

> The CSC is cognizant of this problem and has advised that: Employment goals and target dates should be reasonable and flexible indicators for management action. If goals and timetables are realistic, they will probably be met through appropriate affirmative action. Where they are not met, the reasons for this should be assessed by the agency management to see if the goals or target dates for their achievement should be adjusted, or if additional affirmative actions are needed, including the further commitment of resources to agency recruitment and upward mobility efforts.[13]

In effect, the CSC's desire for realistic approach is the ultimate protector of both the goals-and-timetables approach and the merit system, a fact which is reflected throughout its policy guidelines. For example, the CSC suggests that "to be meaningful, goals and timetables should be developed according to organizational levels and components rather than establishing agency-wide goals which do not take into account local circumstances or occupational differences."[14] Ideally, the national action plans would provide guidance and instructions with respect to the development of goals and the actual goals themselves would "be set at the lowest practicable level in the agency to assure that they are reasonable in terms of their relationship to hiring needs and the skills available in the recruiting area."[15] Lastly, the CSC claims that goals and timetables should normally reflect estimated turnover, accessions, and reductions in force.

The CSC insists that a realistic approach be taken in the establishment of goals. This conservative outlook, however, would militate against "over-enthusiastic" breaches of the merit system. The incremental nature of this approach is reflected in both the limited and even extravagant goals set by several agencies, such as 100 percent female hiring for clerical positions in the Department of Agriculture's Packers and Stockyards Administration. The ideal goal, as envisioned by the CSC, would almost be met even if it were not set, that is, just high enough to motivate supervisors and personnelists to use such traditional affirmative action processes as offering training to minority group members and women and recruiting in minority group areas.

In practice, members of several EEO agency staffs find the CSC's policy guidelines difficult to follow. For example, how does one determine the types of skills which minority group members and women in the available work force possess? Several officials feel that although this might be accomplished in areas where there are good census data, it could not be done in others. In an agency such as the Department of Agriculture, which consists of about 30 semiindependent subunits with different regional maps of their own, obtaining the necessary data and overseeing the setting of goals and timetables is very complex indeed. An HEW official has pointed out that it is difficult to apply the CSC's guidelines because there is no way of knowing the precise degree of turnover, accession, or reduction in the work force, nor where it will take place. This official, moreover, feels that a formula for setting goals is needed that would indicate when and where the approach would be most useful. Some agencies, such as the DOT and the DOD, find it more desirable to establish some goals on a nationwide basis, while others, such as the Department of State, do not employ this approach at all.

Having examined the administrative and policy frameworks for the establishment of goals and timetables, it is now logical, at this point, to turn to an analysis of the nationwide goals that have actually been set.

AGENCY GOALS

Although a thorough analysis of the utilization of goals and timetables is virtually impossible at the present time, one can nevertheless determine whether agencies are using the approach and, if so, how. This has been accomplished by reviewing the affirmative action plans of 22 agencies for calendar or fiscal year(s) 1973 and/or 1974.* Additional interviews were held with directors of EEO or members of their staffs in the department of Agriculture, DOT, HEW, HUD, the Department of the Interior, as well as in the independent VA and the GSA. Extensive interviewing also took place in the CSC's OFEEO.

The information gained in this fashion leads to some important conclusions.

A review of agency EEO national action plans reveals that there is a considerable degree of diversity in the types and extent of goals for the hiring and

---

* The agencies included the Departments of State, Treasury, Justice, Commerce, Labor, Interior, HUD, HEW, Transportation, Agriculture, Army, Navy, Air Force, GSA, EEOC, GPO, Post Office, GAO, CSC, VA, NASA, and the SBA. Taken together, these agencies employ more than 90 percent of the federal work force.

promotion of members of minority groups and women. This is only to be expected in view of the existence of administrative decentalization, which enables agencies and their subunits to formulate goals and timetables on an individual basis, and the ambiguity of policy guidelines governing this process. There is no convenient way of summarizing or describing these variations statistically. The following represents a list of the numerical and percentage goals established for the agencies involved:

GPO (1973): 4 percent increase in the number of women and minority group members in supervisory and "uprate" positions in the Production Department.

EEOC (1974): 30 percent of all new appointments above GS-9 should be women; 5 percent of all new appointees should be Orientals and 5 percent should be native Americans.

GSA (1974): 36 percent of all those hired should be members of minority groups, 30 percent should be women; 54 percent of all those promoted should be minority group members and 44 percent should be women.

Army (1974): increase the number of women in GS 13-15 by 0.5 percent of the total population in those grades; add 5 to 10 minority group members and women to the ranks of the supergrades; 25 percent of all senior-level placements to go to women and 25 percent to go to minority group members.

Navy (1974): the employment of minority group members in all subunits should be equal to at least 75 percent of the percent that is minority in the recruiting area.

Interior (1974): nationwide goal of 12 percent minority in the agency's work force by 1977 (excluding Indians in the Bureau of Indian Affairs); add 50 women to GS-13 level positions.

DOT (1974): action plan endorses the use of goals and in a separate action the department secretary prescribed goals of increasing minority and female employment in the agency by 2.5 percent of the agency's work force.

Air Force (1973): increase minority representation in the work force by 1 percent; increase the number of women and minority group members in grades GS 13-15 by 0.5 percent of the total number of positions in these grades; do the same in supergrade positions.

Agriculture (1974): the average hiring goals established by the bureaus that set goals for the categories included were: professional hires (12 percent minority, 14 percent female); administrative hires (14 percent minority, 30 percent female); support position hires (17 percent minority); clerical hires (28 percent minority, 77 percent female); lower level technician hires (30 percent minority, 44 percent female).

NASA (1974): increase minority employment by 6.1 percent of total agency employment; appoint 80 women and 80 minority group members to professional positions.

Several agencies, including the Departments of the Treasury, Labor, Commerce, Justice, HUD, and HEW, endorsed the strategy of goals and timetables but established no national goals and did not possess or make available consolidated information concerning goals actually set by their regions and field installations. The same was true for the GAO* the CSC, the VA, the SBA, and the Post Office.

Given the decentralized nature of setting goals and the policy framework within which the process operates, one would expect the latter to be conducted in a rather conservative fashion. The easiest approach for agency management (which is more interested in its own agency's mission than in EEO) is to set goals that are modest enough to be achieved without much difficulty. In fact, virtually all EEO officials view EEO as a program and process which must be forced upon largely unreceptive personnel. In the eyes of agency functionaries, the establishment of goals is preferable to their nonexistence, which could create difficulties vis-a-vis the CSC's OFEEO or its regional offices. In most instances, a conservative goal-setting policy is justified under the CSC's policy guidelines and is facilitated, perhaps even anticipated, by the decentralized power structure characteristic of the Federal EEO Program. Furthermore, although it is conceivable that an agency's EEO record might be so poor that a sizeable proportion of its employees would oppose the establishment of overly conservative goals, this has not yet occurred.[16]

On the whole, the nationwide goals established by federal agencies suggest that the CSC's current strategy is unlikely to yield the dramatic results that many of its supporters had hoped for. One may conclude, at least tentatively, that goal setting at the national level has, for the most part, done little to alter the status quo—and has sometimes reinforced it. Although some of the percentage goals are moderately high, the actual number of placements to which they refer are often quite low. In agencies such as DOT and the Air Force, the goals set are almost minuscule compared with the social underrepresentation of minorities and women in some of the grades to which they apply. The same is true of the Army's goal at the GS 13-15 level. The Department of the Interior's goal of 12 percent minority representation in its nationwide work force by 1977 will still leave it, from a social standpoint, with an underrepresentation of minorities in general, and will do little to abate minority concentration in the lowest grades. The Navy's nationwide goal for minority representaion will have the same effect. The goals set by several bureaus in the Department of Agriculture will do little beyond reinforcing a concentration of minority group members and females in low-level positions. In some of these bureaus goals are frankly being set at approximately the same levels at which minority group members and women would be hired in any event. It is not necessary to have a 100 percent female hiring goal in clerical positions in order to accomplish this

---

*The CCR reported that the GAO set a hiring goal of 10 percent for white women. This was lower than their overall employment in the agency. Had this goal been adopted, it would have decreased their proportional representation in the agency. (*Federal Civil Rights Enforcement Effort-1974*, vol. 5, p. 113, n. 374).

end. Finally, although the goals set by NASA and the GPO are perhaps more likely to encourage greater social representation where it is most lacking, these, too, must be viewed as rather modest as compared with the patterns of minority and female underrepresentation that currently exist in these agencies.

Although goal setting generally tends to be conservative, there are instances of a countertrend as well. Given the nature of its mission, the EEOC has established goals that are certain to significantly increase the number of women in its upper levels and Orientals and native Americans throughout its structure.[17] The goals established by some of the bureaus in the Department of Agriculture for professional and administrative positions are likely to encourage meaningful change. Similarly, the GSA's promotion goals will create a steady flow of minorities and women into higher positions. Depending on the actual numbers, the Army's goal of 25 percent of all senior-level placements going to minority group members and women may also have a considerable impact.

Thus, it appears that in general the new approach will not have more than an incremental effect on the racial, ethnic, and sexual composition of the federal service. Given the fact that goals are supposed to be achieved with strict adherence to the merit system, this is perhaps unavoidable. Merit can be circumvented, but not on a wholesale basis. Ultimately a choice between representation and merit may have to be made. Indeed, several EEO officials believe that the chief virtue of the goals-and-timetables approach is not that it yields greater social representation; rather, it is the fact that it puts pressure on managers and supervisors to pay more attention to EEO and to allocate more resources for minority and female training and recruiting. Some agencies, in fact, have begun to openly discriminate in the allocation of training. HEW, for instance, seeks a 50 percent minority and 50 percent female participation in its management intern program. Similarly, the Army tries to reserve 30 percent of all openings for minorities and women in its training programs and its use of Federal Executive Seminar Centers. Whether this approach violates the Equal Employment Opportunity Act's prohibition against discrimination is unclear since the discrimination involved is not necessarily invidious.[18] In any event, it generally does not run afoul of formal merit system constraints. There is no doubt that the effort to include more women and minority group members in training and intern programs is a very indirect way of obtaining greater social representation in the upper levels of the federal service. It may, however, also prove to be one of the surest routes to accomplish this goal. This is especially true where underrepresentation is primarily due to discrimination and disadvantage *in society in general* rather than just within the federal government. Promotion-oriented goals may likewise prove to be of greater utility than hiring goals.

THE FUTURE

Representationists are likely to be dismayed both by the administrative and policy frameworks being utilized to implement goals and timetables and by the nature of the goals actually being set. However, the new strategy is not a dead end and seems destined to dominate the formal side of agency EEO action plans for years to come. This fact alone will probably make the approach increasingly more effective. Pressures for greater implementation of EEO policies are beginning to build. Significantly, the two CSC officials who fought the new approach most forcefully have now retired. Some agency EEO officials have already expressed criticism of the current handling of goals and timetables, and improvements are in the offing.

Among these criticisms, there is widespread consensus that the one-year time frame for action plans and goals is too short. Many believe that it encourages the development of a "paper program" for the CSC's consumption and militates against the creation of an genuinely effective program. Given the fact that it takes an agency such as HEW about five months to write an action plan, it is evident that there is insufficient time remaining to concentrate on implementation. The CSC is aware of this difficulty and is currently exploring the possibility of extending the time frame for action plans without violating the Equal Employment Opportunity Act.

Second, the members of several agency EEO staffs have also expressed a desire for greater centralization in the review of action plans by the CSC. These officials believe that the CSC's regional offices use widely divergent standards in reviewing action plans. This, in turn, makes it difficult for agency headquarters to provide uniform instruction to their regions and field installations. Decentralization also make the latter more responsible to the CSC's regional offices than to their own headquarters, thereby weakening the impact of agency-wide EEO activities and requirements. In the opinion of many practitioners, it would be preferable for agency regional and installation plans to be forwarded along with their national plans to the OFEEO, whereupon the CSC headquarters could call upon CSC regional offices for further investigation and information when it felt this course of action was necessary. The CSC is somewhat sympathetic to these concerns and is presently planning to enlarge the role of the OFEEO in the review of agency action plans.

Finally, a few EEO officials believe that for goals and timetables to be most effective it may be necessary to establish them with specific reference to individual minority groups and women within these groups. For example, a hiring goal of 50 percent minority group members and 50 percent women is ambiguous. There is no guidance in the distribution of members of different minority groups within this framework or for sexual representation within specific racial and ethnic groups. Such a goal could be met by placing black women in 50 percent of all hires, hiring 50 percent minority males and 50 percent nonminority females, or in several other ways. The essence of being considered "minority" is the fact that the individual belongs to a relatively distinct and disadvantaged subculture; different sub cultures should therefore be dealt with on an individual basis. If the ultimate objective of EEO policy is adequate social representation, then goals should be established with this fact clearly in mind.

CONCLUSIONS

Bureaucratic politics can take many forms. In the political struggle between representationists and meritists, each group was able to mobilize sufficient resources to forestall a complete victory by the other group. Representationists made use of several factors in their drive to institute a policy utilizing goals and timetables: 1) the stagnancy of the Federal EEO Program in the late 1960s and early 1970s; 2) widespread dissatisfaction with the CSC's performance in this realm and related demands that the program be transferred to the EEOC; and 3) the emergence of a compensatory civil rights policy. The CSC, the prime spokesman for the merit system, resisted adoption of the new approach until it thought that to continue to do so would mean the loss of the entire Federal EEO Program. Much of its resistance took the form of issuing ambiguous and contradictory policy directives intended to make the agency appear to be open to new concepts while at the same time enabling it to avoid fundamental change.

The contest over goals and timetables did not end with the acceptance by CSC, in May 1971, of this approach. It simply moved from the highly politicized legislative arena to the less visible administrative side of government. What the CSC could not prevent outright it has been able to forestall through administrative mechanisms. Among the latter have been the creation of organizational and policy frameworks which impair the implementation of the new approach and thus protect the merit system from immediate demise. The desire to prevent a weakening of that system stems from the CSC's organizational culture, values, and mission. Thus, a serious loss on the policy front has not yet meant an actual loss in the administrative realm.

A review of the national goals actually established by federal agencies during 1973 and/or 1974 suggests that, on the whole, these goals and the strategy itself, as currently implemented, are not likely to lead to more than incremental change and, in some cases, will do no more than reinforce minority and female concentration and overrepresentation in lower level positions. For the most part, those federal agencies which set nationwide goals tend to do so in ways that are consistent with the personnel actions they would normally take even in the absence of goals.

The basic reason for the CSC's conservative approach is twofold (and is directly related to the nature of the CSC's handling of the implementation of the new policy. First, it is clear that the administrative decentalization characteristic of the establishment and evaluation of goals militates against their rational application. To date, there is little evidence to suggest that either agency headquarters or the CSC's OFEEO, ostensibly the major policy-making units, knows very much about what is going on in the field. Without such knowledge, evaluation becomes impossible, learning feedback unobtainable, and improvement unlikely. In theory, enforcement is largely left to the CSC's regional offices, but agency EEO officials maintain that decentralization at this level results in a haphazard application of divergent standards. This, in turn, makes it difficult for agencies to act as unified organizations in developing coherent EEO programs, In short, the resultant decentralization provides too much autonomy for those generally least interested in EEO.

A second reason why the strategy of using goals and timetables is unlikely to result in substantial changes in the social composition of the federal service in the near future is that policy guidelines for the establishment of goals, as they are currently constituted, are ambiguous and militate against change. For many EEO officials, the use of goals and timetables violates the requirement that personnel actions be made in a nondiscriminatory manner. This has, to some extent, undercut their legitimacy and has made it difficult for EEO officials to obtain a total commitment to use them from managers, supervisors, and personnel specialists. Beyond this problem, which has yet to be fully resolved by the courts, lies the question of whether goals and timetables can be meaningfully utilized within the framework of the merit system. As long as there are open, competitive rankings and a rule of three,* hiring goals and timetables will be limited, in terms of utility, to situations where there is a minority group member or woman among the top three eligibles. Obviously, a major reason for the social underrepresentation of some groups is that this is frequently not the case. Without arguing that federal merit procedures could not be made less discriminatory by eliminating "cultural bias" and adopting other means,† it is likely that any merit system operating in an environment where inequality clearly prevails will be discriminatory in some of its procedures. This can be remedied by offering greater training opportunities within the federal service to those who are disadvantaged in pursuing skills and self-development in the society at large. However, there is an inherent limit to the utility of training, both as a result of financial costs and the number of years of education it may require to prepare individuals for many of the high-level positions in the federal government.

In short, goals and timetables as presently implemented are likely to have only an incremental effect on the establishment of greater social representation in the federal service. To some extent, their implementation could be effected through greater centralization in goal setting and evaluation. They might also prove more effective if they were used extensively to encourage the inclusion of women and members of minority groups in training programs. Ultimately, though, unless American society undergoes a rather radical transformation,

---

*The rule of three permits the individual hiring new employees to select any one of the top three eligibles presented to him or her, as determined by scores and rating on merit examinations.
† See Chapter 6 for several possible solutions to this problem.

a more clearcut choice between greater social representation and the merit system may have to be made. At the most general level, public personnel arrangements are highly political, and the struggle between representationists and meritists is likely to continue in the future.

NOTES

1. See Chapter 2.

2. Letter from the CSC chairman to the staff director of the U.S. CCR, July 24, 1970, p. 2. Hereinafter referred to as the "Hampton Letter."

3. Memorandum issued by President Nixon to the heads of departments and agencies, August 8, 1969 (prepared by the CSC).

4. "Hampton Letter," pp. 1,2.

5. U.S. Commission on Civil Rights, *Federal Civil Rights Enforcement Effort* (Washington, D.C.: U.S. Government Printing Office, 1970), p. 1076.

6. U.S., Congress, House, Committee on Education and Labor; General Subcommittee on Labor, H.R. 1746 (March 4, 1971). 92nd Congress, 1st Session.

7. "Hampton Letter," p. 2. Emphasis added.

8. Letter written by CSC Chairman Robert Hampton to R. Kelley, Assistant Secretary of Defense. The letter received widespread circulation among federal personnel officials. According to the director of the Federal EEO Program, the letter's intentional ambiguity was intended to pacify the DOD and create the impression of flexibility without actually modifying policy. The DOD as well as other agencies apparently felt that little progress would be forthcoming until CSC personnel officials were instructed to hire and promote a specific number of minority group members per year.

9. Letter written by CSC Executive Director Nicholas Oganovic to Adrian Dove, management analyst, OMB, February 3, 1971, p. 6.

10. Civil Service Commission, Federal Personnel Manual System Letter, Chapter 713-22, "EEO Plans," appendix I, no. 9 (October 4, 1973). According to the former director of the FWP, the decision to include women was a direct result of her initiative and was due, in part, to an oversight by the former executive director in approving the letter.

11. This is a more general problem in the federal bureaucracy. See, for example, Elizabeth Drew, "HEW Grapples with PPBS," *Public Interest* 8 (Summer 1967): 9-29. Bureaucratic agencies, like individuals in many walks of life, prefer not to have their performance evaluated and find it politically expedient not to provide the information necessary for doing so. The U.S. CCR, *The Federal Civil Rights Enforcement Effort-1974* (Washington, D.C.: Commission on Civil Rights, 1975), vol. 5, p. 111, n. 369, reported that about 12 percent of all regional plans submitteed in 1973 included goals and timetables. The report, however, did not itemize the contents of each of these plans.

12. "May Memo."

13. CSC, Federal Personnel Manual System Letter, 713-22, appendix I, no. 11.

14. Ibid., no. 10.

15. Ibid., 713-22 (2g).

16. There have been some organized protests by federal employees in the area of civil rights. See, for example, D.H. Rosenbloom, "Some Political Implications of the Drift Toward a Liberation of Federal Employees," *Public Administration Review* 31 (July/August 1971): 420-26; Cary Hershey, *Protest in the Public Service* (Lexington, Mass.: Lexington Books, 1973).

17. The EEOC's goals, however, also raise another question. In 1972 its work force was divided into the following groups: 48.6 percent black, 12.4 percent Spanish-surnameds, and 35.6 percent nonminority. Minority representation was lowest in the supergrades, but nonminorities still filled only 52.9 percent of these positions. Minorities were therefore highly overrepresented in this agency. Its goals for Orientals and native Americans will probably tend to reinforce the underrepresentation of nonminorities. See Civil Service Commission, *Minority Group Employment in the Federal Government,* May 31, 1972, p. 126. (Washington D.C.: Government Printing Office, 1972).

18. If "reverse discrimination" is found to be legitimate by the judiciary in a definitive holding it will probably be on this ground. See *Morton v. Mancari,* 417 U.S. 535, 552 (1974), where it was reasoned that differential treatment in favor of Indians could not be considered "invidious racial discrimination."

6

THE POLITICS OF ADMINISTRATIVE INCREMENTALISM: BLENDING MERIT AND EEO

The politics of federal EEO are presently characterized by a struggle between meritists and representationists. This, as we have seen, is most evident in the area of goals and timetables. Yet there are traces of this fundamental divergence of opinion in virtually all aspects of EEO. In general, meritists are reluctant to introduce changes into the personnel system, believing, perhaps correctly, that it has helped to produce a national bureaucracy that compares very favorably with other public bureaucracies in terms of efficiency, responsiveness, and even representativeness. Meritists do not feel that there is basic conflict between the merit system and equal opportunity, although they do recognize that there is a considerable difference between merit and representation. Thus, the CSC is able to express its mission in the following fashion: "While clearly the purpose of the Commission is to maintain the integrity of the Federal merit system, it is also to assure equal employment opportunity for all persons. . . ."[1] At the same time, however, the CSC is opposed to such representational devices as quotas, which it views as "an approach to personnel management which is not compatible with the basic philosophy of merit system employment. . . ."[2] Consequently, where this type of device (or others, such as goals and timetables, which could lead to its adoption) is not at issue, it is possible for meritists (and the CSC in particular) to attempt to more fully integrate merit and EEO. The CSC's prime consideration, however, will always be maintenance of the merit system; modifications in personnel procedures will therefore be introduced cautiously and slowly. In this area, therefore, the conservative outlook of the "personnel complex,"[3] particularly that of the CSC, comes to the fore.

While meritists consider representational approaches abhorrent, representationists characterize the current implementation of the Federal EEO Program as administratively sluggish and lacking in any sympathy for the plights of members of minority groups and of women. This is particularly true of the CCR, which plays an important role in evaluating the enforcement of federal civil rights policies and has been the most severe governmental critic of the CSC. The CCR is unabashedly representationist. It has adopted the position that, had there been no previous record of discrimination against groups of citizens seeking federal employment,

> the Nation would have discovered that a civil service, operating in a manner consistent with the equal opportunity guarantees embedded in the Constitution, would more likely have the broad range of experience and skills necessary to address society's problems. Moreover, it would more likely generate support for government programs by all groups in society. Because of the growing tendency of elected representatives to delegate and assign legislative and judicial functions to the Federal Bureaucracy, it has become increasingly crucial that the practices which for many years denied equal employment opportunities to citizens because of their race, color, national origin, religion, or sex, and by doing so deprived the Nation of the benefit of their services, be eliminated from public employment procedures.[4]

In the CCR's view, preferential treatment of women and members of minority groups is necessary "to eliminate the vestiges of past, invidious discrimination and to achieve the goal of a truly representative government bureaucracy. . . ."[5] Given this outlook, it is not surprising that the CCR and representationists in general have been highly critical of the CSC's incremental approach to the implementation of the Federal EEO Program. Blending merit and EEO would not be necessary if it were possible to dispense with the former and adopt direct representational appraoaches instead. Several aspects of the Federal EEO Program have, over the years, emerged as sources of political controversy. An analysis of these areas, particularly the CSC's incremental approach, will provide additional insight into the Federal EEO Program and will result in a better understanding of the nature of administrative politics in the federal bureaucracy.

AFFIRMATIVE ACTION THROUGH ACTION PLANS

In terms of its general EEO outlook, the CSC has placed primary emphasis on "traditional" affirmative action as a means of achieving harmony between the merit system and EEO. This can best be understood as a process of removing artificial barriers standing in the way of genuine equal opportunity in the competition for federal positions. Artificial barriers, in turn, can best be conceived of as: 1) those aspects of federal personnel procedures which affect EEO in a negative fashion and do not contribute to overall economy, efficiency, order, or performance; and 2) those characteristics of life in the United States which tend to deny women and members of minority groups who are a part of the Federal EEO Program's constituency the possibility of developing bureaucratic skills in accordance with their natural abilities.

Since September 1966, the affirmative action component of the Federal EEO Program has been operating largely through individual agency action plans. The latter have been defined as "an agency's commitment to assure true equal employment opportunity in all aspects of its operations affecting employees."[6] This approach, utilized to a limited extent by the PCEEO, represents a logical mode of implementing executive orders and legislation in the sense that it makes agency heads responsible for an effective Federal EEO Program within their domain. Such decentralization enables individual agencies to handle their specific EEO problems and also makes it possible to deal with local problems on a local level. On the other hand, it gives agencies a great deal of control over the implementation of EEO and permits them to maintain the status quo if they are so inclined. For example, if an agency is fearful that affirmative action to correct EEO limitations might interfere with its operational programs—which are the source of the agency's prestige, authority, and budget—it might very well do nothing more than the bare minimum in terms of equalizing opportunity.

Since agencies are required to submit their action plans to the CSC for evaluation, it is clear that in practice the success of the action plan approach is dependent upon the individual agency's desire to further the cause of EEO as well as the CSC's ability to provide meaningful advice and to make sure that it is being followed. The CSC's record in reviewing action plans has thus far been mixed. If agency action plans are found to be unsatisfactory by the OFEEO, the agency director of EEO, or the individual who transmitted the plan, is informed of its defects and is expected to correct them. Agency reaction to such criticism has been varied. There have been instances where agencies have submitted virtually useless plans on the assumption that no action would be taken by the CSC; only after receiving a critique from the CSC did they begin to take EEO seriously. In other instances, the CSC's criticism has given additional strength to agency officials who favor intensive EEO efforts but have encountered difficulties in convincing their colleagues to adopt significant measures. Some agencies still continue to submit plans of a questionable nature and more or less ignore the CSC's responses; in addition, plans are often submitted late. There have been a significant number of instances where the CSC has simply failed to provide a timely critique of agency action plans. This is largely due to the fact that, whatever the theoretical importance of affirmative action, in practice officials in the OFEEO and other CSC personnel having considerable EEO responsibilities tend to spend most of their time dealing with individual complaints of discrimination and answering letters from various sources; there have been occasions when officials specifically assigned to action plans have dealt exclusively with complaints and letters for months on end. In addition, even when these officials do get around to writing critiques of the plans, they are often handicapped by a lack of firsthand knowledge of the individual agency's specific EEO situtation and are unable to provide meaningful advice.*

Perhaps the most important benefit resulting from action plans is that they at least force agencies to look at their EEO situation and often serve as a catalyst in initiating constructive reforms. Ideally, action plans should be practical, that is, they should normally include a detailed outline of intended action and specify a time limit. Furthermore, they should encompass all groups receiving insufficient EEO in a particular agency and, at the same time, they "should include specific action items directed at the special problems in assuring equal employment opportunity for women or for particular minorities, e.g., Spanish-speaking Americans, American Indians, and Alaskan natives."[7] The plans should also be developed in such a fashion so that the overall outline can be refined in its application to particular problems at the installation level. In formulating plans, "the ideas of agency managers should be solicited to ensure development of a plan of action which is realistic and relevant to agency employment needs and problems. To assure program credibility, and the responsiveness of EEO activities to various interested parties, consultation with employee, minority, and women's groups to obtain their input is encouraged."[8] Plans should be revised at least once a year, although they have not always been critiqued by the CSC within this time period. Action plans must address the following topics: organization and resources for the administration of EEO; recruitment activities; utilization of present work force; plans and procedures for "upward mobility" and training; participation in community efforts to improve conditions which affect employability; internal evaluation of EEO activities; complaint processing; and special programs for the economically and educationally disadvantaged.

It is evident that if agencies and the CSC could develop comprehensive plans along the guidelines suggested and implement them effectively, they would be making a considerable contribution to the quest for greater EEO. In practice, however, affirmative action plans tend to represent no more than a "paper program," providing a checklist of activities in which agencies ought to engage but seldom do in a meaningful fashion. Indeed, this is necessarily the case given the incremental approach the CSC has adopted vis-a-vis EEO. The pace is slow, no breaches of the merit system are knowingly tolerated, and, as will become evident in the following pages, there is little effective enforcement of plans or serious evaluation of their impact.

COMPLAINTS

No aspect of the Federal EEO Program has been as problematical as the development of a system for the adjudication of complaints of discrimination.

---

*As outlined in Chapter 5, plans are reviewed on a decentralized basis, with national plans going to the CSC's headquarters and others to its regional offices.

A complaint system must be an integral component of a Federal EEO Program because it serves as an enforcement mechanism which, when effective, enables employees themselves to protect their right of equal opportunity whenever they feel it is being violated. At the same time, it provides agencies, supervisory personnel, and the federal service with protection against false accusations of unlawfulness and/or immorality. Complaint systems, moreover, tend to be highly visible; their effectiveness consequently serves as a major indicator of the government's commitment to EEO. A complaint system is also an important factor in determining the degree of administrative credibility that a program fosters among the general public, federal servants, and particularly women and members of certain minority groups.

Complaint systems, however, have tended to be troublesome. It is safe to say that a truly effective complaint system has not yet been devised. The establishment and implementation of complaint systems has been dominated by meritists. From their perspective, complaints involving individual acts of discrimination offer no threat to the merit system, and may even contribute to its improvement. However, general complaints based upon allegations that the personnel system itself is discriminatory in its operation or creates patterns of discrimination could prove damaging from the meritist point of view. Complaints of this nature have consequently either been disallowed or judged under strict meritist (currently CSC) control. Once efforts are initiated to minimize the potential importance of general complaints, the complaint system becomes, for the most part, a remedial rather than a progressive device for acheiving EEO. As a result, the CSC and other organizations holding primary responsibility for the general administration of the Federal EEO Program have tended to downgrade the importance of complaints.

Moreover, there has been considerable reluctance to divorce the adjudication of individual complaints from agency management or to create an independent body to hear complaints. Politically, this is a result of the desire of individual agencies to avoid having their practices in an area as sensitive as EEO aired outside their own organizations. Administratively the policy of permitting agencies to rule on the individual complaints of their own employees is an outgrowth of the CSC's desire to decentralize EEO and to integrate it with personnel procedures as a whole. This approach has been justified on the grounds that since complaints arise within the context of a specific organization's mission and practices, and the agency's management is therefore in the best position to determine the validity of the complaint and to take action when necessary. On the other hand, decentralization of authority has probably contributed to the tendency of complaint proceedings to rule that descrimination has not occurred; in addition, decentralization may also be responsible for a reluctance on the part of employees to file complaints for fear of reprisal and as a consequence of the limited prospects for obtaining benefits.

Individual Complaints

The CSC began to process individual complaints of discrimination before it received the primary responsibility for establishing and coordinating the government-wide Federal EEO Program. As was noted earlier, this is an area in which merit and EEO are compatible and therefore one in which strong policy and vigorous enforcement could be expected. In January 1965, the PCEEO, which preceded the CSC in its current EEO role, delegated authority for the complaint system to the CSC because it found it difficult to resolve cases on a prompt basis. The PCEEO's procedural policy provided that any federal employee or applicant who believed that he or she had been subjected to illegitimate discrimination could file a complaint within 90 days of the alleged discriminatory action. The complaint was then investigated by an EPO who, upon completing the investigation, was instructed to seek an informal resolution. If this failed, the complainant was entitled to an oral hearing before the EPO or his designee. At the hearing, the agency involved was required to produce witnesses who were under its jurisdiction and, when necessary, the rights of cross-examination and confrontation were also available. The findings and recommendations of the hearing examiner were to be transmitted to the agency head or to the PCEEO's executive vice-chairman for study and recommendation. The final decision was to be made by the agency head or his designee. If the employee desired further action, he or she had the right to final review by the executive vice-chairman, provided that this was requested within 30 days after the agency decision. If necessary, the executive vice-chairman could hold another hearing. In some instances, the same official could also review cases on his own initiative. The employee was entitled to be represented, advised, or accompanied by counsel. If an employee failed to appear for the first hearing or did not furnish requested information within 60 days, the case could be closed by the agency. Under this system of delegation of authority, the CSC took on general investigatory functions and its Board of Appeals and Review (BAR) took over some of the functions of the executive vice-chairman.

This system remained more or less in force until April 1966, when the CSC issued new directives. The object of these regulations was to make the system more responsive to the needs of those who believed that they had been subjected to individual, illegal acts of discrimintion. They further encouraged informal settlement and, where that failed, imposed a time limitation on complaint processing of 60 days without a hearing and 90 days in cases in which a hearing was requested. The right to appeal to the BAR was retained.

These changes led, almost immediately, to serious difficulties. The CSC's reform of the complaint procedure encouraged greater expectations on the part of employees and, in turn, resulted in a significant increase in the number of complaints filed. For example, from April 1965 through March 1966, the year before the CSC's revision of the system, there were 918 complaints. Between April 1966 and March 1967, however, agencies received 1,389 formal complaints. This increase, in conjunction with the newly established time limits, contributed to a situation in which a very large proportion of complaint cases were not processed in the allotted time. Thus, by March 31, 1967, almost 40 percent of the cases on hand had passed the required time limits; the average case took 144 days to close. Although, by CSC estimates, about half of these delays could be attributed to complainants, the government's inability to process cases in a prompt fashion led to increasing criticism and reduced the general estimation of the program's effectiveness in the eyes of minority group organizations, employees, and the informed public.

There were other criticisms as well. In the view of many, the major defect in the complaint procedure was that the latter did not provide for a truly impartial review. The agency in which descrimination was alleged to have occurred was in control of the investigation and the initial hearing. This fact, the critics argued, produced an adjudicative conflict of interest. As one critic expressed it:

> The agency (meaning some supervisor) discriminates against a Negro. The agency (meaning some official who will be quickly out of a job if he makes the agency look bad) investigates. The agency (meaning another official who also understands his obligation to protect the image) conducts a hearing. Then the agency (thru still another well-trained official) renders a decision.
> It's a thoroly [sic] stacked-deck process. . . [9]

A related criticism was that agencies only rarely found discrimination to exist. Although they provided relief to employees in about 25 percent of the cases, formal findings of discrimination were made in only about 1.6 percent of all cases.[10] Thus, an agency might find that an employee had a legitimate complaint—he or she was treated unfairly or unreasonably—and would subsequently rectify the situation on the grounds that improper personnel procedure or judgments had been exercised rather than on the basis of discrimination itself. Those critics who viewed the system as a palliative argued that only through findings of discrimination and disciplinary procedures for supervisors guilty of such acts could the government hope to deter prohibited practices within its ranks. In answer to these criticisms, one CSC official reasoned: "We need to recognize that groups that feel downtrodden are going to become increasingly rebellious as conditions improve—as they see some chance of gaining a better deal. We could have the fairest, fastest, and most efficient complaint procedure in the world—but today it would not be good enough."[11] The CSC itself, however, sought to improve the system through further changes.

The CSC's immediate response to mounting criticism was to provide more guidelines for agencies and to provide greater training for those performing EEO functions. A more important change, however, was the development of a new complaint system. Beginning in November 1967 the CSC held meetings to consider possible reforms. In May 1968 its proposals were distributed to agencies, employee organizations, minority group organizations, and other interested parties for comment. The proposals received approval in the public press for being, in the words of John Cramer, "a big step toward divorcing agencies from their oft-criticized dual role of prosecutor-and-judge,"[12] but both agencies and some minority group leaders voiced strong objections. On the one hand, according to a CSC memo, an "overwhelming desire to maintain the investigation and hearing process within the agency" was expressed; on the other hand, it was noted that the idea of moving the compliance phase of the Government is gaining momentum"[13] among individual critics. Finally, on March 18, 1969, the CSC announced new regulations which were to be implemented as of July 1. With some modifications, these rules are still in effect at the present time.

The general objectives of the current system include:

1. To provide maximum opportunity for informal resolution of problems which might result in complaints.
2. To provide an independent investigation of the facts when a formal complaint is lodged.
3. To guarantee a fair an impartial hearing by an independent trained appeals examiner when a hearing is required.
4. To speed up the entire complaint process.[14]

Briefly, the system now functions in the following fashion. An employee who believes that he or she has been subjected to discrimination first discusses the problem on an informal basis with an EEO counselor, a position established under the new regulations. This meeting must take place within 30 days of the alleged act of discrimination. The counselor, who is purportedly free from any restraint, interference, or coercion, is required to seek an informal resolution of the problem within 21 working days. If this fails, as it does in about two-thirds of the cases, the counselor informs the employee of his or her right to file a formal complaint within 15 days. If the employee chooses to do so, the counselor files a report with the EEO officer (another newly created position) and sends a copy to the employee. The EEO officer informs the agency director EEO of the complaint. The latter thereupon orders an investigation to be undertaken by an agency official who is in an echelon or installation which is *not* subordinate to the head of the one in which the complaint arose. In some instances, the CSC uses its own personnel to conduct investigations. These include cases involving a potential conflict of interest; complaints that are highly sensitive or have been given a great deal of publicity; cases in very small agencies; and those instances in which outside organizations have expressed considerable interest. The investigator is required to make an impartial inquiry into the matter, including "a thorough survey of the treatment of members of the group alleged to have been discriminated against as compared with the treatment of other persons by alleged discriminating official ororganization."[15] The statements obtained by the investigator must be made under oath or affirmation and are taken without a pledge of being kept confidential. Upon completion of the investigation, the investigative file is made available to the employee. The agency must again provide another opportunity for informal resolution. If this fails, the employee is notified of the agency's proposed disposition of the case. If unsatisfied, the employee can choose between a hearing before an independent examiner or a decision by the agency head or an individual designated by the latter. In either case, the request must be made within 15 calendar days. About 25 percent of all cases judged on their merits involve hearings. The examiner, who is employed by another agency but certified by the CSC, reviews the file and can request a subsequent investigation. He/she schedules a hearing and requests the presence of necessary witnesses. The hearing is transcribed verbatim. When all the materials in the case have been assembled, the examiner submits the entire complaint file along with his or her findings, and recommendations to the agency head/designee for a final agency decision. If the agency head rejects or modifies the examiner's decision, the reasons for this action must be provided in writing. As might be expected, examiners are more prone to find discrimination than are agency heads. In fiscal year 1974, for instance, although examiners recommended a finding of discrimination in about 17 percent of all cases in which they were involved, agency heads reversed these findings in almost 27 percent of these cases.[16] In general, agency heads found discrimination to exist in about 7 percent of the cases reaching disposition at this stage of the complaint proceedings.[17]

If the complainant is not satisfied with the agency's decision, an appeal may be made to the CSC's ARB within 15 days. In fiscal year 1974, about 30 percent of all agencies' final decisions were appealed. Under the 1972 Equal Employment Opportunity Act, a federal servant also has the right to bring a civil action in a U.S. district court against the head of his or her department, agency, or unit under the following circumstances: 1) a case involving discrimination has been in process in an agency for 180 days without any final decision; 2) an appeal has been pending with the ARB for more than 180 days without a final decision; 3) within 30 days after a final agency or ARB decision with which the employee is dissatisfied. However, such an action does not guarantee anything more than a review of the administrative procedures.

Although the current system for processing individual complaints of discrimination is far superior to past efforts, it nevertheless has received a great deal of criticism. One of its chief drawbacks, in the eyes of critics, is administrative: it takes about 200 days to judge cases on their merits, despite CSC regulations which provide for the resolution of cases within 180 days after filing. Moreover, in some major agencies the process takes well over 300 days.[18] Given the fact that prior to the implementation of the present system the complaint process averaged 144 days with a formal time limit of 90 days, it appears that an outgrowth of more elaborate procedures has been further delay.

In the view of defenders of the system, however, the majority of overdue cases are a direct result of unduly short time limits. Expanding the time frame might encourage even further procrastination and, in any event, would not be politically feasible.

The cause of most delays is not clear. The CSC claims that many employees request postponements so that they can better prepare their cases. Investigations sometimes become highly complex and consequently result in lengthy debates. Agency officials may sometimes try to resolve the complaint informally and, if unsuccessful, may contribute to delay in its formal resolution. There may also be difficulties in scheduling hearings and obtaining examiners. The ARB has also contributed to the lengthiness of the process and at times has taken an average of three to four months to decide those cases pending before it.[19] Where delay is not caused by the complainant, he or she may be victimized and made to suffer serious consequences. These might include lost opportunities for advancement and increased pay; having to work under a supervisor who was charged by the employee with committing acts of discrimination; and an inability to make definite plans concerning one's future in a particular agency or the federal service as a whole.

Delay may also be partially responsible for another aspect of the complaint system which has received substantial criticism. It appears that employees are reluctant to use the system itself. At the lower levels some employees may be discouraged from doing so by EEO counselors. Thus, only about 11 percent of the 75,000 employees counseled during the 1972-74 period went on to file formal complaints.[20] This means that the overwhelming number of potential complaints are either resolved informally or aborted at the counseling stage. Because informal resolution occurs in only about 37 percent of these instances, many observers, including some officials in the OFEEO, believe that a substantial proportion of potential cases are dropped at this level because counselors discourage employees from pursuing them. In most cases there may be no basis for a complaint. Even where sufficient grounds do exist, however, there are reasons why a conscientious counselor might be wise to advise an employee not to press his or her case. First, as was previously noted, there is the problem of inconvenience and delay. Second, the possibility of reprisal always lurks in the background; it may often be wise not to press one's claims. More importantly, there is no guarantee that even a favorable decision will result in rectification or remedy. This last point requires further elaboration.

Table 15 presents various types of corrective action resulting from formal complaint cases in fiscal 1970/71, the latest years for which data of this type are available. It shows that over a two-year period, the most common "relief" provided was the improvement of agencies' personnel practices. Yet such improvements might do nothing to benefit the complainant either directly or indirectly. Hence it is possible for an employee to invest a considerable amount of time, energy, and money (for legal representation) in a complaint, win his or her case, and nevertheless fail to receive any tangible benefit. Nor, as the data

TABLE 15

Corrective Action in Formal Complaint Cases, Fiscal 1970/71

Action	Number of Cases	
	1970	1971
Priority consideration for next promotion	5	3
Training opportunity received	18	16
Promotion received	45	49
Requested reassignment/transfer received	32	19
Reappointment/reinstatement	15	15
Removal of adverse material from file	14	8
Initial appointment received	4	1
Agency improved personnel practices	82	48
Job reclassified/position reviewed	11	5
Quality and/or within-grade increases given	3	1
Adverse action reduced and/or rescinded	12	9
Position upgraded	9	–
Leave approved	2	1
Priority consideration for next promotion and job reclassified	1	–
Adverse action rescinded, complainant reinstated	1	–
Supervisor given necessary training	1	6
Illegal promotions rescinded or reposted	3	1
Other	–	16
Total	258	198

Source: Data made available by U.S. CSC, OFEEO. See also, M. Weldon Brewer, *Behind the Promises* (Washington D.C.: Public Interest Research Group, 1972), Table IV, p. III-39; Table V, p. III-40.

suggest, is this possibility remote. The CSC's rationale for this state of affairs is that it is often impossible to provide a benefit for the complainant without injuring another party. For example, if a white is promoted over a black as a result of discrimination by a supervisor, it is considered inappropriate to demote the white who benefited from this action, because he or she did not engage in discrimination. However, when this logic is coupled with cases averaging 200 days, it is easy to see that those who benefit from discrimination against others are likely to keep on doing so by virtue of their acquired experience, higher salaries, seniority, and eligibility for further advancement. In fact, although the Equal Employment Opportunity Act specifically authorizes retroactive relief, recently only 3 percent of all corrective action was retroactive in nature.[21] Nevertheless, it should also be emphasized that Table 15 indicates that successful complainants may receive substantial rewards, including promotion and requested reassignment or transfer. It is rare, however, that those super-visors guilty of discrimination are subjected to disciplinary action.

In passing, it should be noted that if lower level employees are discouraged by counselors from pursuing their complaints, those in the upper third of the GS are even more unlikely to use the complaint process. This is not so much a result of a lack of women and members of minority groups in these positions—although in general this is the case—rather, it is a consequence of the fact that to claim that there is discrimination in the upper reaches of the federal service is to violate a cardinal rule of the bureaucratic culture against exposing the deficiencies of the agency's leadership. Such a complaint would inevitably militate against future promotion or acceptance by into the top ranks of management, if only because it would be interpreted as displaying "poor judgment."

The complaint process has also been criticized on two other grounds: 1) it places an unfair burden of proof on the complainant, and 2) the officials involved are pro-management. Although the existence of discrimination is more frequently found to exist now than in the past, such findings are still limited to about 13 percent of all cases, this despite the fact that corrective action is taken in about 32 percent of the complaints reaching a formal resolution stage within agencies. The CSC has generally defended this record on the grounds that discrimination is often subtle and difficult to prove. In the words of M. Weldon Brewer, a forceful critic,

> More credible reasons than the difficult-to-prove rationale for the low number of discrimination findings are: the lack of the use of the principle of following precedent in adjudication; lack of devices for discovery, subpoena or similar modes of information gathering; the placing of the burden of proof on the complainant to show that discrimination occurred; the nature of the informal evidentiary rules followed; the nature of the pressures, feared and actual, upon complainants, their witnesses, and their representatives [who may also be agency employees]; the positions, backgrounds, and biases of the officials who gather the evidence and decide the complaint; the fact that hearings are closed to the public; and the lack of representation, or the poor quality of representation, for the complainant.[22]

It is hardly encouraging for potential complainants to know that it is they who must prove the existense of discrimination. The agency, moreover, has a far greater advantage in terms of resources. The CCR has charged, for instance, that there are grounds for "a reasonable person to believe that the complaints examiner is instructed to apply a standard which gives the benefit of the doubt to the allegedly discriminatory agency."[23] The agency has more extensive knowledge of past personnel practices and current regulations than do the vast majority of employees, it also has legal counsel specialized in EEO cases, in contrast to the inferior legal representaiton of individual complainants. The agency can also call upon a vast number of employees in preparing its case. In addition to these advantages, it should not be forgotten that the agency itself may make the final decision.

Even under the best of procedural circumstances, however, one is not likely to get a fair hearing if the judges are biased. This, perhaps, has been the most damaging criticism of the complaint process. Cases are decided by the heads of agencies and members of the CSC's ARB. Moreover, counselors, investigators, and examiners play an important role in the development of cases, and it is not at all clear whether these officials are aligned on the side of management. Investigators are usually employees of the agency. Although it is required that they be employed in a unit other than the one in which the complaint arose, it is evident that their future careers are very much linked to the agency itself. Examiners are theoretically independent of agency control and are trained by the CSC. By and large, they tend to take a management perspective and, in fact, are paid for their services by the agency in which the hearing is held. Counselors are most likely to be sympathetic to employees, but even here there is a tendency for them to be identified with agency management, upon whom their careers ultimately depend. Thus, one study of counselors in two installations found that:

> [T]he EEO counselor usually has a relatively high grade [GS-9 or GS-11]. . . . Most complaints, however, come from employees from the lower grade ranges, with the bulk in the below GS-5 grade range. Thus the employee approaches an EEO counselor who, because of his relatively high grade, is identified with management, and it is management who is viewed by the complaining employee as responsible for his situation. The element of mutual trust, essential to any successful counseling situation, is, therefore, vitiated from the beginning by the selection of counselors with grades significantly higher than their clientele.[24]

The ARB has aroused the most criticism for being pro-management. Indeed, it has been so unsympathetic to the plight of individual employees that it has become something of an embarrassment to the CSC. In the words of one civil rights activist, it has become "the epitome of entrenched bureaucracy; totally insensitive to how the people are suffering under a system of discrimination. They just don't know what discrimination is and they are unwilling to admit that there is discrimination."[25] In fiscal 1974 the ARB upheld agency decisions which found no discrimination to exist or rejected complaints in 75 percent of all cases which were appealed; the ARB reversed agency decisions in only 5.5 percent of all cases.[26] The remaining cases were either remanded to agencies for further processing or dropped by the complainant. In the words of the CCR:

The Board reviews the record to determine if it shows that the complainant was subjected to disparate treatment. It does not consider discrimination in the form of disparate impact [which could lead to a reevaluation of personnel policy]. If disparate treatment is shown, the burden is then shifted to the agency to come forward with evidence that the treatment was justified by some lawful purpose, such as [Civil Service] Commission or agency qualification standards. An agency's decision finding no discrimination will be upheld if the evidence in the record supports the conclusion that the disparate treatment was justified. The Board does not follow or refer to judicial decisions interpreting the substantive or procedural requirements of [the Civil Rights Act of 1964 as modified by the Equal Opportunity Act of 1972], nor does it follow the rule of *stare-decisis* with regard to its own prior decisions.

Although it is well settled under . . . law that the complainant need not show direct proof of intentional discrimination and that a statistical disparity shifts the burden to the employer to show evidence of non-discrimination, the Board does not apply this standard.[27]

These criticisms of the complaint process certainly carry a great deal of weight. However, it is important not to lose sight of the fact that the present complaint system represents a vast improvement over past systems. Indeed, in the view of one federal court the CSC "promulgated comprehensive regulations that are particularly well calculated to ensure ready reception and prompt, fair disposition of discrimination claims."[28] Although difficulties still remain to be ironed out, many of these (delays, for example) are of a technical nature and do not require major policy changes. Ultimately, though, a much larger question remains to be resolved. The CSC has designed a complaint process that is capable of rooting out the disparate or unfair treatment of individuals based on race, color, ethnicity, religion, or sex, but it has also sought to make certain that the system will not inquire into or render decisions concerning the legitimacy of ostensibly neutral treatment (such as that resulting from merit examinations) that has an adverse impact on women or members of an ethnic, racial, or religious group. In other words, the processing of individual complaints of discrimination is designed to prevent breaches of the merit system rather than to remedy the adverse impact that the application of that system might have on specific social groups. A separate approach exists for dealing with the latter, one which is tightly controlled by the CSC.

General Complaints

General complaints are usually filed on behalf of a class of people by individuals or third parties, such as civil rights organizations, against personnel practices rather than against individual officials deemed to be guilty of engaging in discriminatory practices. For example, a specific merit examination may tend to exclude a higher proportion of blacks than whites from federal employment and might therefore be challenged in a general complaint alleging that the test is "culturally biased" and illegitimately discriminatory. Similarly, recruitment and rating practices that place a heavy emphasis on prior experience might be challenged on the grounds that they have an adverse and unwarranted impact on women. It should be evident that complaints of this nature pose a considerable threat to meritists and the CSC as an organizational entity. Past practices and present-day administration suggest that the merit system has not been neutral in its racial, ethnic, and sexual impact on specific groups. Under current judicial guidelines,[29] public personnel practices which have a harsh impact on women and members of minority groups may be legally and constitutionally valid only if it can be demonstrated that they are related to some rational purpose of the government. However, such a proof is often difficult to come by, especially (as noted in Chapter 2) when the validity of examinations, promotion procedures, and rating devices are at issue. Even when personnel techniques are rationally related to a legitimate government purpose, it may be very difficult to prove that this is the case. Since anyone looking at the social composition of the federal service can make a *prima facie* case that the merit system is discriminatory, it is vulnerable to attack and might prove virtually impossible to defend successfully.

The CSC is cognizant of this threat and has consequently developed a separate system for hearing general complaints. These procedures place the complainant at a considerable disadvantage and enable agencies and the CSC to maintain control over decisions. In complaints of this nature, the agency is required to establish a file and notify the complainant of its decision. The decision may be appealed to the CSC, where the commissioners may rule on the case. When the complaint involves a personnel practice which is required by the CSC, it may be brought directly to the latter. The extent to which this system permits agencies and the CSC to determine the outcome of general complaints is evidenced by the following: 1) there is no requirement that an investigation, impartial or otherwise, be held; 2) there is no requirement that a hearing be held; 3) there is no right of appeal to the CSC's ARB; 4) the complainant is not permitted access to the file until after the case has been closed; 5) there is no time limit on the decision-making process; and 6) CSC regulations do not acknowledge the complainant's right to bring such cases up as civil actions in federal court. Moreover, the CSC has not publicized the existence of the general complaint process; it is therefore safe to assume that many employees and other interested individuals are unaware of the fact that they may challenge discriminatory practices in this fashion. Available evidence suggests that it is possible, but very difficult, to win a general complaint.*

---

*The CSC began the practice of maintaining data on such cases (filed nationally) in July 1975. During the first quarter of that fiscal year, 25 general complaints were filed.

SELECTION AND PROMOTION

Perhaps no aspect of the federal personnel system has been more severely criticized by representationists and other proponents of greater EEO than that associated with initial selection and subsequent advancement in the bureaucracy. As might be expected in view of the politics of EEO and the CSC's agency culture, the latter's reponse has been to gradually institute a series of incremental personnel reforms which do not seriously threaten the merit system. These reforms have done little to redress the balance of minority and female under-representation in the upper half of the GS. The CSC's efforts in this area have demonstrated both the complexity and difficulty of increasing social bureau-cratic representation in U.S. society under the current merit system.

Examinations

Many observers believe that a major cause of the proportional under-representation of members of minority groups and women in the upper levels of the federal service can be found in the examination process. For example, the CCR has concluded:

> In some instances, heavy emphasis on verbal skills—often not related to the requirements of the job—has tended to screen out minority group members denied an adequate basic education. Similarly, the premium placed on higher education as an aid in evaluating candidates for promotion, has drastically curtailed upward mobility for many black and brown employees. In recent years, the inherent cultural bias in "objective" tests has come to be recognized.[30]

Other observers have charged that federal recruitment processes are rife with unrealistic prerequisites which compound the effects of societal discrimination against women and members of minority groups.

There are several kinds of examinations, some of which are written and/or contain a significant degree of cultural bias, thus making them discriminatory in their effects. In general, the CSC has staunchly defended the examination process. Several of its officials have even argued that some exams must contain a substantial amount of cultural bias if they are to be useful measuring devices. From the perspective of the current EEO problem, the two most important examinations have been the Federal Service Entrance Examination (FSEE, pronounced "FC") and the Professional and Administrative Careers Examination (PACE). The FSEE was used from 1955 until 1974. It covered 200 different types of managerial, technical, and professional occupations and accounted for between 10,000 and 14,000 placements each year. The FSEE purportedly measured both verbal and quantitative ability and was heavily dependent upon a candidate's educational background. Upon passing the exam, entry could be at the GS-5 or GS-7 level, depending upon the candidate's educational and employment background. In either case, the entrant was likely to be placed in a position where advancement could be readily expected. The exam consequently served as a gatekeeper for both the career service as a whole and the upper ranks of the GS. Although the CSC has maintained that the exam was valid, it was clearly discriminatory in its impact on minorities. For example, according to some sources, the passing rate for blacks was about 12 percent, whereas it was 60 percent for whites.[31] As the exam came under increasing attack for its adverse impact on EEO, the CSC initiated a process whereby some individuals were allowed to bypass the exam entirely. From 1967 until 1974 (the year the FSEE was replaced by PACE) it was possible, under the Outstanding Scholar Program, to be appointed to a federal position through the FSEE register without having taken the exam. In order to have done so, an individual must have received a B.A. or B.S. degree within the previous two years and have either maintained a 3.5 out of a possible 4.0 grade point average or graduated in the top 10 percent of his or her class. This program made it possible for some potential entrants—especially those educated at black colleges and other minority group institutions of higher education—to avoid "culture shock" on the FSEE. Only about 5 percent of those appointed from the FSEE register per year, however, entered the federal service in this manner; the program consequently had little impact on the overall social composition of the federal service. It is not known how such entrants fared in terms of promotions.

In 1971 a suit was brought against the FSEE by black interns in HUD whose employment was terminated or whose promotion was denied as a result of their failure to pass the exam.[32] The validity and constitutionality of the examination were upheld at the district court level. In the court's view, the plaintiffs failed to demonstrate that the exam had a discriminatory impact. The CSC proved that the exam had an acceptable degree of "rational validity" and developed its argument in three steps:

1. Identification of the duties and responsibilities of the job.
2. Identification of the qualification standards on knowledge, skills, and ability considered necessary for job performance.
3. Development of appraisal procedures for measuring the qualification standards.

This type of validity analysis cannot predict different levels of job performance; many observers therefore consider it to be unsatisfactory. In fact, "rational validity" is at odds with the EEOC's requirements for private employment. When the latter agency joined those challenging the FSEE on appeal,[33] a cry arose that the federal government was imposing more rigorous EEO standards on private employers than upon itself. Politically, such a charge could have devastating effects upon the EEOC's ability to implement EEO in the private sphere, and it has long been agreed that the government must excel in this area before it can rationally expect others to cooperate in eradicating discrimination from American society. The court of appeals reversed the lower court and ruled that it was incumbent upon the CSC to demonstrate that a more substantial validation procedure was infeasible before the constitutionality and legality of the exam could legitimately be upheld.

These events make it possible to once again gain an insight into the nature of bureaucratic politics in the federal government. Fragmentation, different missions and clienteles, and positions in the governmental structure provide the bases upon which agencies may disagree vehemently over considerable stakes. One government agency joins a group challenging the practices of another unit, in the hopes of furthering its ideology and enhancing its political position. Here the conflict was played out before the judiciary, which itself may reach divergent conclusions. Administrative pluralism reigns supreme and there is absent even a trace of a hierarchical authority to provide unity in government.

The specific impact of this litigation on EEO became moot in 1974 when the CSC abandoned the FSEE and implemented the PACE in its stead. Although the latter applies to the same kinds of positions and also serves as a gatekeeper to both the career service and the upper levels, it is substantially different. It tests for the following:

1. ability to understand and use written language
2. ability to derive general principles from particular data
3. ability to analyze data and derive conclusions
4. ability to understand, interpret, and solve problems presented in quantitative terms
5. ability to derive conclusions from incomplete data, supplemented by general knowledge
6. ability to discover the logical sequence of a series of events

These abilities are deemed central to performance in six occupational categories covering more than 50 job titles in the federal service. Unlike the FSEE, PACE permits evaluation of candidates in the context of a particular type of job. This is accomplished by placing a different weight on each of the separate abilities in accordance with their presumed relative importance for functioning well in specific positions.

As was discussed in the second chapter, establishing the validity of examinations can be extremely difficult, and although PACE offers far more flexibility than FSEE and represents a considerable improvement over it, there is no concrete evidence that it will be either nondiscriminatory or highly valid. The CSC plans to do intensive studies on these questions during the coming years. It will not, however, attempt to ascertain the examination's predictive validity, because it views this as legally unfeasible and professionally unnecessary. Instead, efforts will be made to determine whether there is a substantial relationship between the job performance of those already employed in the federal service and the scores they obtained on the exam. According to the PACE selection process, college grade point average may be taken into account but cannot constitute a substitute for the exam itself.

One of the problems involved in assessing the validity of PACE and other selection devices is that the scores of those actually appointed may be so similar that the differences between them cannot possibly account for differences in actual job performance. For instance, in a review of the CSC's "unassembled" exams, that is, rating processes making use of prior experience, responsibility, and education and having no written component, the GAO found that a minor variation in score could affect a candidate's standing by 50 places or more. In addition, ratings resulting from these devices, which are used primarily for lateral entry into the upper third of the GS, proved unreliable in the sense that reratings of the same individuals led to significant fluctuations in their scores. The GAO therefore concluded that the "rule of three" was likely to exclude qualified individuals and suggested that it be modified to permit selection from among a wider range of candidates.[34]

Proposals of this nature reach to the heart of the politics of EEO and are central to the meritist political problem. In the eyes of the civil service reformers, as we have seen, the primary objective of competitive examinations was to prevent political favoritism. If they also yielded more efficient and effective administration practices and could be defended on these terms, so much the better. But reform of the civil service was considered a step towards total political reform. Now that the spoils system is a thing of the past, meritists find it institutionally imperative to defend the reformers' ideology, and representationists demand empirical proof of its validity. Because civil rights and equality are currently among the central political problems facing the nation, meritists are unavoidably placed in a disadvantageous position. Selection devices, which are, in the broadest sense, political devices, will eventually be adapted to suit the political realities of the times. Goals and timetables, as we have seen, represent one proposed modification of the merit system which would make it more compatible with the political needs of the polity today; their integration with a system of selection from among all those passing examinations, rather than from among only the best qualified, is on the present political horizon. Such a system is currently being used in at least one state (Michigan) and is strongly supported by representationists. It would permit public employers more flexibility in attempting to expand their level of social representation. There appears to be little substance to the fear that it would lead to a return of the spoils system. Moreover, because meritists are basically unable to demonstrate that the best qualified really are better qualified and will perform more satisfactorily on the job, it can be argued neither that efficiency and effectiveness will suffer nor that such a process will necessarily discriminate against those who are most qualified. Interestingly enough, the NCSL, which was founded in 1881 by the civil service reformers and has played an important role in the "personnel complex" ever since, has recently endorsed such an approach,[35] a move which constitutes a major breach in the ranks of the meritists.

Promotion

From the perspective of the current EEO problem, the nature of promotion policy and procedure is of great importance. Although the government can attract women and members of minority groups from outside the federal service to fill positions in the upper grades, most of these slots have traditionally been filled through the career system. Yet the promotion process has been heavily criticized by representationists and others on the grounds that it does little to prevent bias or to develop the skills of culturally and/or economically disadvantaged employees. Politically, the conflict between meritists and representationists in this area is well known: the former argue that no special efforts should be made to promote members of minority groups and women as a class, while the latter demand that they be given preferential treatment in the allocation of training and advancement opportunities.

Prior to 1959, there was no overall merit promotion program. In some agencies promotions were largely made on the basis of personal choice; discrimination against minority group members and women was widespread. In 1959 a government-wide merit promotion policy was instituted to deal with this and other personnel problems. Under the new policy, agencies were required to adopt systematic procedures to ensure that promotions were based on merit principles. By almost all accounts the policy was a failure. Agencies did not adequately explain their new programs to employees and supervisory personnel, evaluation techniques were unsatisfactory, and there was a failure to use competitive selection for promotions to many positions where this method would have been desirable. Consequently, in September 1966 the CSC established a task force to consider a revamping of the merit promotion policy. In April 1967 a draft of proposed changes was circulated to agencies for comment. An interagency advisory group workshop was also held on "merit promotion and performance appraisal." After receiving comments and criticism on the draft proposals from interested individuals and those who attemped the workshop, the CSC made some policy revisions and circulated the new proposals to agencies, interested groups, and Federal Executive Boards in the CSC's regional offices. In August 1968 a new merit promotion policy was inaugurated, one which is currently in operation. It was designed to assure that promotions are based solely on merit criteria. Various elements of the new policy—including 1) evaluation processes and methods, 2) determining important elements of job performance, 3) selecting instruments for evaluating employees, 4) arranging employees in order of merit, and 5) guidelines for use of written tests—have been set down in considerable detail.[36]

The new merit promotion policy does not completely prevent discrimination and cronyism from affecting promotions, but it certainly makes it much more difficult for officials to engage in these practices. According to one CSC official, "Although we can't make some people think right, we can at least make them act right."* By and large, CSC officials believe that the new policy is effective. In the final analysis, however, some degree of individual judgment and discretion will continue to exist in evaluations and other personnel decisions relevent to promotion; discrimination against members of minority groups and women will therefore still be possible. The CCR has concluded:

> Evaluations and promotions ultimately come down to matters of subjective judgment. Personal preferences, preconceptions and biases come into play. Recognizing the imperfect nature of merit ratings and the importance of allowing some flexibility, the revised Federal Merit Promotion Policy suggests that candidates be considered from as broad an area as "practicable" (with agency-wide consideration normally for promotion to GS-14 and above), with final selection made from an "adequate number" (e.g., 3-5) of the best qualified candidates. The principle of freedom to select from among the best qualified is expressly recognized.[37]

The character of promotions is therefore directly related to the quality of supervisory personnel, and the CSC has taken measures to increase the latter's sensitivity to EEO requirements. In the past, supervisors at the lower levels (where most minority group employees are employed) have been criticized for being "more apt than other segments of the American population to carry into their jobs the customary beliefs and biases shared by white Americans in the middle and lower middle ranges of this country's social and economic spectrum"[38]; they are therefore more likely to engage in discriminatory practices. The CSC has tried to overcome any tendency in this direction through training and other techniques. The merit promotion policy requires that all first-line supervisors be provided with "suitable initial training" emphasizing EEO, either before or soon after assuming their new responsibilities. There are also incentive programs to reward supervisors whose EEO records are impressive. Moreover, supervisory ratings include an evaluation of their performance in the EEO area. There is also an EEO component in almost all general management and supervisory courses given by the CSC. These elements, in conjunction with Society's changing attitudes, are believed to be effective in reducing discrimination. At the present time, however, most complaints of discrimination

---

*Statement of Bernard Rosen to author, March, 1971. Rosen was then Deputy Executive Director, later became Executive Director of CSC.

continue to be based on a failure to be promoted; there is consequently evidence to prove that room for improvement still exists.

Promotion is related to employee development, and employee training is another aspect of the personnel system which, in the eyes of some critics, leaves something to be desired from the point of view of EEO. For example, Roger Wilkins, James Frazier, Jr., and others have argued:

> When minorities reach the upper echelons of their particular job categories as clerks, typists, messengers, etc., there are no significant means for those with ability and desire to enter other areas leading to rewarding careers. For those who wish to pursue greater self-development, the Federal Government should be the catalyst. There should be aggressive, on-going training programs for improving morale, promoting self-help and productivity, and good citizenship generally.[39]

Under limitations imposed by federal statute, however, "the possibilities for large-scale in-service training for Federal employees are virtually precluded."[40] The CSC, moreover, has not instituted any long-term programs. It is responsible for the development and coordination of training programs and may, along with other agencies, provide some in-service training to develop an employee's skills and basic knowledge so that his or her ability to perform required functions will consequently be improved. Nongovernment facilities, however, may be utilized to a more limited extent and training cannot be provided solely for the purpose of obtaining an educational degree in order to qualify for appointment to a particular position. The cost of training is largely borne by the departments and agencies themselves.

In April 1967 the CSC established a Bureau of Training to improve training techniques for EEO and other purposes. The Bureau of Training provides increased coordination and promotes interagency cooperative training programs. It also provides the following training courses of its own at various training centers throughout the nation: executive development; general and personnel management; communications; office skills; automatic data processing; financial management and planning, programming, and budgeting. About one-third of the total number of federal employees have been exposed to training programs. The CCR, however, has concluded that "it seems fair to assume, even in the absence of precise data by race, that minority group employees do not share equitably in benefits of Federal training programs."[41]

The CSC has taken additional measures to increase the amount of training available to minority group employees. The most important of these has been a policy of upward mobility for lower level employees.[42] The policy applies to all employees in grades 1-7 in the GS and similar pay plans.* The new policy calls for all of the following:

1.   career systems to increase opportunities for advancement, utilization, training, and education
2.   career development plans for lower grade employees
3.   career counseling and guidance
4.   training opportunities
5.   personnel procedures to assist upward mobility
6.   occupational analysis and job restructuring
7.   qualifications standards facilitating upward mobility
8.   communication of information concerning the upward mobility program to employees.

It is believed that under this new policy many underutilized employees will be promoted and those employees with the potential for advancement will be trained for higher positions. At the present time, upward mobility is a major CSC strategy for change. Although it may be too early to accurately assess its impact, at least, in theory, the program cannot be considered a significant EEO improvement because it fails to address the EEO problem in the upper grades where it is currently most acute.

It should be evident from this discussion that although meritists have, in the promotion issue, adopted an approach that stresses employee development and is aimed at preventing discrimination against women and members of minority groups, the programs and procedures developed will contribute little to achieving greater social representation in the upper levels of the federal service. Indeed, the only representationist approach of any consequence is that of setting goals and timetables for promotions. As we have seen, in its current form this policy is not likely to lead to fundamental change. Hence promotions remain a major stumbling block from the perspective of EEO and representative bureaucracy.

PROGRAM EVALUATION

Program and policy evaluations are a critical aspect of public administration. Policymakers and line administrators must have information concerning the operation of programs. Otherwise they lack the feedback necessary to modify

---

*In 1973 about 53 percent of all full-time employees in these pay plans were situated in these grades, of which approximately 24 percent were minority group members. About 77 percent of all minority group members were to be found in these grades.[43] In addition, about half of all white-collar employees in these grades were women.

and implement their policies and strategies. As was previously demonstrated, the lack of feedback in the use of goals and timetables, while politically useful from the CSC's perspective, has had the effect of drastically impairing the utility of this approach. Similarly, as a partial result of inadequate feedback several aspects of the Federal EEO Program, including the complaint system and promotion processes, are not geared to resolving the current EEO problem. Indeed a lack of information concerning the implementation of programs is not confined to EEO—it is a fundamental characteristic of federal administration. As Elizabeth Drew has written:

> Those who picture Washington as one mass of files and computers containing more information than they would like will be comforted by the experiences of program-planners in attempting to evaluate on-going programs. Whatever the files and computers do contain, there is precious little in them about how many and whom the programs are reaching, and whether they are doing what they are supposed to do.[44]

Such a state of affairs is largely due to the nature of bureaucratic politics. Few agencies find it desirable to divulge information about what or how well they are doing in their jobs, and the best way to assure that such information will not find its way into the hands of hostile congressmen and rival agencies is not to gather it in the first place. This attitude has had a significant impact on the Federal EEO Program.

Surveys

Periodic surveys of minority group employees were initiated in 1961; similar surveys for female employment have been conducted since 1966. It is obvious that in the absence of data concerning the racial, ethnic, and sexual composition of the federal service, it is extremely difficult to formulate sweeping strategies for change. Surveys have, in fact, become the major means of measuring progress in the EEO realm, and such strategies as "upward mobility for lower level employees" have partly been based upon the findings obtained in these periodic surveys. In general, surveys have aimed at providing accurate knowledge concerning the bureaucratic representation of specific groups and making it possible "to pinpoint and eliminate discrimination that may exist in specific areas and thus provide a practical means for affirmative action."[45] As with other aspects of the Federal EEO Program, however, surveys tend to raise some problems. For example, the CSC has theorized that they foster the objectives of representationists:

> One of the most frequent comparisons made . . . is that of the ratio of employment of a minority group in an installation to

the ratio present in the surrounding area. Such information is valuable as an indicator of the need for analysis and for possible action.
Too often, such a finding is interpreted by agencies as representing
a goal in itself against which their program will be evaluated.[46]

This holds true, even under the policy of using goals and timetables, because the
latter are based upon the "skills composition" of the potential work force rather
than its social composition. In addition, it is also evident that the method of
presentation chosen for some parts of the surveys (especially the summaries)
has often been selected more for public relations purposes than for enlightenment. A reluctance to provide data on the breakdown of racial and ethnic groups
according to sex has also proved to be a serious shortcoming; it has made it
impossible to accurately ascertain which groups have benefited most from
EEO activities. Indeed, only limited data along these lines for the year 1972
have been made public by the CSC.

From 1961 through 1965 surveys were conducted under the aegis of the
PCEEO. They were made on the basis of visual identification (that is, employees
were classified according to what their supervisor considered them to be).
This system, however, had inherent limitations. Visual identification failed to
provide the most meaningful data concerning American Indian and Spanish-
surnamed employment, which, given the CSC's special interest in EEO for
these groups, would have been useful to possess. Moreover, the system of visual
identification precluded obtaining data on religious affiliation and national origin. This, in effect, meant that members of disadvantaged, but not readily identifiable, religious or ethnic groups could not be helped by EEO to the same extent
that members of more identifiable groups were aided. A final drawback to this
survey method was that only gross data were collected by grade level and group
status; there was thus no specific identification of individual employees. This
made it impossible to update the data by means of automatic data processing
(ADP) as well as other techniques. It also precluded the generation of data for
a whole range of personnel actions, including promotion rates, discharges,
adverse actions, and so forth. Nor was it possible to take such factors as education and age into account.

In 1965 the CSC decided to replace the supervisory visual identification
system with one relying upon self-identification. Cards requesting employees
to identify themselves as American Indian, Negro, Oriental, Spanish-American,
or other were distributed. The cards also requested the employee's name, date
of birth, and social security number. A note to employees stated:

> The Federal Government and your employer want to be sure
> that every individual whatever his race or national origin gets fair
> and equal treatment. To do this, we need to know how many
> minority group employees there are, what kinds of jobs they hold,
> what grade level their jobs are, and other things that will show

whether or not there is discrimination. Minority group records are being set up for this purpose. . . . Your answers will be kept confidential and will not be used against you in any way.[47]

No employee was required to fill out a card, but "appropriate" follow-up procedures were authorized to obtain information from employees who gave incomplete answers. A similar means was used to ascertain the status of new employees and agencies were allowed to continue the old system if they so desired.

The new system, which was used in the 1966 employee census, was a failure.[48] Not all employees participated, and the racial and ethnic composition of 8.2 percent of the federal civilian work force was not known. The census also revealed that there were 26,022 individuals claiming to be American Indians actively employed at the time, an inflated figure resulting, it appears, from the false answers of some individuals who evidently wanted to obstruct the new system. The disproportionate number of State Department employees claiming to be American Indians gave rise to talk of a "Foggy Bottom tribe." On the basis of the national census of 1960, it turned out that 126 percent of the American Indian population of the District of Columbia was employed by the federal government![49] Aside from generating inaccurate data, the system also generated a good deal of hostility both within and without the federal service.

At approximately the same time that the decision to use the self-designation system was made, Senator Ervin and other legislators were becoming increasingly more sensitive to the problems of invasion of personal privacy—espeically with regard to federal employees, who were for many years subjected to intensive, long-term investigations as part of loyalty-security and suitability procedures. Ervin became a natural outlet for complaints about the system and received a significant number of protests from federal servants. Aside from the issue of invasion of privacy, many employees objected to the new system because they feared that it would lead to either a quota system or "reverse discrimination."[50] As a result of protests by Ervin and other interested individuals, in August 1967 the CSC decided to discontinue the self-designation procedure and return to the visual identification system.[51] In September the Senate passed Senator Ervin's "Bill of Rights for Federal Employees" (S.1035) by a vote of 79 to 4.[52] The bill forbade the use of racial, religious, or ethnic questionnaires and, although it never became law, it made the self-identification approach untenable.

The basic need to obtain more useful data concerning minority group employment, however, continues to be felt. At the present time, an automatic data-processing system designed for this purpose is in use. This has been made possible through improvements in system capabilities and as a result of social changing attitudes, the latter reflecting a greater tolerance of racial and ethnic classification—not on the basis of self-designation—in personnel records. For example, several officials in the American Civil Liberties Union (ACLU) now support the maintenance of racial and other data if the objective is to implement programs for greater EEO.[53] Sexual classification, of course, has long been an accepted practice. The AFP system is able to develop a full array of information concerning minority group members, including promotions, grade allocations, separations, transfers, and appointments. CSC officials maintain that the data will not be used in individual actions and will be protected against misuse by complex system safegrards.

Although the CSC now has an improved informational capability, there is little evidence to suggest that it has put the latter to use in evaluating the operation of the Federal EEO Program. Surveys continue to be the best tool for measuring the impact of the program. Although they are now issued more frequently, their format remains unchanged. In summarizing their contents and the findings of other studies, the CSC makes every effort to present the Federal EEO Program in the best light—it is politic to do so. At the same time, however, analysis of the data reveals that little progress is being made in the upper levels of the federal service. As a result, the gulf between meritists and representationists continues to grow.

Agency Self-Evaluation

During the course of its development, individual departments and agencies have expressed a great desire to retain control of several aspects of the Federal EEO Program. Such decentralization provides them with greater freedom in the area of personnel affairs and helps them avoid bad publicity. This is especially true with respect to the complaint process, but it also applies to the establishment of goals and timetables and other affirmative action procedures. Although it is often charged that these administrative arrangements create a conflict of interest, in practice both the CSC and most of the agencies it oversees find it politically advisable to stress decentralization and agency autonomy. From an administrative angle, it stands to reason that once agencies are required to develop their own affirmative action plans, they should also be held responsible for studying and evaluating their impact.

Executive Order 11478 (Nixon) requires that agencies engage in some degree of self-evaluation. The CSC has issued guidelines to aid agencies in this process. These guidelines suggest that, at the very least, the self-evaluation process should be detailed enough to assure agency management that the implementation of EEO plans is in accordance with merit system principles and reaches all relevant social groups. Suggested self-evaluation methods include: on-site visits by management; written reports by subordinate levels; statistical analysis of the agency's work force; periodic reviews of complaints and appeals; interviews with employees and supervisors; reviews of information submitted by other organizations, such as civil rights groups; and so forth. The major areas covered by this self-evaluation process include:

1. the clarity of policy directives
2. the content of action plans
3. the organization of the EEO function
4. program communications and publicity
5. the use of statistical data
6. manpower planning and position management
7. the nature of agency qualifications and requirements
8. recruitment and placement procedures
9. employee training and development
10. promotion and advancement procedures
11. analysis of separations
12. assimilation and equal treatment for all work-force members.

Agencies are also required to evaluate the rate of progress in achieving their EEO goals.

On the whole, it appears that self-evaluation, as presently constituted, is not a viable method for developing a general assessment of the impact of the Federal EEO Program. It appears that some agencies do not engage in any serious effort at self-evaluation and others do not report the results of their studies. More importantly, from the point of view of the politics of EEO,

> The Commission's guidelines on EEO program evaluation presume that the basic ingredients required by the Commission to be included in an affirmative action plan are effective if implemented and, therefore, limit evaluation to determining to what extent the steps have been followed. It is as if a doctor were prescribing aspirin to a cancer patient simply by determining to what extent aspirin doses were being administered.[54]

Moreover, from a representationist perspective, the self-evaluation process is defective because it is designed both to make certain that the merit system is not being violated as well as to learn more about the implementation of EEO.

CSC Inspections

The CSC also engages in program evaluation by means of two types of inspections of agency EEO activities. Politically, unless agency shortcomings become widely publicized, CSC inspections pose little threat to meritists. In general, the thrust of these activities is aimed at securing faithful adherence to merit principles in the execution of EEO.

Community Reviews and Evaluations

An important technique in attempting to overcome barriers to greater EEO (even though it has been discontinued) is the use of community reviews. The concept of such reviews grew out of political events which occurred in 1963. During civil rights demonstrations in Birmingham, Alabama, it was alleged that federal as well as private employment patterns in that area were discriminatory. Attorney General Robert Kennedy went to Birmingham to urge businessmen to hire more blacks. The businessman argued that the government should put its own house in order before telling others what to do. It became obvious to Kennedy that it would be highly desirable for the government to set a better example in the EEO realm. He consequently asked CSC Chairman Macy to analyze the federal employment situation in the Birmingham area and to take whatever action he deemed necessary to further the Federal EEO Program. A representative of the CSC's BRE was soon sent to Birmingham to work with regional officials on this issue. Their analysis of the situation represented the CSC's first community review of agency programs and soon became a model for future studies.

A review of federal employment in Birmingham quickly ascertained that there was a need for far-reaching improvement in the area of EEO. Although the city was about one-third black, it was found that, excluding the Post Office and the VA, the proportion of black federal civil servants was less than 1 percent. On the face of it, the record of federal employment of blacks in Birmingham was poorer than the rest of Alabama, where about 11 percent of all federal servants were black. This direct review of the employment situation demonstrated the desirability and utility of concentrated examination and analysis of personnel procedures in the field. It was found that even where immense EEO problems existed, some rapid improvements could still be made. The decision was reached to immediately take three steps: first, to announce new examinations where there was a need for personnel and the existing registers were old; second, to announce new examinations even though the registers were comparatively new if it could not be proven conclusively that the exams had been widely publicized to all segments of the community; third, it was decided to identify members of minority groups working at levels below their qualifications in the hope of promoting them.

The Birmingham review proved to be so productive and useful in such a short period of time that the decision was reached to employ the basic concept elsewhere. By the first week in July 1963, similar reviews were underway in three other cities in the Atlanta civil service region; by the end of June 1964, community reviews had been organized in 71 communities of varying size and social composition throughout the nation.

As more reviews were made, they became more highly refined. The community review program gradually developed three major purposes. First, the program aimed at developing better communication between the CSC and the heads of installations and officers in the field and providing a greater opportunity for "ascertaining the extent to which local operating units were reflecting the directives from higher headquarters and the manner in which the personnel system was being operated."[55] Second, the program enabled CSC officials to ensure that boards of civil service examiners were "operating in such a manner as to provide full opportunity for everyone in the community to compete for Federal jobs."[56] Finally, the community review program provided an opportunity to inspect the "personnel activities carried on by the installations themselves in connection with the President's Equal Employment Opportunity Program."[57] During the review sessions, discussions were also held with representatives of minority groups and other community groups in an effort to gain a better understanding of their attitudes and of community problems in general.

The community reviews proved to be of great utility. As was mentioned in Chapter 2, they led to several important findings concerning the formulation and implementation of EEO policy. Their effect on Federal units in the field was also beneficial. They enabled the latter to develop a greater sensitivity to the needs of minority groups and the goals of a successful Federal EEO Program and to develop a greater understanding of their own shortcomings. Many changes favoring equality of opportunity were instituted. The reviews were considered by many to be a dynamic addition to the EEO program. In short, they increased the level of understanding in the EEO realm by analyzing the relationship between societal conditions and federal personnel practices, thus suggesting significant reforms.

By 1967, however, they had more or less run their course and their utility began to decrease significantly. In true "bureaucratic" fashion, they became so highly refined that they took up too much time to be useful and taxed the CSC's resources too heavily. The lengthy community review held in Los Angeles dealt a *coup de grace* to the program and it was decided to adopt a modified approach. A new format was developed and implemented, but before long funds dwindled and it was decided to forego the reviews, which had largely served their purpose.

Inspections

Although community reviews are no longer utilized, agency EEO activities are still examined by the CSC's BPME and by CSC units in the regional offices. The examination is conducted both as part of a general inspection of agency personnel practices and in a more specialized fashion. These inspections reach about 15 percent of all government installations per year. Inspection guidelines state that "compliance and corrective action need not be based solely on unlawful employment practices that result from intent to discriminate but may be aimed at the discriminatory effects of institutional practices upon minorities and women as a group."[58] However, in actual practice the CSC's inspections are largely aimed at uncovering breaches of the merit system and other personnel requirements. Moreover, the CSC has failed "to investigate the possibility of an adverse impact on minorities and women resulting from personnel practices which the Commission identifies as merit system violations."[59] As a result, it is safe to conclude that none of the evaluation techniques currently in use are likely to lead to the adoption of fundamental changes in the Federal EEO Program. Indeed, they appear to be designed to protect the merit system rather than to implement the government's EEO activities.

CONCLUSIONS

The nature of bureaucratic politics in the federal government has encouraged the CSC to adopt an incremental course of action in implementing the Federal EEO Program. Throughout almost every phase of the program, it has made an effort to "blend" EEO into the framework of the merit system.

This administrative strategy yields at least two political advantages. First, it limits the visibility of the program and thereby makes it less likely that it will be transferred to another agency. EEO has become intertwined with a host of other personnel activities, including promotions, training, and information gathering. It has also been decentralized to the extent that countless officials in a myriad of agencies now have substantial EEO responsibilities. Hence, the program is somewhat amorphous and, in some respects, actually consists of several diverse programs, thus making reorganization difficult.

Second, the CSC's mode of implementation places the merit system above EEO. The latter consequently has to accommodate the former; the CSC's instructions and inspection efforts are intended to assure that this remains the case. Although the CSC's administrative approach has drawn considerable criticism over the years, the agency has thus far been able to return control of Federal EEO Program. This is partly due to the fact that the CSC's organizational strategy has made it difficult to conceive of successfully transferring the program to another agency. However, the CSC has also been willing to adopt incremental reforms of the personnel system; these have gradually led to improvements in the EEO area. Progress has been more substantial where there is no inherent conflict or tension between EEO and merit. On the other hand, with respect to such areas as general complaints, placing the operation of the Federal EEO Program in the hands of the CSC has militated against the adoption of forceful regulations that could pose a challenge to the personnel system as it currently exists. To the extent, therefore, that the personnel system is itself not neutral in its impact on EEO only limited change in the direction of a more socially representative bureaucracy is to be expected. Hence, at the broadest level the CSC's implementation of the Federal EEO Program again demonstrates that organizational choices are also political choices and that administrative approaches may well be politically motivated.

NOTES

1. Communication by CSC Chairman Robert E. Hampton to John A. Buggs, Staff Director, U.S. CCR, May 2, 1975, chap. 6, p. 2.

2. Ibid., Chapter 1, p. 2.

3. See Chapter 4, *supra*.

4. U.S. Commission on Civil Rights, *The Federal Civil Rights Enforcement Effort—1974* (Washington, D.C.: Commission on Civil Rights, 1975), vol. 5, p. 6.

5. Ibid., p. 61.

6. U.S. Civil Service Commission Bulletin, 713-12 (December 30, 1969), p. 1.

7. Ibid., p. 2. Until 1969, separate plans for women were required as well.

8. Ibid., p. 3.

9. John Cramer, "Taking the Plaint from Complaint," Washington *News,* May 15, 1968.

10. Memo from Chief of Personnel Management Section, CSC, to file, October 19, 1969.

11. Ibid.

12. Cramer, "Taking the Plaint from Complaint."

13. Civil Service Commission memo from A. Rachal, Jr., to I. Kator, June 18, 1968.

14. Civil Service Commission *Civil Service News,* March 18, 1969, p. 1.

15. Civil Service Commission, Bureau of Training, "Steps in Conducting the Investigation" (1970?), p. 3.

16. Commission on Civil Rights, *The Federal Civil Rights Effort Enforcement—1974,* p. 79, no. 272.

17. Ibid., p. 79. According to the most recent CSC figures, agency heads found evidence of discrimination in about 6 percent of all cases terminated at this stage during fiscal 1974/75. In 1975, discrimination was found in 12.8 percent of all cases judged upon their merits. Hampton/Buggs memo, chap. 4, p. 9.

18. Commission on Civil Rights, *The Federal Civil Rights Enforcement Effort—1974,* p. 80.

19. See M. Weldon Brewer, *Behind the Promises* (Washington, D.C.: Public Interest Research Group, 1972), Chapter 2, pp. 29-30.

20. Commission on Civil Rights, *The Federal Civil Rights Enforcement Effort—1974,* p. 67, n. 221. In fiscal 1975 the figure was 15 percent.

21. Ibid., p. 85.

22. Brewer, *Behind the Promises,* Chapter 3, p. 9.

23. Commission on Civil Rights, *The Federal Civil Rights Enforcement Effort—1974,* p. 79.

24. Quoted by Brewer, *Behind the Promises,* Chapter 4, p. 8.

25. U.S., Congress, Senate, Committee on Labor and Public Welfare, Subcommittee on Labor, Hearings on S. 2453, 91st Cong., 1st sess., (August 11, 12, 1969; September 10, 16, 1969), p. 84.

26. Commission on Civil Rights, *The Federal Civil Rights Enforcement Effort—1974,* pp. 81-82.

27. Ibid., pp. 82-83.

28. *Penn v. Schlesinger,* 497 F2d 970 (1974): 490 F2d 700, 711 (1973).

29. See D. H. Rosenbloom and C.C. Obuchowski, "Public Personnel Examinations and the Constitution: Emergent Trends," *Public Administration Review* 37 (January/ February 1977): 9-18.

30. Civil Service Commission, *Federal Civil Rights Enforcement Effort. 1970* (Washington, D.C.: Commission on Civil Rights, 1970), p. 82.

31. See *Douglas v. Hampton,* 512 F2d 976 982 (1975).

32. *Douglas v. Hampton,* 338 F. Supp. 18 (1972).

33. *Douglas v. Hampton,* 512 F2d 976 (1975).

34. See Commision on Civil Rights, *The Federal Civil Rights Enforcement Effort—1974,* pp. 54-55 for a more detailed discussion.

35. Ibid., p. 57; see, also, J.J. Couturier, "The Model Public Personnel Administration Law," *Public Personnel Review* 32 (October 1971): 202-09.

36. See Commission on Civil Rights, *Federal Civil Rights Enforcement Effort—(1970)* pp. 95-96.

37. Ibid., pp. 96-97. Freedom of choice, however, can both help and harm minority group members and women.

38. Roger Wilkins, James Frazier, Jr., et al., "The Equal Employment Opportunity Posture of the U.S. Federal Government" (unpublished report, [1969]), p. 8.

39. Ibid., p. 6.

40. Commission on Civil Rights, *Federal Civil Rights Enforcement Effort—(1970)* p. 103. My discussion is based on pp. 101-06 of this study.

41. Ibid., p. 106.

42. U.S. Civil Service Commission, "Upward Mobility for Lower Level Employees: Suggested Goals and Actions," May 7, 1970.

43. U.S. Civil Service Commission, *Study of Minority Group Employment* (Washington, D.C.: Government Printing Office, 1974).

44. Elizabeth Drew, "HEW Grapples with PPBS," *Public Interest* 8 (Summer 1967): 11.

45. Civil Service Commission, "Establishing and Maintaining a Record of Minority Group Status," Federal Personnel Manual System Letter, Chapter 293-5, Exhibit B, Attachment 2 (March 4, 1966).

46. "Reporting on Equal Employment Opportunity," CSC Operation Letter, 273-372 (November 18, 1966).

47. Ibid., Exhibit A.

48. See U.S. Civil Service Commission, *Study of Minority Group Employment in the Federal Government* (Washington, D.C.: U.S. Government Printing Office, 1966).

49. Interagency Group, Chart Presentation, January 19, 1967. In the words of the chairman of the CSC, "We tried a self-identification census, and that did not work because people who were not [American] Indians identified themselves as [American] Indians. There was a resistance to self-identification." U.S., Congress, Senate, Committee on Labor and Public Welfare, Subcommittee on Labor, Hearings, "Equal Employment Opportunity Enforcement Act," 91st Cong., 1st sess., on S. 2453 p. 134.

50. Memorandum from the director of the CSC Bureau of Policies and Standards (BPS) to CSC Chairman John Macy, "Fifth Progress Report on Complaints About Minority Status Self-Determination," November 8, 1966.

51. Federal Personnel Manual System Letter, Chapter 713-5 (August 24, 1967).

52. U.S., Congress, Senate, *Congressional Record,* 90th Cong., 1st sess., 1967, 113, p. 19: 25456.

53. Statement of the director of the CSC Bureau of Manpower Information Systems [BMIS], September 15, 1970.

54. Commission on Civil Rights, *The Federal Civil Rights Enforcement Effort—1974,* pp. 95-96.

55. U.S. Civil Service Commission BRE, *Equal Opportunity in Federal Employment, May 15, 1963—June 30, 1964* (September 1964), p. 2.

56. Ibid.

57. Ibid., p. 32.

58. Federal Personnel System Supplement (Int.), 273-73 (March 1974), p. 66; cited in CCR, *The Federal Civil Rights Enforcement Effort—1974,* p. 123.

59. Commission on Civil Rights, *The Federal Civil Rights Enforcement Effort—1974,* p. 133.

7

BUREAUCRATIC POLITICS, PUBLIC PERSONNEL ADMINISTRATION, AND DEMOCRACY

The foregoing analysis of the Federal EEO Program illustrates several general features of bureaucratic politics. For one thing, it indicates that federal agencies exist and interact in a highly politicized environment. A variety of demands and pressures are placed upon them; these come from individuals (presidents, legislators, and journalists) as well as from organizations (interest groups, other agencies, legislative committees, and courts). At the same time, agencies are constrained by the norms of the political community as a whole and by those traditional administrative practice. Moreover, whether agencies are basically consolidative (reactive) or innovative (proactive), they must be well organized internally if they are to cope successfully with stress derived from external sources. Hence, agencies develop ideologies and cultures, and join with other organizational units into complexes. These processes serve to pattern agency responses to new and continuing problems, generate internal and external support, and provide a protective shield against encroachment by hostile outsiders. As a result, organization and reorganization become devices that may be employed to achieve political rather than administrative ends.

Merit and representation are the basic ideologies of the major protagonists in the realm of federal EEO. The CSC and other members of the personnel complex generally find themselves in opposition to agencies such as the CCR and the EEOC. The latter are frequently joined by various civil rights and women's organizations, and sometimes by congressional committees as well.

The struggle for domination of federal personnel administration occurs on several levels. With regard to policy, representationists have made considerable gains. The CSC, after being threatened with loss of the Federal EEO Program and consequently of control over federal personnel policy in general, reluctantly acceded to a policy of goals and timetables for the hiring and promotion of women and members of minority groups. The merit system is officially no longer either completely "color-blind" or ostensibly socially neutral. Current federal personnel policy embraces representation as a desirable goal.

On the implementation level, however, a different state of affairs prevails. Here the CSC, which has been unable to dominate on the policy level, has developed a solid defense of its traditional values, culture, and mission. Forced to accept some representationist demands, the CSC has sought to lessen their impact in the daily administrative routine. This has largely been accomplished by means of organizational "tools," including the decentralization of information feedback and program implementation. It has also issued policy "clarifications" that have sometimes militated against the achievement of formal policy objectives. Other agencies remain largely in control of their own EEO activities. The CSC's general oversight tends to insure that the merit system is not violated or even successfully challenged.

Finally, there is the publicity level. Both meritists and representationists have turned out reams of information intended to show how desirable their approaches really are. Each side regularly—and rightly—accuses the other of distortion. The CSC makes every effort to issue only those statistics which "prove" that the Federal EEO Program is working well, while the CCR engages in historical fantasy in an attempt to demonstrate that the civil service reformers sought the establishment of a representative bureaucracy. Each hopes to convince appropriate political officials of the desirability of its cause. Thus far neither side has achieved a complete victory; it may be possible to continue the incremental approach of blending representation and merit indefinitely. Such an outcome would be a logical result of the pluralistic politics surrounding this policy area. On the other hand, change in the social composition of the upper levels of the federal service has been very slow and current EEO policy appears unlikely to make these levels more representative of the nation's population in the near future. A choice between merit and representation may eventually be required. Moreover, there is reason to believe that federal personnel policy is drifting towards a new conceptualization which places heavy emphasis on the value of representation. Before discussing this development, it is necessary to briefly examine the nature of bureaucratic politics in the EEO arena.

BUREAUCRATIC POLITICS

The organizational development and policy evolution of the Federal EEO Program supports several propositions concerning bureaucratic politics:

1. "Every organization's social functions strongly influence its internal structure, and vice versa."[1] Thus, although he CSC originally sought to integrate the EEO function with its other operating functions, it was finally compelled to create the OFEEO; later, the FWP and the SSP were made into relatively distinct organizational units as well.

2. "The quantity and detail of reporting required by monitoring bureaus tends to rise steadily over time, regardless of the amount or nature of the activity being monitored."[2] This proposition is supported by the CSC's experience with community reviews and agency action plans. The former ultimately became so detailed that they had to be abandoned because they could not be completed within a time period which would maximize their utility. Action plans continue to grow on a yearly basis; many of them have become voluminous. In the view of some agency EEO officials in agencies this has tended to make EEO a "paper" program.

3. "Every large organization is in partial conflict with every other social agent it deals with."[3] This is basically true of the CSC's relationship with organizations interested in EEO. In this pluralistic policy arena, the CSC has come into conflict with women's and civil rights gorups, legislative committees, as well as the CCR and the EEOC. Yet on occasion it has also gained the support of these organizations. Although the CSC can generally count on support from members of the personnel complex, it has entered into some degree of conflict with the NCSL over the crucial issue of how to select public employees.

4. "As bureaus grow older . . . [O]fficials shift their emphasis from carrying out the bureau's social functions to insuring its survival and growth as an autonomous institution."[4] This is, in part, an accurate description of the CSC's organizational development over a period of time. Originally its primary social function was to remove the spoils system from the federal bureaucracy. Once this had been accomplished, it began to stress the objectives of efficient and economic federal administration. Today the CSC sees in the merit system the key to its own survival; it has therefore been reluctant to attively pursue the social objectives associated with the Federal EEO Program. Indeed, it considers rigorous implementation of the program a threat both to its already limited support from other agencies and to the uniqueness of its mission.

5. "Leaders of all large organizations are opposed to detailed investigations of the behavior of their organizations by outsiders."[5] Thus, the CSC has traditionally been wary of investigations of the Federal EEO Program by the CCR, congressional committees, and individual scholars; on occasion it has even obstructed such activities.

6. "Organizations constantly involved in potentially threatening situations do not respond in force to every signal of potential or even actual danger received from their own agents, but refrain from beginning significant responses until these alarm signals become very loud and are being received from multiple sources."[6] This is quite characteristic of the CSC's response pattern. EEO is an inherently threatening activity because of the tension between the merit system and greater bureaucratic representation. The CSC characteristically introduces change or strong protective measures only after criticism of its administration has mounted and gained a sympathetic hearing in Congress. Modifications of the complaint system and the adoption of the policy of using goals and timetables are typical of this response pattern.

7. "In bureaus with 'remote' social functions, innovation is more likely to be stimulated by rivalry with functionally overlapping competitiors in their own nation than by substantive developments regarding their social function *per se.* "[7] This is very true of the CSC, which adopted its major EEO innovations as a result of rivalry with the EEOC and the CCR.

8. "The rate at which innovations will be suggested by bureau members will be greater . . . [t]he greater the external pressure for change, especially if bureau members at all levels of the hierarchy interact with the 'outsiders' generating such pressure."[8] To some extent, this proposition is an accurate description of the CSC's behavior in the EEO realm. Most agency contacts with outsiders involve members of the personnel complex and other federal agencies basically in support of the CSC's administration, which protects traditional personnel values and permits other operating units to exhibit a great deal of autonomy. However, a number of CSC officials, including the director of FWP, the director of Federal EEO, and the director of SSP, engage in a considerable degree of interaction with members of women's and civil rights groups; these officials are most likely to propose meaningful reforms and have been most sympathetic to these clientele groups.

9. "Every bureau ideology:

a) emphasizes the positive benefits of the bureau's activities and de-emphasizes their costs.

b) Indicates that further expansion of the bureau's services would be desirable and any curtailment thereof would be undesirable.

c) emphasizes the benefits that the bureau provides for society as a whole, rather than its services to particular 'special interests.'

d) stresses the high present level of the bureau's efficiency.

e) emphasizes its achievements and future capabilities and ignores or minimizes its failures and inabilities."[9]

These characteristecs are highly descriptive of the CSC's ideology. The agency presents the merit system as something vital to the nation as a whole. It stresses its low cost in comparison to its benefits, seeks to integrate other functions (such as EEO) with it, and portrays its activities in the most favorable light possible. On the whole, the CSC's EEO activities match the dominant public administrative and political science models of bureaucratic policy making in the federal government. The agency is best thought of as a system which responds to internal and external pressures. Its responses consist of policies, regualtions, support-building, public relations, and occasionally even "stonewalling." In most instances, the CSC seeks to determine the impact of these responses on its environment, although it avoids making this feedback public unless it is favorable. In some instances, however, such as the case involving implementation of goals and timetables, the CSC makes an effort to prevent the generation of organized feedback. This in itself is a policy intended to protect the agency against attack from representationists and to weaken the goals-and-timetables approach. Although the CSC's internal organization and goal consensus are strong, on occasion it has had to adjust to the demands of high-ranking insiders, such as the directors of FWP and SSP. In the realm of EEO it has also suffered considerable turnover, partly as a result of dissatisfaction with its Federal EEO Program. The politics of EEO, therefore, are best summed up in the pluralist interpretation of American politics: several competing organizational units interact, primarily before a legislative "umpire," and policy is made and modified as an outgrowth of this process. In the long run, the public interest will hopefully be served and power will not reside in the hands of a single individual or organization prone to making arbitrary decisions.

Yet both this model and the propositions concerning bureaucratic behavior presented earlier ignore an important facet of bureaucratic politics. People can make a difference, both individually and collectively, to the extent that they condition the nature of organizations. The policy outcomes of bureaucratic politics are influenced by structural and organizational elements, but they are also affected by the talents, values, objectives, and ideologies of individual bureaucrats. Organizations have a "human side" and changes in personnel can lead to changes in policy as well. This raises one of the most fundamental questions facing modern democratic nations. If public policy is to be made by non-elected, bureaucratic officials, how can one safeguard the principle of popular rule? As was suggested in Chapter 2, one possible answer is through the creation of a representative bureaucracy. However, the answer for which our society is currently opting is a much broader one; from the perspective of EEO, it is one on which virtually assures the eventual victory of representationists.

TOWARDS A NEW PUBLIC PERSONNEL ADMINISTRATION

The crux of the political problem created as a result of the bureaucratization of public life in democratic societies is the inherent conflict between the two. They each require different values and structural arrangements. For instance, bureaucracy requires hierarchy, unity, long-term positions, command, secrecy and the assumption that some citizens are more qualified than others to take part in public policy making. Democracy, on the other hand, requires equality, plurality, rotation in office, liberty, openness, and the assumption that all citizens are qualified to participate in politics. Yet no modern democracy is likely to govern effectively, let alone survive, unless it has a well-developed bureaucratic component capable of pernetrating the economic, social, and political life of society. Originally the problem was thought to be one of control, but control has been possible only to a limited extent. Moreover, control solutions have generally not enhanced bureaucratic efficiency.

The Scientific Management (SM) approach provides an enlightening example. The Scientific Management Movement (SMM), which followed close on the heels of civil service reform and had much in common with it, went further in attempting to secure efficiency. It sought smooth-running, efficient production and organization. With regard to government SM urged an incorporation of the dichotomy between politics and administration into the organization of public bureaucracy. Its advocates believed that politics and administration could not be combined without a resulting inefficiency and, consequently, that efficiency was the foremost value of administration. In their view, politics interfered with the efficient organization of public bureaucracy, and they became, in the words of Harold Seidman,

> preoccupied with the anatomy of Government organization and concerned primarily with arrangements to assure that (1) each function is assigned to its appropriate niche within the Government structure; (2) component parts of the executive branch are properly related and articulated; and (3) authorities and responsibilities are clearly assigned.[10]

Such a mode of organization would not only be more efficient, it would also contribute to the general direction of administration by political executives. In the United States, this argument was best expressed by the Brownlow Commission,[11] which advocated a consolidation of the executive branch and the establishment of organizational units which would enable the president to control, direct, and coordinate the bureaucracy. The president would serve as the manager-in-chief; other political elements would, for the most part, be excluded from the organization and operation of the federal bureaucracy.

Although the SM approach contributed to the rational organization of public administration in the United States, it nevertheless failed to come to grips with bureaucratic politics and did not grasp the extent to which administrative agencies wield influence over their politically appointed heads. Thus, there is ample testimony from cabinet members[12] and presidents[13] concerning their inability to control bureaucratic agencies and, on occasion, even to influence them substantially. The nature of bureaucratic politics at the national level is such that it leaves little room for command. Consequently, formal channels of authority, while far from meaningless, are insufficient to control policy outcomes. In addition, the Executive Office of the President, the creation of which was strongly endorsed by the Brownlow report, has created a significant control problem of its own, as was evidenced by the Watergate affair. Ultimately, control solutions are unlikely to prove satisfactory because they fail to recognize the extent to which administration is entangled with political issues and ignore the fact that these are not necessarily dealt with by political executives. Control solutions are also likely to ignore the divergence between formal arrangements and the dynamics of informal organizations.

Once the shortcomings of SM became apparent, attention was focussed on noncontrol solutions to the problems posed by the bureaucratization of democracy. In the United States, the foremost among these solutions has been the politics of pluralism. Here efficiency is consciously sacrificed in favor of duplication, competition, and a system of checks and balances. Public administration is viewed as politics, and policymaking in the public interest becomes the ultimate objective. The overriding assumption is that public bureaucracies can be structured so as to advance the politics of interest carried out through competition. Ideally, interest groups would state their needs and preferences before government agencies, which, acting as impartial and expert judges, would adopt the policies best suited to serve the public interest. These choices would subsequently be subject to modification by the legislature. Such a system ostensibly maximizes the amount of information available to administrators before making their decisions.

In what Theodore Lowi has called the "interest group liberal"[14] version of pluralism, on the other hand, government agencies are not impartial judges supervised by legislators, but rather advocates of the causes of special interests. In this view, agencies are essentially controlled by interest groups and become part of policy-interest complexes, including private groups, public agencies, and legislative committees.

Although both of these models contain elements of bureaucratic politics in the United States and both can increase bureaucratic responsiveness through the participation of relevant groups in policymaking processes, neither is totally satisfactory. Not all segments of the citizenry have an equal opportunity or ability to organize or to be effectively represented by groups or complexes. A lack of competition sometimes characterizes the relationships existing among interest groups—which is precisely why they tend to blend into complexes. In the view of some consequently, the politics of pluralism discriminates against the more disadvantaged segments of society and cannot consistently yield policies for achieving social equity.[15] Moreover, groups and complexes tend to represent constituencies only on specific levels of interest, and generally ignore broader elements in their political thinking.[16] Finally, the duplication inherent in pluralist administration creates problems of coordination and negatively affects the general public's image of the federal bureaucracy.

At the present time, another noncontrol approach to the resolution of the tension existing between democracy and bureaucracy is emerging. Unlike pluralism and other approaches, it deemphasizes structural arrangements and places a heavy emphasis on public personnel administration. The major elements of this approach have been formulated in separate policy spheres as a result of different kinds of pressures, but they are interrelated in a logical fashion. Moreover, representation is of crucial importance to their integration.

Liberation

The constitutional position of public employees in the United States has historically been governed by what has become known as the "doctrine of privilege."[17] According to this line of reasoning, it was generally accepted that since there was no constitutional right to public employment and since such employment was voluntary rather than compulsory, public employees had few constitutional rights which could not be legitimately abridged by the state in its role as employer. This approach was best expressed in Justice Holmes' classic statement, "The petitioner may have a constitutional right to talk politics, but he has no constitutional right to be a policeman."[18] It has now been rejected in favor of an approach which begins "with the premise that a state [of the federal government] cannot condition an individual's privilege of public employment on his non-participation in conduct which under the Constitution is protected from direct interference by the state."[19] Moreover, according to the current conception, "whenever there is a substantial interest, other than employment by the state, involved in the discharge of a public employee, he can be removed neither on arbitrary grounds nor without a procedure calculated to determine whether legitimate grounds do exist."[20] As a result of this change, a public employee's right to free speech, religion, association, and petition has been upheld, as has his or her protection against self-incrimination and unconstitutional searches and seizures. It is also required that a public employee be provided with equal protection of the law and procedural safeguards in adverse actions.

This change in the constitutional law governing the status of public employees has made it possible for the latter to play a much larger role in public debate. For example, during the 1960s there were several public protests by federal employees against the war in Southeast Asia, the Nixon administration's position on civil rights, and racial inequality within the federal bureaucracy. Indeed, on at least one occasion a federal employee testified before a congressional committee, supplying it with information that proved to be highly detrimental to his own agency.[21] Although there have been some efforts to discipline employees engaging in such activities, these have generally not been successful; given the current judicial rulings, it is difficult to see how they could be.

The "liberation of federal employees can have several beneficial effects on democracy. On the broadest level, civil servants can play a substantial role in the political and administrative "enlightenment" of a political community. A knowledgeable citizenry, of course, is generally considered a prerequisite to achieving effective democracy. Thus, Herbert J. Storing has argued that "the special kind of practical wisdom that characterizes the civil servant points to a more fundamental political function of the bureaucracy, namely to bring to bear on public policy its distinctive view of the common good or its way of looking at questions about the common good."[22]

Specifically, middle- and high-level public employees tend to have a good deal more technical knowledge about what is feasible and how goals may be achieved; they are more politically neutral, in a partisan sense, than most public officials, and they often know more than anyone else about the programs and policies they are implementing. They may also be knowledgeable about the formulation of these policies and have an extensive understanding of their aims. As a result, they are in a unique position to contribute to public debate and can encourage the development of a more informed public opinion. They possess the facts, the expertise, and frequently the objective outlook enabling them to become a significant counterforce to inaccurate, misleading, or meaningless political rhetoric and news management techniques. Their participation in public debate provides a counterweight to the tendency to devitalize or weaken democratic political systems, a tendency which stems from a belief that the electorate cannot really judge policy options or the actions of politicians because they do not possess sufficient information about them. The latter view encourages uninformed citizen participation through voting based upon the candidates' apparent personalities and vague statements about the political good and how it can be attained. In a very real sense, only civil servants and national statesmen are in a position to counteract this tendency.

At the same time that "liberation" is beneficial, it also tends to increase the problem of hierarchical control and destroys the myth of bureaucratic neutrality. Additional kinds of changes are being instituted to remedy these problems.

Organizational Democracy

Another feature of the emerging public personnel administration encompasses (1) full-fledged participation by middle-level civil servants in general bureaucratic policymaking and (2) the participation of all employees in decision-making processes involving the organization of work and the nature of public personnel administration.

Taking the latter element first, it has been increasingly argued that expanding the role of rank-and-file employees in the structuring of work processes and the formulation of personnel procedures tends to produce greater efficiency. Moreover, there are now enough advocates, analyses, and successful examples of this approach to lead some individuals to conclude that in the work place, at least, "democracy is inevitable."[23] Although the various arguments in favor of this approach are too complex to review in their entirety, they may nevertheless be quickly summarized.

Basically, the impetus for the democratization of organized work can be traced back to the well-known Hawthorne experiments (Western Electric Researches).[24] Individuals here and, later, researchers associated with the early Human Relations Approach,[25] demonstrated that productivity could be increased by involving employees in decisions concerning the organization of work processes, allowing them to develop self-leadership, encouraging the development of informal groups among employees, and avoiding strict and punitive supervision. This type of approach has recently been advocated by such organizational theorists as Douglas McGregor, George Berkley, and Warren Bennis, among others.[26] In *The Human Side of Enterprise*, for example, McGregor argues that traditional management practices of direction and control, whether of the "hard," "soft," or "firm-but fair" varieties, simply fail to generate adequate commitment to organizational objectives in a developed and affluent society. Drawing upon Maslow's concept of a hierarchy of needs, he concludes that traditional management fails because direction and control are unsatisfactory methods of motivating people whose physiological and safety needs are reasonably satisfied and whose social, egoistic, and self-fulfillment needs are predominant. McGregor has called traditional, more authoritarian personnel practices "Theory X" and has contrasted them with "Theory Y." In his view, motivation, efficiency, and productivity are increased where employees participate in management, which is open and interested in their outlook, power and responsibility are decentalized, nonspecialization (job enlargement) is emphasized, and employee evaluation is primarily self-evaluation.

In speculating about the nature of future personnel organizations, Bennis likewise concluded that they will be more participative. Hitting upon many of the same points as McGregor, he argues that hierarchy and specialization, as they now exist, will be supplanted:

> People will be differentiated not vertically, according to rank and role, but flexibly and functionally according to skill and professional training.
> Adaptive, problem-solving, temporary systems of diverse specialists linked together by co-ordinating and task evaluating specialists in an organic flux—this is the organizational form that will gradually replace bureaucracy as we know it.[27]

Berkley, who is in general agreement with McGregor's "Theory Y" and Bennis's approach, is more empirical in his orientation. He cites examples of "the new administration at work,"[28] including several private firms in the United States and elsewhere. Even more impressive, however, are the general patterns emerging in some European democracies. According to Berkley:

> Both Sweden and West Germany, along with Norway and Holland, have enacted laws giving workers the right to elect representatives to the boards of directors of their companies. West Germany at the start of 1974 was preparing new legislation to enlarge

this right. It would allow employees of the [country's] 650 largest firms to elect half of the directors of these companies.[29]

Sweden is presently considering legislation which "would give workers a share in virtually all the decisions private industry has traditionally reserved for management—from the appointment of directors to pricing policies and mergers."[30] Nor are such examples confined to the private sector.

Although the United States has been somewhat resistant to the "Theory Y" approach, the 1960s saw the development of a whole new era with regard to labor relations in the federal service. Prior to this date, there was little support for, and much opposition to, the development of effective labor organizations and labor relations in the government. In 1962, however, President Kennedy issued an executive order which gave labor organizations the right to "be represented at discussions between management and employees or employee representatives concerning grievances, personnel policies and practices, or other matters affecting general working conditions . . . [and to] meet at reasonable times [with agency representatives] and confer with respect to personnel policy and practices. . . . "[31] In addition, federal employees were provided with greater protection in adverse actions and had a better opportunity to participate in grievance proceedings.[32]

Although the specific procedures governing the new relationship between federal employees and agency management have undergone continuous modification, it is clear that unions currently play a much greater role in determining the nature of working conditions and personnel practices in the federal service. Moreover, they have provided a base upon which advocates of greater participation have, in the words of Cary Hershey, attempted to "organize employees around their work grievances and, from the institutional base of a strong organization of workers, to seek changes in their agencies' working conditions, personnel practices, and substantive policies."[33] Significant examples of a more participatory approach have also occurred in the actual organization of work in some bureaus of the Social Security Administration.[34]

Greater employee participation in policymaking is another aspect of the new public personnel administration, but it is one which is less advanced. Although theoretical propositions and empirical analyses are less prevalent in this area, it is nevertheless possible to construct an argument for greater internal participation in policy making and to cite some examples of its application. At the heart of this approach is the belief that public bureaucracies make and implement public policy and that policy arrived at democratically, as opposed to hierarchically, will be more satisfactory because it will be more pluralisitc in its representation of different perspectives and values. This is of particular importance where a bureaucracy is highly representative in a social sense, since it would allow social representatives a greater opportunity to become active representatives.

Moreover, where democratic values are strong, policy that is arrived at democratically is generally considered to be more legitimate.* In a sense, a negative presentation of this argument makes an even stronger case for active representation. Democracy may not always yield effective policy, but hierarchical policymaking will create even more serious disadvantages. Hierarchy leads to elitism and offers no guarantee that the elite rulers will be responsive either to the public at large or to political authorities. Hierarchy also contradicts such basic democratic values as egalitarianism and respect for the dignity of the individual. It places greater value upon the opinions of some on the basis of status rather than content, whereas democracy assumes that all citizens are competent to develop and articulate political ideas. Furthermore, hierarchy militates against a free and open exchange of ideas and information and, given the fact that middle-level employees often have a great deal of expertise and knowledge concerning the policy areas in which they work, hierarchy consequently critically weakens the quality of imput vis-a-vis decision-making processes. Lastly, in some political systems, such as that found in the United States, hierarchy is contrary to dominant political practices because it concentrates power rather than fragments it. Only by opening up policy-making processes to participation by middle-level employees can information, a diversity of ideas and values (including those stemming from social background), adherence to democratic values, and legitimacy be maximized and elitist, nondemocratic tendencies minimized.

Some participation along these lines already exists in Western Europe; there is a movement in this direction in the United States. With regard to the former, Berkley writes: "As for the public sector, worker participation in many areas of policy formulation and decision-making has also gone forward. In Great Britain, West Germany and Scandinavia, rank-and-file representatives sit on a variety of policy boards and commissions throughout their respective bureaucracies."[35]

In the U.S. federal service both management and employee organizations support such an approach, although there are important differences between them. Thus, a former executive director of the CSC has written: "The more complex the system, the larger is the proportion (not just the absolute number) of its members who make professional contributions and participate in policy formulation and decision-making. Participative management, in this relative sense is coming less from behavioral science theory than from the intrinsic requirements of bigness and complexity."[36]

---

* The importance of this general approach can be observed in the United States. In November 1975, when President Ford fired Secretary of Defense James Schlesinger, several members of Congress expressed concern that this act would lessen the diversity of opinion within the Cabinet and would have undesirable effects on policy formulation within the presidential "establishment."

During the late 1960s a protest movement arose within the ranks of the federal service. As the heart of the controversy was the proposition that middle-level employees should have more influence in the determination of public policy. One organization advocating such a state of affairs, Federal Employees for a Democratic Society, had an ideal vision of how the federal bureaucracy should operate. It suggested that:

1. Employees would have a voice in the basic policy formulation of their agency and in decisions affecting the programs they administer and conditions under which they work . . .
2. Privileges of class and status should be eliminated whenever they create barriers among workers . . .
3. The hierarchy within the Federal bureaucracy must be reduced to a minimum . . .
4. Workers should be allowed to refuse to perform work which is contrary to their consciences or their sense of justice[37]

On at least one occasion the participatory ideal was nearly achieved on an institutional basis. In 1970 HEW Secretary Robert Finch agreed to discuss his personal leadership, department priorities, and national policies with 600 HEW employees. The discussion was to be relayed by closed-circuit television cameras to the cafeterias in HEW buildings in the Washington, D.C., metropolitan area. The meeting never took place. Finch became ill and subsequently resigned his post in favor of one in the Executive Office of the President.[38]

THE EMERGING PUBLIC PERSONNEL ADMINISTRATION AND THE QUESTION OF REPRESENTATION

Our analysis of the Federal EEO Program indicates that social representation has emerged as a fundamental value in public personnel administration, one which must be maximized. Although the CSC is opposed to representationist objectives and techniques where they conflict with traditional merit principles, it has nevertheless agreed that a socially representative bureaucracy is desirable. More importantly, representationists have made considerable inroads vis-a-vis federal personnel administration, especially in the area of goals and timetables. In addition, merit exams have been under attack in courts and elsewhere; in some cases the judiciary has proposed representationist remedies for illegitimately discriminatory examinations. The emergence of several other aspects of the new public personnel administration will inevitably increase the importance of social representation and will certainly lead to an even more representationist personnel administration.

Specifically, once federal employees have been "liberated," they will not only be technically competent but also politically active; they will play a larger role in the formulation of public policy and the public debate surrounding it. Once the veneer of neutrality has been discarded, it seems likely that representation will have to be stressed in order to legitimize beaureucratic power in a democratic political community.

Organizational democracy enhances the role of employees with regard to the structuring of work and the making of public policy. It lessens the chances of control by politically appointed executives and thereby limits the possibility of the creation and preservation of an effective link between the will of the electorate and the operations of bureaucratic agencies. Here, too, representation would afford a greater degree of legitimacy. In short, bureaucratic power is more easily tolerated in democracies if it is wielded by a representative group, preferably a microcosm of society at large.

In conclusion, one should stress the fact that the emerging public personnel administration seems destined to favor representation even if it is only symbolic. In theory, however, "liberation" and organizational democracy afford social representatives new opportunities to be active representatives. The emerging public personnel administration may therefore contribute to a resolution of the tension between democracy and bureaucracy by making the latter a far more representative and responsive institution. In any event, these personnel developments will undoubtedly have a major impact on future federal EEO policy. It appears likely that although this policy area will continue to be beset by considerable conflict, the CSC will come under increasing pressure to embrace the representationist ideal. Indeed, it may well be that in the United States today, as was the case a century ago, public personnel administration again stands at the brink of contributing to major political reforms.

NOTES

1. Anthony Downs, *Inside Bureaucracy* (Boston: Little, Brown, 1967), p. 262.
2. Ibid.
3. Ibid., p. 263.
4. Ibid., p. 264.
5. Ibid., p. 266.
6. Ibid., p. 274.
7. Ibid., p. 275.
8. Ibid.
9. Ibid., p. 279.
10. Harold Seidman, *Politics, Position, and Power* (New York: Oxford University Press, 1970), p. 5.
11. U.S., President's Committee on Administrative Management, *Administrative Management in the Government of the United States* (Washington; D.C.: Government Printing Office, 1937).
12. See J. Bartlett and D.N. Jones, "Managing a Cabinet Agency," *Public Administration Review* 34 (January/February 1974): 62-70.
13. See Richard Neustadt, *Presidential Power* (New York: John Wiley, 1960) for specific examples. Neustadt argues that presidential power is largely the power to persuade.
14. See Theodore Lowi, *The End of Liberalism* (New York: Norton, 1969), pp. 68-93.

15. See H. George Frederickson, "Toward a New Public Administration," in *The Dimensions of Public Administration,* 2nd ed., ed. Joseph A. Uveges, Jr. (Boston: Holbrook Press, 1975), pp. 54-74.

16. See Grant McConnell, *Private Power and American Democracy* (New York: Knopf, 1966), pp. 91-118, 342-45.

17. See David H. Rosenbloom, *Federal Service and the Constitution* (Ithaca, N.Y.: Cornell University Press, 1971) for a detailed analysis of the changing constitutional position of federal employees; idem, "Some Political Implications of the Drift Toward a Liberation of Federal Employees," *Public Administration Review* 31 (July/August 1971): 420-26.

18. *McAuliffe v. New Bedford,* 155 Mass. 216, 220 (1892).

19. *Gilmore v. James,* 274 F. Supp. 75, 91 (1967).

20. *Birnbaum v. Trussell,* 371 F2d 672, 678 (1966). For a comprehensive discussion of this issue, see David H. Rosenbloom and Jennifer A. Gille, "The Current Constitutional Approach to Public Employment," *Kansas Law Review* 23 (Winter 1975): 249-75.

21. See *Fitzgerald v. Hampton,* 467 F2d 755 (1972).

22. Herbert J. Storing, "Political Parties and the Bureaucracy," in *Political Parties, U.S.A.,* ed. Robert A. Goldwin (Chicago: Rand McNally, 1961), p. 154.

23. See Warren Bennis and Philip Slater, "Democracy is Inevitable," *Harvard Business Review* 42 (March/April 1964): 51-9.

24. For a discussion of this experiment, see George C. Homans, "The Western Electric Researches," in *Readings on Modern Organizations,* ed. Amatai Etzioni (Englewood Cliffs, N.J.: Prentice Hall, 1969), pp. 99-114.

25. See Amatai Etzioni, *Modern Organizations,* Chapter 4 for a convenient discussion.

26. See Douglas McGregor, *The Human Side of Enterprise* (New York: McGraw-Hill, 1960); idem, *Leadership and Motivation* (Cambridge, Mass.: MIT Press, 1966); idem, *The Professional Manager* (New York: McGraw-Hill, 1967); Warren Bennis and Philip Slater, *Harvard Business Review* 42 (March/April 1964): 51-9. Warren Bennis, "Beyond Bureaucracy," *Transaction* 2, (July/August 1965), 31-5; George E. Berkley, *The Administrative Revolution* (Englewood Cliffs, N.J.: Prentice Hall, 1971); idem, *The Craft of Public Administration* (Boston: Allyn and Bacon, 1975).

27. Bennis, "Beyond Bureaucracy," p. 35.

28. Berkley *The Craft of Public Administration,* pp. 478-86.

29. Ibid., p. 479.

30. The New York *Times,* October 26, 1975, Sect. 4, p. 7.

31. Executive Order 10988, U.S., *Federal Register,* 27: pt. 1 551, 553 (January 17, 1962).

32. Executive Order 10987, ibid., p. 550 (January 17, 1962).

33. Cary Hershey, *Protest in the Public Service* (Lexington, Mass.: Lexington Books, 1973), p. 50.

34. See Berkley, *The Craft of Public Administration,* pp. 482-3.

35. Ibid. p. 480.

36. Bernard Rosen, "The Developing Role of Career Managers," *Civil Service Journal* 13 (January/March 1973) p. 31.

37. Hershey, *Protest in the Public Service,* p. 51, note a.

38. The New York *Times,* May 18, 1970, p. 20.

BIBLIOGRAPHY

I. Books and Pamphlets

Aronson, Sidney. *Status and Kinship: Standards of Selection in the Administrations of John Adams, Thomas Jefferson, and Andrew Jackson*. Cambridge, Mass.: Harvard University Press, 1964.

Bendix, Reinhard. *Higher Civil Servants in American Society*. Boulder, Colo.: University of Colorado Press, 1949.

Berkeley, George E. *The Administrative Revolution*. Englewood Cliffs, N.J.: Prentice-Hall, 1971.

————. *The Craft of Public Administration*. Boston, Mass.: Allyn and Bacon, 1975.

Bernstein, Marver. *The Job of the Federal Executive*. Washington, D.C.: Brookings Institution, 1958.

Brewer, M. Weldon. *Behind the Promises*. Washington, D.C.: Public Interest Research Group, 1972.

Chapman, Brian. *The Profession of Government*. London, England: Unwin University Books, 1959.

Clark, Kenneth. *Dark Ghetto*. New York: Harper and Row, 1965.

Cunningham, Nobel E., Jr. *The Jeffersonian Republicans in Power*. Chapel Hill, N.C.: University of North Carolina Press, 1963.

Donovan, J., Ed. *Recruitment and Selection in the Public Service*. Chicago, Ill.: Public Personnel Association, 1968.

Downs, Anthony. *Inside Bureaucracy*. Boston, Mass.: Little, Brown, 1967.

Dubois, W.E.B. *Dusk of Dawn*. New York: Harcourt, Brace, 1940.

Eaton, Dorman B. *The Civil Service in Great Britain*. New York: Harper and Bros., 1880.

Frederickson, H. George. "Toward a New Public Administration." In *The Dimensions of Public Administration*, 2nd ed., ed. Joseph A. Uveges, Jr. Boston, Mass.: Holbrook Press, 1975, pp. 54-74.

Gellhorn, Walter. *Security, Loyalty, and Science*. Ithaca, N.Y.: Cornell University Press, 1950.

Goodnow, F. *Politics and Administration*. New York: Macmillan, 1900.

Gulick, Luther. "Science, Values, and Public Admininstration." In *Papers on the Science of Administration,* ed. Luther Gulick and L. Urwick. New York: Institute of Public Administration, 1937, pp. 189-95.

Hall, Richard. *Organizations: Structure and Process.* Englewood Cliffs, N.J.: Prentice-Hall, 1972.

Harrington, Michael. *The Other America.* Baltimore, Md.: Penguin, 1964.

Hayes, Laurence J. *The Negro Federal Government Worker.* Washington, D.C.: Howard University Press, 1941.

Herring, E. Pendleton. *Federal Commissioners.* Cambridge, Mass.: Harvard University Press, 1936.

Hershey, Cary. *Protest in the Public Service.* Lexington, Mass.: Lexington Books, 1973.

Homans, George C. "The Western Electric Researches." In *Readings on Modern Organizations,* ed. Amitai Etzioni. Englewood Cliffs, N.J.: Prentice-Hall, 1969, pp. 99-114.

Jackson, Andrew. *The Correspondence of Andrew Jackson,* 7 vols. ed. J.S. Bassett. Washington, D.C.: Carnegie Institution, 1926. Vol. IV.

Kesselman, Louis C. *The Social Politics of FEPC.* Chapel Hill, N.C.: University of North Carolina Press, 1948.

Kilpatrick, Franklin P., Milton C. Cummings, Jr., and M. Kent Jennings. *The Image of the Federal Service.* Washington, D.C.: The Brookings Institution, 1964.

Kingsley, J. Donald. *Representative Bureaucracy.* Yellow Springs, Ohio: Antioch Press, 1944.

Krislov, Samuel. *The Negro in Federal Employment.* Minneapolis, Minn.: University of Minnesota Press, 1967.

—————. *Representative Bureaucracy.* Englewood Cliffs, N.J.: Prentice-Hall, 1974.

Link, Arthur S. *Wilson: The New Freedom.* Princeton, N.J.: Princeton University Press, 1956.

Lipset, Seymour M. "Bureaucracy and Social Change." In *Reader in Bureaucracy,* ed. Robert K. Merton, et al. New York: Free Press, 1952, pp. 221-32.

Litwack, Leon F. *North of Slavery.* Chicago, Ill.: University of Chicago Press, 1961.

Long, Norton. "Power and Administration." In *Bureaucratic Power in National Politics,* ed. F. Rourke. Boston, Mass.: Little, Brown, 1965, pp. 14-23.

Lowi, Theodore. *The End of Liberalism.* New York: Norton, 1969.

Lubell, Samuel. *The Future of American Politics.* New York: Anchor, 1955.

McConnell, Grant. *Private Power and American Democracy.* New York: Knopf, 1966.

McGregor, Douglas. *The Human Side of Enterprise.* New York: McGraw-Hill, 1960.

————. *Leadership and Motivation.* Cambridge, Mass.: MIT Press, 1966.

————. *The Professional Manager.* New York: McGraw-Hill, 1966.

McMillin, Lucille. *Women in the Federal Service.* Washington, D.C.: U.S. Government Printing Office, 1941.

Mead, Margaret, and F.B. Kaplan, eds. *American Women.* New York: Scribner's, 1965.

Menzel, Johanna, ed. *The Chinese Civil Service.* Boston, Mass.: D.C. Heath, 1963.

Mosher, Frederick. *Democracy and the Public Service.* New York: Oxford University Press, 1968.

National Committee on Segregation in the Nation's Capital. *Segregation in Washington.* Chicago, Ill.: National Committee on Segregation in the Nation's Capital, 1948.

Neustadt, Richard. *Presidential Power.* New York: John Wiley, 1960.

Nigro, Felix. *Public Personnel Administration.* New York: Henry Holt, 1959.

Norgen Paul H., and Samuel Hill. *Toward Fair Employment.* New York: Columbia University Press, 1964.

Pfiffner, John, and Robert Presthus. *Public Administration.* New York: Ronald Press, 1967.

Presthus, Robert. *The Organizational Society.* New York: Random House, 1962.

Richardson, James D., ed. *A Compilation of the Messages and Papers of the Presidents of the United States, 1789-1897.* 10 vols. Washington, D.C.: U.S. Government Printing Office, 1896-1899. Vol. II.

Rosenbloom, David H. *Federal Service and the Constitution.* Ithaca, N.Y.: Cornell University Press, 1971.

Rossi, Peter H., et al. *The Roots of Urban Discontent.* New York: John Wiley, 1974.

Ruchames, Louis. *Race, Job and Politics: The Story of FEPC.* New York: Columbia University Press, 1953.

Sayre, Wallace S. "Introduction: Dilemmas and Prospects of the Federal Government Service." In *The Federal Government Service,* ed. Wallace Sayre. Englewood Cliffs, N.J.: Prentice-Hall, 1965, pp. 1-6.

Schurz, Carl. *Congress and the Spoils System.* New York: George G. Peck, 1895.

————. *Speeches, Correspondence, and Political Papers of Carl Schurz.* 6 vols. ed. Frederick Bancroft. New York: Putnam's, 1913. Vol. II.

Seidman, Harold. *Politics, Position, and Power.* New York: Oxford University Press, 1970.

Stahl, O. Glenn. *Public Personnel Administration.* New York: Harper and Row, 1962.

Storing, Herbert J. "Political Parties and the Bureaucracy." In *Political Parties, U.S.A.,* ed. Robert A. Goldwin. Chicago, Ill.: Rand McNally, 1961, pp. 137-58.

United Public Workers of America. *Jim Crow Discrimination Against U.S. Employees in the Canal Zone.* N.p., n.d.

—————. *The Story of Discrimination in Government.* N.p., [1948].

Van Riper, Paul P. *History of the United States Civil Service.* Evanston, Ill.: Row, Peterson, 1958.

Warner, W. Lloyd, et al. *The American Federal Executive.* New Haven, Conn.: Yale University Press, 1963.

Wasby, Stephen. *Political Science—the Discipline and Its Dimensions.* New York: Scribner's, 1970.

Weber, Max. *From Max Weber: Essays in Sociology,* trans. and ed. H.H. Gerth and C.W. Mills. New York: Oxford University Press, 1958.

White, Leonard D. *The Jeffersonians.* New York: Free Press, 1965.

—————. *The Republican Era.* New York: Free Press, 1965.

Wilkins, Roger, James Frazier, Jr., et al. "The Equal Employment Opportunity Posture of the U.S. Federal Government." Unpublished report, [1969?].

Yarmolinsky, Adam. *Case Studies in Personnel Security.* Washington, D.C.: Bureau of National Affairs, 1955.

II. Journals and Periodicals

Aptheker, Herbert. "Segregation in Federal Government Departments: 1928." *Science and Society* 28 (Winter 1964): 86-91.

The *Baltimore Afro-American,* 1968.

Bartlett, J.W., and D.N. Jones. "Managing a Cabinet Agency." *Public Administration Review* 34 (January/February 1974): 62-70.

Bennis, Warren. "Beyond Bureaucracy." *Transaction* 2 (July/August 1965), 31-35.

Bennis, Warren, and Philip Slater. "Democracy Is Inevitable." *Harvard Business Review* 42 (March/April 1964): 51-59.

Couturier, J.J. "The Model Public Personnel Law." *Public Personnel Review* 32 (October 1971): 202-09.

Cramer, John. "Taking the Plaint from Complaint." Washington *News,* May 15, 1968.

Davis, John A. "Nondiscrimination in the Federal Services." *Annals of the American Academy of Political and Social Science* 244 (March 1946): 65-74.

Dresang, Dennis L. "Ethnic Politics, Representative Bureaucracy and Development Administration: the Zambian Case." *American Political Science Review* 68 (December 1974): 1605-17.

Drew, Elizabeth. "HEW Grapples with PPBS." *Public Interest* 8 (Summer 1967): 9-27.

Federal Times, 1970.

Grabosky, Peter, and David H. Rosenbloom. "Racial and Ethnic Integration in the Federal Service." *Social Science Quarterly* 56 (June 1975): 71-84.

Harrison, Evelyn. "The Working Woman: Barriers in Employment." *Public Administration Review* 24 (June 1964): 78-85.

Hellriegel, Don, and Larry Short. "Equal Employment Opportunity in the Federal Government: A Comparative Analysis." *Public Administration Review* 32 (November/December 1972): 851-58.

International Herald Tribune, April 27, 1972: p. 3.

Markoff, Helene. "The Federal Women's Program." *Public Administration Review* 32 (March/April 1972): 144-51.

Maslow, Will. "FEPC—A History in Parliamentary Maneuver." *University of Chicago Law Review* 13 (June 1946): 407-44.

Meier, Kenneth. "Representative Bureaucracy: An Empirical Analysis." *American Political Science Review* 69 (June 1975): 526-42.

Meier, K. J., and L. Nigro. "Representative Bureaucracy and Policy Preferences." *Public Administration Review* 36 (July/August 1976): 458-69.

Nachmias, David, and David H. Rosenbloom. "Measuring Bureaucratic Representation and Integration." *Public Administration Review* 33 (November/December 1973): 590-97.

New York *Times.* October 7, 1968, p. 1; May 18, 1970, p. 20; June 25, 1972, p. 28; April 23, 1974, p. 20; October 26, 1975, sect. 4, p. 7.

Nikoloric, L.A. "The Government Loyalty Program." *American Scholar* 19 (Summer 1950): 285-98.

Reissman, Leonard. "A Study of Role Conceptions in Bureaucracy." *Social Forces* 27 (March 1949): 305-10.

Rosen, Bernard. "The Developing Role of Career Managers." *Civil Service Journal* 13 (January/March 1973): 26-31.

Rosenbloom, David H. "A Note on the Social Class Composition of the Civil Service, 1789-1837." *Polity* 5 (Fall 1972): 136-38.

—————. "Some Political Implications of the Drift Toward a Liberation of Federal Employees." *Public Administration Review* 31 (July/August 1971): 420-26.

Rosenbloom, David H., and Jennifer A. Gille. "The Current Constitutional Approach to Public Employment." *Kansas Law Review* 23 (Winter 1975): 249-75.

Rosenbloom, David H., and Carole C. Obuchowski. "Public Personnel Examinations and the Constitution: Emergent Trends." *Public Administration Review* 37 (January/ February 1977): 9-18.

Schurz, Carl. "What is Reform?" *Harper's Weekly,* July 1, 1893, p. 614.

Subramanian, V. "Representative Bureaucracy: A Reassessment." *American Political Science Review* 61 (December 1967): 1010-19.

Wilson, Woodrow. "The Study of Administration." *Political Science Quarterly* 56 (December 1941): 481-506.

Wolgemuth, Kathleen Long. "Woodrow Wilson's Appointment Policy and the Negro." *Journal of Southern History* 24 (November 1958): 457-71.

III. Public Documents

U.S. Civil Service Commission. *Annual Report,* 8, 1891.

—————. *Annual Report,* 80, 1963.

—————. *Civil Service News,* March 18, 1969.

—————. *Consolidated Report of Inspection Findings on the Status of Women in the Federal Service, April 30, 1962-April 30, 1964.* Washington, D.C.: U.S. Civil Service Commission, 1964.

—————. *Federal Personnel Manual System. Installment for Basic Manual* 135 (May 29, 1970).

—————. *Federal Personnel Manual System Letter.* "EEO Plans." 713-22, October 4, 1973.

—————. *Federal Personnel Manual System Letter.* "Establishing and Maintaining a Record of Minority Group Status." 293-95, March 4, 1966.

—————. *History of the Federal Civil Service, 1789 to the Present.* Washington, D.C.: U.S. Government Printing Office, 1941.

—————. *Minority Group Employment in the Federal Government.* Washington, D.C.: U.S. Government Printing Office, 1966-75.

—————. *The Opening Door.* Washington, D.C.: CSC, 1962.

—————. *Operations Letter.* "Reporting on Equal Employment Opportunity." 273-372, November 18, 1966.

—————. *Steps in Conducting the Investigation.* Bureau of Training. N.d.

—————. *Study of Employment of Women in the Federal Government.* Washington D.C.: U.S. Government Printing Office, 1969-74.

—————. *Upward Mobility for Lower Level Employees: Suggested Goals and Actions.* May 7, 1970.

U.S., Civil Service Commission, Bureau of Recruiting and Examining. *Equal Opportunity in Federal Employment, May 15, 1963-June 30, 1964.* (September 1964).

U.S., Civil Service Commission Fair Employment Board. *Fair Employment in the Federal Service.* Pamphlet 44, 1951.

U.S., Civil Service Commission. *Civil Service News,* March 18, 1969; October 6, 1975; April 26, 1976.

U.S., Civil Service Commission. *Federal Civilian Manpower Statistics Monthly Release,* 1971-76.

U.S., Commission on Civil Rights. *Federal Civil Rights Enforcement Effort.* Washington, D.C.: U.S. Government Printing Office, 1970.

—————. *The Federal Civil Rights Enforcement Effort—1974.* Washington, D.C.: Commission on Civil Rights, 1975.

U.S., Congress, House Committee on Education and Labor, General Subcommittee on Labor. *Equal Employment Opportunity Enforcement Procedures.* H.R. 1746, 92nd Cong., 1st sess., 1971.

U.S., Congress, Senate Committee on Labor and Public Welfare, Subcommittee on Labor. *Equal Employment Opportunity Enforcement Act.* 91st Cong. 1st sess., 1969.

U.S., Congress, Senate. *Congressional Record,* 76th Cong., 3d sess., 1940, 86, pt. 11: 12640.

—————. *Congressional Record,* 90th Cong., 1st sess., 1967, 113, pt. 19: 25456.

U.S., Fair Employment Practice Committee. *Final Report.* Washington, D.C.: U.S. Government Printing Office, 1947.

U.S. Federal Register, 5, 1940, pt. 4: 4445; 6, 1941, pt. 2: 3109; 13, 1948, pt. 7: 4311; 20, 1955, pt. 1: 409; 26, 1961, pt. 3: 1977; 26, 1961, pt. 12: 12059; 27, 1962, pt. 1: 550; 27, 1962, pt. 1: 551; 30, 1965, pt. 9: 12319; 32, 1967, pt. 10: 14303; 34, 1969, pt. 8: 12985.

U.S., President, Office of the White House Press Secretary, news release, November 5, 1970.

U.S., President, Richard M. Nixon, Memorandum for the Heads of Departments and Agencies, August 8, 1969.

U.S., President's Committee on Administrative Management. *Administrative Management in the Government of the United States.* Washington, D.C.: U.S. Government Printing Office, 1937.

U.S., President's Committee on Government Employment Policy. *Fourth Report.* Washington, D.C.: U.S. Government Printing Office, 1961.

U.S., *Statutes at Large,* vols. 2, 42, 50, 53, 54, 78, 86.

IV. Court Cases

Bailey v. Richardson, 182 F2d 46 (1950).

Birnbaum v. Trussell, 371 F2d 672 (1966).

Bridgeport Guardians v. Bridgeport CSC, 482 F2d 1333 (1973).

Carter v. Gallagher, 452 F2d 315 (1971).

Chance v. Board of Examiners, 458 F2d 1167 (1972).

Douglas v. Hampton, 338 F. Supp. 18 (1972); 512 F2d 976 (1975).

Fitzgerald v. Hampton, 467 F2d 755 (1972).

Gilmore v. James, 274 F. Supp. 75 (1967).

Kirkland v. New York State Dept. of Correctional Services, 374 F. Supp. 1361 (1974); 520 F2d 420 (1975).

McAuliffe v. New Bedford, 155 Mass. 216 (1892).

Morton v. Mancari, 417 U.S. 535 (1974).

Penn v. Schlesinger, 497 F2d 970 (1974).

Washington v. Davis, 48L. Ed. 2d 597 (1976).

Western Addition Community Organization v. Alioto, 330 F. Supp. 536 (1971).

Vulcan Society v. CSC, 360 F. Supp. 1265 (1973).

V. U.S. Civil Service Commission Memoranda and Miscellaneous Communications

"Implementation of the Commission's Responsibilities under Executive Order 11246 in Equal Employment Opportunity." Internal memorandum from the Executive Director of the Civil Service Commission to the Commission, November 2, 1965.

Letter from the Civil Service Commission Chairman to the Staff Director of the U.S. Commission on Civil Rights, July 24, 1970.

Memorandum from the Civil Service Commission Chairman, May 20, 1970.

Memorandum from Civil Service Commission Chairman Robert E. Hampton to John A. Buggs, Staff Director, U.S. Commission on Civil Rights, May 2, 1975.

Memorandum from Chief of Personnel Management Section, Civil Service Commission, to file, October 19, 1969.

Memorandum from the Director of the Civil Service Commission Bureau of Policies and Standards to Civil Service Commission Chairman John Macy. "Fifth Progress Report on Complaints about Minority Status Self-determination." November 8, 1966.

Memorandum from A. Rachal, Jr., Civil Service Commission, to I. Kator, June 18, 1968.

Oganovic, Nicholas J., Executive Director, Civil Service Commission, letter to Adrian Dove, Management Analyst, Office of Management and Budget, February 3, 1971.

Statement of Assistant Executive Director of the Civil Service Commission on H.R. 6288, April 7, 1970.

Statement of the Director of the Civil Service Commission Bureau of Manpower Information Systems, September 15, 1970.

ABOUT THE AUTHOR

DAVID H. ROSENBLOOM is an Associate Professor of Political Science at the University of Vermont. He specializes in research on public bureaucracy and has concentrated much of his work on the federal service.

Before joining the University of Vermont, Professor Rosenbloom taught at the University of Kansas and Tel Aviv University. He was also an American Society for Public Administration Fellow with the Office of Federal Equal Employment Opportunity of the U.S. Civil Service Commission, a position which enabled him to gain firsthand experience and many insights into the subject matter of the present study.

Professor Rosenbloom received his Ph.D degree from the University of Chicago. He wrote his dissertation on the constitutional status of public employees in the United States, subsequently published under the title, *Federal Service and the Constitution.* His work on this area was relied upon by the Supreme Court in its disposition of *Elrod v. Burns* (1976). Dr. Rosenbloom has also published more than twenty articles and research notes dealing with public bureaucracy in the United States and Israel. These have appeared in such Journals as *Public Administration Review, Social Science Quarterly, Polity, Western Political Quarterly, Midwest Review of Public Administration, Public Personnel Management, Indian Journal of Public Administration, Chinese Journal of Administration, University of Kansas Law Review,* and *Law Review Digest.*

OCCUPATIONAL CHOICES AND TRAINING NEEDS: Prospects for the 1980s
Leonard A. Lecht

PUBLIC PERSONNEL MANAGEMENT: The Heritage of Civil Service Reform
Jay M. Shafritz

A SURVEY OF CHINESE-AMERICAN MANPOWER AND EMPLOYMENT
Betty Lee Sung

WOMEN IN ACADEMIA: Evolving Policies Toward Equal Opportunities
edited by
Elga Wasserman
Arie Y. Lewin
Linda Bleiweiss